Quick and Easy
HEART HEALTHY RECIPES

Quarto.com

© 2025 Quarto Publishing Group USA Inc.
Text © 2009 Dick Logue

First Published in 2025 by New Shoe Press, an imprint of The Quarto Group,
100 Cummings Center, Suite 265-D, Beverly, MA 01915, USA.
T (978) 282-9590 F (978) 283-2742

Essential, In-Demand Topics, Four-Color Design, Affordable Price
New Shoe Press publishes affordable, beautifully designed books covering evergreen, in-demand subjects. With a goal to inform and inspire readers' everyday hobbies, from cooking and gardening to wellness and health to art and crafts, New Shoe titles offer the ultimate library of purposeful, how-to guidance aimed at meeting the unique needs of each reader. Reimagined and redesigned from Quarto's best-selling backlist, New Shoe books provide practical knowledge and opportunities for all DIY enthusiasts to enrich and enjoy their lives.

Visit Quarto.com/New-Shoe-Press for a complete listing of the New Shoe Press books.

New Shoe Press titles are also available at discount for retail, wholesale, promotional, and bulk purchase. For details, contact the Special Sales Manager by email at specialsales@quarto.com or by mail at The Quarto Group, Attn: Special Sales Manager, 100 Cummings Center, Suite 265-D, Beverly, MA 01915, USA.

ISBN: 978-0-7603-9086-3
eISBN: 978-0-7603-9087-0

The content in this book was previously published in *1001 Heart-Healthy Recipes* (Fair Winds Press 2013), *500 High-Fiber Recipes* (Fair Winds Press 2009), and *500 Low-Cholesterol Recipes* (Fair Winds Press 2009) all by Dick Logue.

Library of Congress Cataloging-in-Publication Data available

The information in this book is for educational purposes only. It is not intended to replace the advice of a physician or medical practitioner. Please see your health-care provider before beginning any new health program.

Quick and Easy
HEART HEALTHY RECIPES

Eat Well and Maintain Health with Recipes High in Fiber and Low in Sodium and Cholesterol

DICK LOGUE

NEW SHOE PRESS

Contents

INTRODUCTION: What Do We Mean By Heart Healthy?   7

CHAPTER 1: BREAKFASTS   11

CHAPTER 2: SNACKS AND NIBBLES   24

CHAPTER 3: MAIN DISHES: POULTRY   39

CHAPTER 4: MAIN DISHES: BEEF   54

CHAPTER 5: MAIN DISHES: PORK   64

CHAPTER 6: MAIN DISHES: FISH AND SEAFOOD   74

CHAPTER 7: MAIN DISHES: VEGETARIAN   86

CHAPTER 8: SOUPS AND STEWS   98

CHAPTER 9: BREADS   111

CHAPTER 10: DESSERTS   121

CHAPTER 11: SAUCES, CONDIMENTS, MIXES, AND SPICE BLENDS   132

ABOUT THE AUTHOR   140

INDEX   140

What Do We Mean By Heart Healthy?

First let's define exactly what we mean by heart-healthy recipes and how this collection is different from other cookbooks you may have or have seen. Heart-healthy diets are aimed at preventing or reducing a number of risk factors that can lead to heart attacks and heart disease. Among the more important ones are coronary artery disease, high cholesterol and high blood pressure.

The American Heart Association lists seven key items for maintaining cardiovascular health. They are:

- Don't smoke
- Maintain a healthy weight
- Engage in regular physical activity
- Eat a healthy diet
- Manage blood pressure
- Take charge of cholesterol
- Keep blood sugar, or glucose, at healthy levels.

You can easily see that while they list diet as a separate factor, what you eat affects everything on the list except smoking and exercise. If you start digging into the details of dietary recommendations for staying a healthy weight, maintaining a healthy blood pressure and cholesterol level, and managing blood sugar levels you immediately find that the same recommendations are key to many or all of them. Common themes at such diverse web sites as the Centers for Disease Control and Prevention, the U.S. Department of Agriculture, the American Heart Association, the Mayo Clinic and WebMD include:

- Limit the amount of unhealthy fats such as saturated fats and trans fats that you eat
- Choose lean sources of protein
- Eat more whole grains
- East more fruits and vegetables
- Limit your sodium intake
- Limit your cholesterol intake.

Given the importance of the topic, there are of course a number of heart-healthy cookbooks available. I have quite a few myself and some of them have a number of really good recipes. But what I've found in looking at them is that most of them focus on one or another aspect of heart healthy cooking and tend to ignore the others. So you'll find a book that has pages of great information on lower fat substitutions, but still includes a number of high sodium ingredients for which there are equally easy-to-find substitutions. Another book may focus on including more whole grains, but have recipes that are high in saturated fat. It seemed to me that what was needed was one book that took all the aspects of heart-healthy cooking into consideration and gave you enough recipes that you could always find what you were looking for: a one stop shop for heart-healthy cooking. That is what this book is. It contains healthy versions of some things that may already be family favorites like fried chicken, meatloaf, and pizza as well as things that you may not have thought about, such as roasted chickpeas and bean pie.

A Little Bit about Me

Some of you may already know me from my Low-Sodium Cooking website and newsletter or from my other books focused on low-sodium and other heart-healthy recipes. For those who don't, perhaps a little background information might be useful.

I started thinking about heart-healthy cooking after being diagnosed with congestive heart failure in 1999. One of the first, and biggest, things I had to deal with was the doctor's insistence that I follow a low-sodium diet . . . 1,200 mg a day or less. At first, like many people, I found it easiest to just avoid the things that had a lot of sodium in them. But I was bored. And I was convinced that there had to be a way to create low-sodium versions of the foods I missed. So I learned all kinds of new cooking things. I researched where to get low-sodium substitutes for the things that I couldn't have anymore, bought cookbooks, and basically redid my whole diet. And I decided to share this information with others who may be in the same position I had been in. I started a website, www.lowsodiumcooking.com, to share recipes and information. I sent out an email newsletter with recipes that now has more than 20,000 subscribers. And I wrote my first book, *500 Low Sodium Recipes*.

Perhaps the best way to start telling you who I am is by telling you who I'm not. I'm not a doctor. I'm not a dietician. I'm not a professional chef. What I am is an ordinary person just like you who has some special dietary needs. I have enjoyed cooking most of my life. I guess I started it seriously about the time my mother went back to work when I was twelve or so. In those days, it was simple stuff like burgers and hot dogs and spaghetti. But the interest stayed. After I married my wife, we got pretty involved in some food-related pursuits—growing vegetables in our garden, making bread and other baked goods, canning and jelly making, that kind of thing. She always said that my "mad chemist" cooking was an outgrowth of the time I spent in college as a chemistry major, and she might be right. So creating the kind of food that people said couldn't be done, low in sodium and high in taste, was a fun challenge for me.

Along the way, I also learned about other things that make a diet heart healthy. I became more aware of cholesterol, fiber, and other things that make some foods better for your heart than others. I began incorporating what I'd learned into the recipes. So you will find that the recipes here are not only low in sodium, but they also tend to be low in saturated fat, contain whole grains and other high-fiber foods, and tend to focus on fresh ingredients. This all actually comes together nicely, because in many cases the same foods that fit one of those requirements also support others.

How Is the Nutritional Information Calculated?

The nutritional information included with these recipes was calculated using the AccuChef program. It calculates the values using the latest U.S. Department of Agriculture National Nutrient Database for Standard Reference. I've been using this program since I first started trying to figure out how much sodium was in the recipes I've created. It's inexpensive, easy to use, and has a number of really handy features.

For instance, if I go in and change the nutrition figures for an ingredient, it remembers those figures whenever I use that ingredient. AccuChef is available online from www.accuchef.com. They offer a free trial version if you want to try it out and the full version costs less than twenty dollars.

Of course, this implies that these figures are estimates. Every brand of tomatoes, or any other product, is a little different in nutritional content. These figures were calculated using products that I buy here in southern Maryland. If you use a different brand, your nutrition figures may be different. Use the nutritional analysis as a guideline in determining whether a recipe is right for your diet.

CHAPTER 1

Breakfasts

I'm a great believer in the idea that breakfast is the most important meal of the day. I need something in the morning to get me going and keep me going until lunch. Even though traditional breakfast meat tends to be high in fat and sodium, we have some options for you like a low fat turkey sausage with only 35 mg of sodium per serving. Along with lots of egg dishes we have a great selection of whole grain pancakes, fruit breakfasts and smoothies.

Turkey Breakfast Sausage

I've been back at the chemistry table—I mean, kitchen counter—trying various recipes for sausage again. This is my favorite so far. It contains about 5% of the sodium, 10% of the fat, and one-third of the calories of the average store-bought sausage.

1 pound (455 g) ground turkey

¼ teaspoon (0.5 g) black pepper

¼ teaspoon (0.5 g) white pepper

¾ teaspoon (0.6 g) dried sage

¼ teaspoon (0.4 g) ground mace

½ teaspoon (1.5 g) garlic powder

¼ teaspoon (0.8 g) onion powder

¼ teaspoon (0.5 g) ground allspice

1 teaspoon (5 ml) olive oil

Combine all ingredients, mixing well. Fry, grill, or preheat oven to 325°F (170°C, or gas mark 3) and cook on a greased baking sheet to desired doneness.

—Yield: 8 servings

NUTRITIONAL ANALYSIS

PER SERVING: 69 calories (20% from fat, 77% from protein, 2% from carbohydrate); 13 g protein; 1 g total fat; 0 g saturated fat; 1 g monounsaturated fat; 0 g polyunsaturated fat; 0 g carbohydrate; 0 g fiber; 0 g sugar; 106 mg phosphorus; 9 mg calcium; 1 mg iron; 35 mg sodium; 153 mg potassium; 5 IU vitamin A; 0 mg ATE vitamin E; 0 mg vitamin C; 41 mg cholesterol; 43 g water

Snowy Day Breakfast Casserole

My wife came up with this one winter when we were snowed in. It has since become a standard in our house, just the sort of thing you need to sit in front of the fire with.

2 slices low sodium bacon

3 potatoes, shredded

½ cup (80 g) onion, chopped

¼ cup (37 g) green bell pepper, chopped

4 eggs

¼ cup (30 g) low fat Cheddar cheese, shredded

Preheat oven to 350°F (180°C, or gas mark 4). Fry bacon in a large skillet. Remove bacon to a paper towel–covered plate to drain. Add potatoes, onion, and green pepper to skillet and sauté until potatoes are crispy and onion soft. Stir in crumbled bacon. Transfer to greased 8-inch (20-cm) square baking dish. Pour eggs over. Sprinkle with cheese. Bake until eggs are set, about 20 minutes.

—Yield: 4 servings

NUTRITIONAL ANALYSIS

PER SERVING: 292 calories (14% from fat, 22% from protein, 63% from carbohydrate); 17 g protein; 5 g total fat; 1 g saturated fat; 1 g monounsaturated fat; 1 g polyunsaturated fat; 47 g carbohydrate; 5 g fiber; 4 g sugar; 314 mg phosphorus; 101 mg calcium; 4 mg iron; 221 mg sodium; 1310 mg potassium; 299 IU vitamin A; 5 mg ATE vitamin E; 33 mg vitamin C; 207 mg cholesterol; 308 g water

Breakfast Skillet

This was originally a Sunday-morning breakfast in late summer. At that time of year, I usually have extra peppers from the garden, and this recipe used up a few of them.

1 tablespoon (15 ml) olive oil

¼ cup (40 g) onion, finely chopped

¼ cup (38 g) red bell pepper, finely chopped

½ cup (105 g) frozen hash brown potatoes, thawed

3 eggs, beaten

Heat oil in a large skillet over medium heat. Sauté onion and red bell pepper until tender. Add hash browns and cook until potatoes are softened and beginning to brown, stirring occasionally. Pour eggs over vegetables and continue to cook for 5 minutes, or until set, stirring occasionally.

—Yield: 2 servings

NUTRITIONAL ANALYSIS

PER SERVING: 195 calories (47% from fat, 26% from protein, 26% from carbohydrate); 13 g protein; 10 g total fat; 2 g saturated fat; 6 g monounsaturated fat; 2 g polyunsaturated fat; 13 g carbohydrate; 1 g fiber; 2 g sugar; 149 mg phosphorus; 61 mg calcium; 3 mg iron; 180 mg sodium; 129 mg potassium; 922 IU vitamin A; 0 mg ATE vitamin E; 30 mg vitamin C; 300 mg cholesterol; 154 g water

Vegetable Omelet

This can be either a breakfast or the main part of an evening meal.

1 tablespoon (15 ml) olive oil

2 ounces (55 g) mushrooms, sliced

¼ cup (40 g) onion, diced

¼ cup (37 g) green bell peppers, diced

¼ cup (28 g) zucchini, sliced

½ cup (90 g) tomato, diced

4 eggs

2 tablespoons (30 g) fat-free sour cream

2 tablespoons (30 ml) water

2 ounces (55 g) Swiss cheese, shredded

Add olive oil to a large skillet and sauté mushrooms, onion, green bell pepper, zucchini, and tomato until soft, adding tomato last. Whisk together eggs, sour cream, and water until fluffy. Coat an omelet pan or skillet with nonstick vegetable spray and place over medium-high heat. Pour egg mixture into pan. Lift the edges as it cooks to allow uncooked egg to run underneath. When eggs are nearly set, cover half the eggs with the cheese and sautéed vegetables and fold the other half over. Continue cooking until eggs are completely set.

—Yield: 2 servings

NUTRITIONAL ANALYSIS

PER SERVING: 263 calories (46% from fat, 41% from protein, 13% from carbohydrate); 25 g protein; 13 g total fat; 3 g saturated fat; 6 g monounsaturated fat; 3 g polyunsaturated fat; 8 g carbohydrate; 2 g fiber; 4 g sugar; 386 mg phosphorus; 369 mg calcium; 3 mg iron; 309 mg sodium; 246 mg potassium; 962 IU vitamin A; 6 mg ATE vitamin E; 25 mg vitamin C; 395 mg cholesterol; 259 g water

Cinnamon Apple Omelet

A little different version of an omelet. I remember years ago there were often recipes for omelets with jelly or other sweet fillings, but you don't see them much any more. This one makes me think they are still a good idea.

1 tablespoon unsalted butter, divided

1 apple, peeled and sliced thin

½ teaspoon cinnamon

1 tablespoon (15 g) brown sugar

3 eggs

1 tablespoon cream

1 tablespoon sour cream

Melt 2 teaspoons butter in egg pan. Add apple, cinnamon, and brown sugar. Sauté until tender. Set aside. Whip eggs and cream until fluffy; set aside. Clean egg pan. Melt remaining butter, pour in egg mixture. Cook as you would for an omelet. When eggs are ready to flip, turn them, then add to the center of the eggs the sour cream and on top of that the apple mixture. Fold it onto a plate.

—Yield: 2 servings

NUTRITIONAL ANALYSIS

PER SERVING: 129 g water; 252 calories (57% from fat, 17% from protein, 25% from carb); 11 g protein; 16 g total fat; 8 g saturated fat; 5 g monounsaturated fat; 1 g polyunsaturated fat; 16 g carbohydrate; 1 g fiber; 14 g sugar; 181 mg phosphorus; 73 mg calcium; 2 mg iron; 126 mg sodium; 211 mg potassium; 695 IU vitamin A; 187 mg vitamin E; 3 mg vitamin C; 379 mg cholesterol

Spinach Quiche

This versatile dish can work for breakfast, lunch, or dinner.

8 slices low-sodium bacon

1 cup (160 g) chopped onion

4 eggs, beaten

1 cup (235 ml) light cream

1 cup (235 ml) skim milk

1 tablespoon flour

1/8 teaspoon nutmeg

12 ounces (340 g) frozen spinach, thawed and chopped

4 ounces (115 g) mushrooms, sliced

1 cup (115 g) shredded Monterey Jack cheese

1 cup (115 g) shredded Cheddar cheese

1 prepared piecrust

Cook together bacon and onion. Crumble bacon. Mix all ingredients together. Pour into piecrust in quiche-baking dish. Bake at 325°F (170°C, gas mark 3) for 50 minutes. Let stand 10 minutes before serving.

—Yield: 8 servings

NUTRITIONAL ANALYSIS

PER SERVING: 141 g water; 296 calories (65% from fat, 25% from protein, 11% from carb); 19 g protein; 22 g total fat; 12 g saturated fat; 7 g monounsaturated fat; 1 g polyunsaturated fat; 8 g carbohydrate; 2 g fiber; 2 g sugar; 338 mg phosphorus; 382 mg calcium; 2 mg iron; 379 mg sodium; 387 mg potassium; 5775 IU vitamin A; 174 mg vitamin E; 3 mg vitamin C; 177 mg cholesterol

Breakfast Wraps

For those days when you want a little something different for breakfast. This is similar to the breakfast burritos served at several fast food restaurants, but with a lot less fat.

1 medium potato

½ pound (225 g) Turkey Breakfast Sausage (see recipe page 12)

½ cup (80 g) onion, chopped

1 teaspoon (2.6 g) chili powder

¼ teaspoon (0.5 g) cayenne pepper

2 eggs, beaten

6 flour tortillas

½ cup (58 g) low fat Cheddar cheese, shredded

Boil or microwave potato until tender. Peel and cut into cubes. Brown sausage in a frying pan. Add chopped onion, chili powder, and cayenne pepper and cook for 10 minutes. Drain and discard any fat. Add potato and eggs. Stir until eggs are set. Divide mixture evenly among warmed tortillas, top with shredded cheese, and roll up tortillas to enclose mixture.

—Yield: 6 servings

NUTRITIONAL ANALYSIS

PER SERVING: 269 calories (36% from fat, 22% from protein, 42% from carbohydrate); 15 g protein; 11 g total fat; 4 g saturated fat; 3 g monounsaturated fat; 2 g polyunsaturated fat; 28 g carbohydrate; 2 g fiber; 2 g sugar; 211 mg phosphorus; 116 mg calcium; 2 mg iron; 524 mg sodium; 190 mg potassium; 254 IU vitamin A; 7 mg ATE vitamin E; 16 mg vitamin C; 95 mg cholesterol; 108 g water

Frittata

A frittata is an Italian-style omelet, with the filling mixed in with the eggs. It's cooked without turning and then the top set under the broiler. This version does not have any of the meat and potatoes that they often have, providing you with a filling weekend breakfast low in sodium, fat, and carbohydrates.

¼ cup (60 ml) olive oil

2 baking potatoes, peeled and thinly sliced

1 cup (160 g) thinly sliced onion

2 cups (226 g) thinly sliced zucchini

1 cup (150 g) red bell pepper, cut in ½-inch (1-cm) cubes

1 cup (150 g) green bell pepper, cut in ½-inch (1-cm) cubes

12 eggs

2 tablespoons chopped fresh parsley

Preheat oven to 450°F (230°C, gas mark 8). Pour oil into 12-inch (30-cm) square or round baking dish. Heat oil in oven for 5 minutes, then remove. Place potatoes and onion over bottom of dish and bake until potatoes are just tender, 20 minutes. Arrange zucchini slices over potatoes and onion, then sprinkle peppers over all. Beat eggs. Add chopped parsley to eggs. Pour eggs over vegetables. Bake until eggs are set and sides are "puffy," about 25 minutes. Top should be golden brown. Serve hot or at room temperature.

—Yield: 6 servings

NUTRITIONAL ANALYSIS

PER SERVING: 293 g water; 364 calories (50% from fat, 19% from protein, 31% from carb); 18 g protein; 20 g total fat; 5 g saturated fat; 11 g monounsaturated fat; 3 g polyunsaturated fat; 29 g carbohydrate; 5 g fiber; 5 g sugar; 320 mg phosphorus; 92 mg calcium; 4 mg iron; 172 mg sodium; 918 mg potassium; 1606 IU vitamin A; 156 mg vitamin E; 87 mg vitamin C; 474 mg cholesterol

Sausage Frittata

We like this for breakfast on those rare occasions when the entire family is around, but it also makes a good dinner with a salad and a slice of freshly baked bread.

4 eggs

¼ cup (60 ml) skim milk

8 ounces (225 g) Turkey Breakfast Sausage (see recipe page 12)

½ cup (75 g) green bell pepper, chopped

4 ounces (115 g) low fat Cheddar cheese, shredded

Preheat broiler. Combine eggs and milk in medium bowl; whisk until well blended. Set aside. Place a 12-inch (30-cm) broiler-proof nonstick skillet over medium-high heat until hot. Add sausage; cook and stir for 4 minutes or until no longer pink, breaking up sausage with spoon. Drain sausage on paper towels; set aside. Add pepper to same skillet; cook and stir for 2 minutes, or until crisp-tender. Return sausage to skillet. Add egg mixture; stir until blended. Cover; cook over medium-low heat for 10 minutes, or until eggs are almost set. Sprinkle cheese over frittata. Broil for 2 minutes, or until cheese is melted and eggs are set. Cut into wedges.

—Yield: 4 servings

NUTRITIONAL ANALYSIS

PER SERVING: 245 calories (54% from fat, 40% from protein, 6% from carbohydrate); 24 g protein; 14 g total fat; 6 g saturated fat; 4 g monounsaturated fat; 3 g polyunsaturated fat; 4 g carbohydrate; 0 g fiber; 1 g sugar; 339 mg phosphorus; 193 mg calcium; 2 mg iron; 626 mg sodium; 198 mg potassium; 385 IU vitamin A; 6 mg ATE vitamin E; 32 mg vitamin C; 241 mg cholesterol; 137 g water

Vegetable Frittata

This meatless version is packed with nutrient-dense veggies.

½ cup (75 g) red bell pepper, diced

½ cup (80 g) onion, chopped

1 cup (70 g) broccoli florets

8 ounces (225 g) mushrooms, sliced

1 cup (113 g) zucchini, sliced

6 eggs

1 tablespoon (0.4 g) dried parsley

¼ teaspoon (0.5 g) black pepper

2 ounces (55 g) Swiss cheese, shredded

Spray a large oven-proof skillet with nonstick vegetable oil spray. Stir-fry the red bell pepper, onions, and broccoli until crisp-tender. Add the mushrooms and zucchini and stir-fry for 1 to 2 minutes more. Stir together the eggs, parsley, and pepper, and pour over vegetable mixture, spreading to cover. Cover and cook over medium heat for 10 to 12 minutes, or until eggs are nearly set. Sprinkle cheese over the top. Place under the broiler until eggs are set and cheese is melted.

—Yield: 4 servings

NUTRITIONAL ANALYSIS

PER SERVING: 140 calories (26% from fat, 51% from protein, 22% from carbohydrate); 18 g protein; 4 g total fat; 1 g saturated fat; 1 g monounsaturated fat; 2 g polyunsaturated fat; 8 g carbohydrate; 2 g fiber; 4 g sugar; 283 mg phosphorus; 209 mg calcium; 3 mg iron; 216 mg sodium; 321 mg potassium; 1618 IU vitamin A; 6 mg ATE vitamin E; 50 mg vitamin C; 306 mg cholesterol; 220 g water

Pasta Frittata

This makes a wonderful meatless meal. It's kind of like macaroni and cheese, only a little fancier.

2 tablespoons (30 ml) olive oil

1 cup (150 g) red bell pepper, diced

1 cup (160 g) onion, chopped

2 cups (100 g) cooked pasta

¼ cup (25 g) grated Parmesan

4 eggs

Heat a 10-inch (25-cm) nonstick skillet that is broiler safe. When the pan is hot, add the oil, then sauté red bell pepper and onion for 2 to 3 minutes, stirring frequently. Add the pasta to the pan, mixing well. When ingredients are thoroughly combined, press down on pasta with spatula to flatten it against the bottom of the pan. Let it cook a few minutes more. Whisk grated Parmesan into the eggs. Pour egg mixture over the top of the pasta, making sure the eggs spread evenly. Gently lift the edges of the pasta to let egg flow underneath and completely coat the pasta. Let the eggs cook for 6 to 9 minutes. Slide the pan into a preheated broiler and finish cooking until eggs are set.

—Yield: 4 servings

NUTRITIONAL ANALYSIS

PER SERVING: 360 calories (29% from fat, 20% from protein, 51% from carbohydrate); 18 g protein; 12 g total fat; 3 g saturated fat; 6 g monounsaturated fat; 2 g polyunsaturated fat; 46 g carbohydrate; 3 g fiber; 5 g sugar; 242 mg phosphorus; 125 mg calcium; 2 mg iron; 213 mg sodium; 169 mg potassium; 1421 IU vitamin A; 7 mg ATE vitamin E; 51 mg vitamin C; 206 mg cholesterol; 128 g water

Easy Breakfast Strata

This is another great fix-ahead breakfast. We usually have some variation of this on special holidays when there is a lot to do in the morning, but we want a special family breakfast.

1 pound (455 g) sausage

8 eggs

10 slices whole wheat bread, cubed

3 cups (710 g) skim milk

2 cups (225 g) shredded Cheddar cheese

10 ounces (280 g) frozen chopped broccoli, thawed

2 tablespoons (28 g) unsalted butter, melted

2 tablespoons (16 g) flour

1 tablespoon dry mustard

2 teaspoons basil

In large skillet, brown sausage, drain. In large bowl, beat eggs. Add remaining ingredients and mix well. Spoon into 13 × 9-inch (33 × 23-cm) baking pan coated with nonstick vegetable oil spray. Cover and refrigerate 8 hours or overnight. Preheat oven to 350°F (180°C, gas mark 4). Bake 60 to 70 minutes or until knife inserted near center comes out clean.

—Yield: 8 servings

NUTRITIONAL ANALYSIS

PER SERVING: 181 g water; 379 calories (49% from fat, 25% from protein, 26% from carb); 24 g protein; 21 g total fat; 11 g saturated fat; 6 g monounsaturated fat; 2 g polyunsaturated fat; 24 g carbohydrate; 2 g fiber; 3 g sugar; 449 mg phosphorus; 462 mg calcium; 3 mg iron; 593 mg sodium; 396 mg potassium; 1293 IU vitamin A; 243 mg vitamin E; 15 mg vitamin C; 281 mg cholesterol

Breakfast Potatoes

Sometimes called O'Brien potatoes, this is a traditional breakfast kind of dish, but it works just as well as a side dish at dinner.

4 potatoes

1 cup (160 g) onion, chopped

¼ cup (37 g) green bell peppers, chopped

1 tablespoon (14 g) unsalted butter

½ teaspoon (1 g) freshly ground black pepper

Boil or microwave potatoes until almost cooked through. Drain. Coarsely chop potatoes and combine with onion and green bell pepper. Melt butter in a heavy skillet. Add potato mixture. Sprinkle black pepper over the top. Fry until browned, turning frequently.

—Yield: 6 servings

NUTRITIONAL ANALYSIS

PER SERVING: 201 calories (10% from fat, 10% from protein, 81% from carbohydrate); 5 g protein; 2 g total fat; 1 g saturated fat; 1 g monounsaturated fat; 0 g polyunsaturated fat; 42 g carbohydrate; 5 g fiber; 4 g sugar; 161 mg phosphorus; 34 mg calcium; 2 mg iron; 37 mg sodium; 1174 mg potassium; 141 IU vitamin A; 23 mg ATE vitamin E; 28 mg vitamin C; 5 mg cholesterol; 229 g water

Latkes

These are delicious any time of day.

4 potatoes

1 tablespoon finely chopped onion

1 egg

½ cup (60 g) bread crumbs

2 tablespoons (28 ml) canola oil

Peel and grate potatoes. Squeeze in a kitchen towel to remove excess moisture. Mix all ingredients together. Heat oil in heavy skillet. Drop batter onto hot skillet in ¼-cup measures and flatten with fork into pancakes. Cook until browned. Turn over and finish cooking.

—Yield: 4 servings

NUTRITIONAL ANALYSIS

PER SERVING: 11 g water; 139 calories (61% from fat, 10% from protein, 29% from carb); 3 g protein; 9 g total fat; 1 g saturated fat; 5 g monounsaturated fat; 3 g polyunsaturated fat; 10 g carbohydrate; 1 g fiber; 1 g sugar; 47 mg phosphorus; 32 mg calcium; 1 mg iron; 42 mg sodium; 47 mg potassium; 84 IU vitamin A; 22 mg vitamin E; 0 mg vitamin C; 53 mg cholesterol

TIP

Serve with butter, sour cream, or applesauce.

Zucchini Pancakes

These make a great side dish with almost any kind of meat, but I have to admit to having them for breakfast a time or two also. Maybe that's just because I get desperate when the garden is really producing zucchini.

4 cups (452 g) shredded zucchini

4 eggs

½ cup (62 g) flour

⅛ teaspoon black pepper

¼ teaspoon garlic powder

¼ cup chopped fresh parsley

3 tablespoons (45 ml) canola oil

Wash zucchini and trim the ends. Grate or grind into a bowl. Squeeze dry. In a bowl, combine the zucchini and all the other ingredients except the oil. Heat the oil in a heavy skillet over medium heat. Drop zucchini mixture by heaping table-spoons into hot oil. Flatten them a little, fry until golden brown on bottom. Turn and brown second side. Drain on paper towels. (If mixture is thin, add more flour.)

—Yield: 6 servings

NUTRITIONAL ANALYSIS

PER SERVING: 110 g water; 168 calories (58% from fat, 16% from protein, 26% from carb); 7 g protein; 11 g total fat; 2 g saturated fat; 6 g monounsaturated fat; 3 g polyunsaturated fat; 11 g carbohydrate; 1 g fiber; 2 g sugar; 116 mg phosphorus; 37 mg calcium; 2 mg iron; 62 mg sodium; 293 mg potassium; 560 IU vitamin A; 52 mg vitamin E; 17 mg vitamin C; 158 mg cholesterol

Whole Wheat Buttermilk Pancakes

A great tasty, old-fashioned pancake. Reminds me of the kind of breakfasts my grandmother made.

1 cup (120 g) whole wheat pastry flour

½ teaspoon baking soda

¼ teaspoon cinnamon

1¼ cups (295 ml) buttermilk

2 eggs

3 tablespoons (45 ml) canola oil

Blend dry ingredients. Blend wet ingredients except oil. Mix the two mixtures together. Will be slightly lumpy. Heat oil in cast-iron skillet. Pour one-quarter of the batter into pan. When pancake bubbles, turn, cook 1 to 2 minutes.

—Yield: 4 servings

NUTRITIONAL ANALYSIS

PER SERVING: 93 g water; 266 calories (48% from fat, 15% from protein, 38% from carb); 10 g protein; 15 g total fat; 2 g saturated fat; 8 g monounsaturated fat; 4 g polyunsaturated fat; 26 g carbohydrate; 4 g fiber; 4 g sugar; 226 mg phosphorus; 116 mg calcium; 2 mg iron; 121 mg sodium; 275 mg potassium; 159 IU vitamin A; 44 mg vitamin E; 1 mg vitamin C; 122 mg cholesterol

Cornmeal Pancakes

Another of those old-fashioned breakfast meals. Do you suppose that I keep saying that because people ate healthier food in the good old days?

1 cup (235 ml) boiling water

¾ cup (105 g) cornmeal

1¼ cups (295 ml) buttermilk

2 eggs

1 cup (120 g) whole wheat pastry flour

1 tablespoon baking powder

¼ teaspoon baking soda

¼ cup (60 ml) canola oil

Pour water over cornmeal, stir until thick. Add buttermilk; beat in eggs. Mix flour, baking powder, and baking soda. Add to cornmeal mixture. Stir in canola oil. Bake on hot griddle.

—Yield: 7 servings

NUTRITIONAL ANALYSIS

PER SERVING: 89 g water; 233 calories (40% from fat, 12% from protein, 48% from carb); 7 g protein; 11 g total fat; 1 g saturated fat; 6 g monounsaturated fat; 3 g polyunsaturated fat; 29 g carbohydrate; 3 g fiber; 3 g sugar; 190 mg phosphorus; 182 mg calcium; 2 mg iron; 280 mg sodium; 184 mg potassium; 127 IU vitamin A; 25 mg vitamin E; 0 mg vitamin C; 69 mg cholesterol

Multigrain Pancakes

These are great pancakes, thicker and full of much more flavor than regular ones.

1½ cups (180 g) whole wheat pastry flour

¼ cup (35 g) cornmeal

¼ cup (20 g) rolled oats

2 tablespoons oat bran

2 tablespoons wheat germ

2 tablespoons (18 g) toasted wheat cereal, such as Wheatena

1 teaspoon baking soda

½ teaspoon baking powder

1 teaspoon vanilla extract

1½ cups (355 g) skim milk

2 egg whites

Mix all dry ingredients. Add milk and vanilla to make batter. Thicker batter makes thicker pancakes. Set aside to rest for a half an hour. Beat egg whites until stiff peaks form. Gently fold into batter after it has rested. Spoon onto moderate griddle and cook until bubbles break. Turn and cook until done. Bake more slowly than with regular pancakes because of the heavy batter.

—Yield: 6 servings

NUTRITIONAL ANALYSIS

PER SERVING: 70 g water; 195 calories (6% from fat, 20% from protein, 74% from carb); 10 g protein; 1 g total fat; 0 g saturated fat; 0 g monounsaturated fat; 1 g polyunsaturated fat; 37 g carbohydrate; 5 g fiber; 1 g sugar; 249 mg phosphorus; 127 mg calcium; 2 mg iron; 101 mg sodium; 316 mg potassium; 154 IU vitamin A; 40 mg vitamin E; 1 mg vitamin C; 1 mg cholesterol

Oat Bran Pancakes

Why should breakfast be boring or unhealthy? Try these pancakes and you will not be bored.

1 cup (100 g) oat bran

½ cup (60 g) flour

2 teaspoons (9 g) sugar

2 teaspoons (9.2 g) baking powder

1 cup (235 ml) skim milk

1 tablespoon (15 ml) canola oil

1 egg white

Heat griddle over medium-high heat. Spray lightly with nonstick vegetable oil spray. Stir first 4 ingredients together. Combine remaining ingredients, add to the oat bran mixture, and mix well. Spoon batter onto griddle and cook until bubbles form on the tops. Turn over and cook until done.

—Yield: 4 servings

NUTRITIONAL ANALYSIS

PER SERVING: 171 calories (24% from fat, 15% from protein, 61% from carbohydrate); 6 g protein; 5 g total fat; 1 g saturated fat; 2 g monounsaturated fat; 1 g polyunsaturated fat; 27 g carbohydrate; 2 g fiber; 4 g sugar; 205 mg phosphorus; 251 mg calcium; 5 mg iron; 336 mg sodium; 105 mg potassium; 263 IU vitamin A; 71 mg ATE vitamin E; 2 mg vitamin C; 1 mg cholesterol; 64 g water

Breakfast Couscous

We usually think of couscous as a dinner item, perhaps with curry or some other savory topping. But this sweeter version makes a great breakfast.

¼ cup (55 g) unsalted butter, divided

¼ teaspoon cinnamon

¼ teaspoon cardamom

2¼ cups (535 ml) orange juice

½ cup (75 g) currants

1½ cups (263 g) whole wheat couscous

¼ cup (35 g) chopped cashews

Melt 2 tablespoons butter, add spices, and cook 2 minutes. Add juice and currants. Bring to a boil. Mix in couscous and add remaining butter. Cover. Remove from heat and let stand 5 minutes. Fluff with fork and put in bowl. Add cashews. Serve.

—Yield: 4 servings

NUTRITIONAL ANALYSIS

PER SERVING: 144 g water; 466 calories (31% from fat, 9% from protein, 59% from carb); 11 g protein; 16 g total fat; 8 g saturated fat; 5 g monounsaturated fat; 1 g polyunsaturated fat; 69 g carbohydrate; 4 g fiber; 0 g sugar; 180 mg phosphorus; 47 mg calcium; 2 mg iron; 11 mg sodium; 473 mg potassium; 496 IU vitamin A; 95 mg vitamin E; 71 mg vitamin C; 31 mg cholesterol

Banana-Peach-Blueberry Smoothie

Smoothies make a quick and easy breakfast, and they are packed with nutrition. The fiber and protein will help to keep you from being hungry as the morning goes on.

2 cups (490 g) peach low-fat yogurt

1 cup (145 g) blueberries

2 cups (300 g) sliced banana

Mix all ingredients in a blender and serve.

—Yield: 2 servings

NUTRITIONAL ANALYSIS

PER SERVING: 415 g water; 485 calories (7% from fat, 10% from protein, 83% from carb); 13 g protein; 4 g total fat; 2 g saturated fat; 1 g monounsaturated fat; 0 g polyunsaturated fat; 108 g carbohydrate; 8 g fiber; 81 g sugar; 325 mg phosphorus; 354 mg calcium; 1 mg iron; 133 mg sodium; 1296 mg potassium; 282 IU vitamin A; 27 mg vitamin E; 28 mg vitamin C; 12 mg cholesterol

Chocolate-Raspberry Smoothie

How could anyone not like the taste of chocolate and raspberries for breakfast?

1 cup (235 ml) skim milk

½ cup (141 g) chocolate syrup

3 cups (750 g) frozen raspberries

Pour the milk and chocolate syrup into a blender. Slowly add the raspberries, 1 cup at a time, and blend for 15 to 30 seconds after adding each cup. Do not overmix, as this will thin the drink down. Serve immediately.

—Yield: 2 servings

NUTRITIONAL ANALYSIS

PER SERVING: 268 g water; 146 calories (9% from fat, 18% from protein, 73% from carb); 7 g protein; 2 g total fat; 0 g saturated fat; 0 g monounsaturated fat; 1 g polyunsaturated fat; 29 g carbohydrate; 12 g fiber; 8 g sugar; 191 mg phosphorus; 222 mg calcium; 1 mg iron; 74 mg sodium; 502 mg potassium; 311 IU vitamin A; 75 mg vitamin E; 50 mg vitamin C; 2 mg cholesterol

TIP

Substitute other frozen fruit for the raspberries (strawberry, banana, etc.).

Raspberry-Banana Smoothie

Another great-tasting smoothie. The raspberries give this one a special boost in fiber.

2 cups (250 g) fresh raspberries

2 cups (300 g) sliced banana

2 cups (475 ml) skim milk

¼ cup (60 g) low-fat vanilla yogurt

1 tablespoon (20 g) honey

Combine all ingredients in a blender or food processor and process until smooth.

—Yield: 2 servings

NUTRITIONAL ANALYSIS

PER SERVING: 496 g water; 397 calories (5% from fat, 13% from protein, 83% from carb); 14 g protein; 2 g total fat; 1 g saturated fat; 0 g monounsaturated fat; 1 g polyunsaturated fat; 88 g carbohydrate; 14 g fiber; 42 g sugar; 361 mg phosphorus; 394 mg calcium; 2 mg iron; 149 mg sodium; 1444 mg potassium; 684 IU vitamin A; 150 mg vitamin E; 55 mg vitamin C; 5 mg cholesterol

Bananaberry Breakfast Shake

So why not a shake for breakfast? Besides, it's really just a smoothie.

1 cup (145 g) strawberries

1 cup (150 g) sliced banana

1½ cups (355 ml) skim milk

1 cup (230 g) vanilla yogurt

1 tablespoon (20 g) honey

Place all ingredients in a blender. Process until well blended.

—Yield: 2 servings

NUTRITIONAL ANALYSIS

PER SERVING: 417 g water; 336 calories (7% from fat, 17% from protein, 76% from carb); 15 g protein; 3 g total fat; 1 g saturated fat; 1 g monounsaturated fat; 0 g polyunsaturated fat; 67 g carbohydrate; 4 g fiber; 43 g sugar; 415 mg phosphorus; 492 mg calcium; 1 mg iron; 192 mg sodium; 1129 mg potassium; 508 IU vitamin A; 127 mg vitamin E; 58 mg vitamin C; 10 mg cholesterol

Oat Bran–Berry Smoothie

Adding oat bran to a smoothie is probably not something you'd thought about doing. But it really works, adding flavor, texture, and lots of good nutrition.

1 cup (235 ml) cranberry juice

1 cup (255 g) strawberries, frozen

8 ounces (225 g) vanilla yogurt

2/3 cup (66 g) oat bran

1 cup ice cubes

Place all ingredients except ice in blender. Cover. Blend on high about 2 minutes or until smooth. Gradually add ice, blending on high until smooth. Serve immediately.

—Yield: 2 servings

NUTRITIONAL ANALYSIS

PER SERVING: 267 g water; 246 calories (9% from fat, 13% from protein, 79% from carb); 8 g protein; 2 g total fat; 1 g saturated fat; 1 g monounsaturated fat; 0 g polyunsaturated fat; 50 g carbohydrate; 3 g fiber; 22 g sugar; 251 mg phosphorus; 241 mg calcium; 5 mg iron; 135 mg sodium; 449 mg potassium; 217 IU vitamin A; 58 mg vitamin E; 60 mg vitamin C; 6 mg cholesterol

Cranberry Orange Smoothie

If you have a little cranberry sauce left, this is a tasty way to use it.

½ cup (135 g) cranberry sauce

½ cup (120 ml) orange juice

1 cup (230 g) plain nonfat yogurt

1 cup (225 g) banana, sliced

½ cup (120 ml) skim milk

Combine all ingredients in a blender and process until smooth.

—Yield: 2 servings

NUTRITIONAL ANALYSIS

PER SERVING: 326 calories (3% from fat, 13% from protein, 84% from carbohydrate); 11 g protein; 1 g total fat; 0 g saturated fat; 0 g monounsaturated fat; 0 g polyunsaturated fat; 72 g carbohydrate; 4 g fiber; 49 g sugar; 297 mg phosphorus; 346 mg calcium; 1 mg iron; 152 mg sodium; 963 mg potassium; 283 IU vitamin A; 40 mg ATE vitamin E; 33 mg vitamin C; 4 mg cholesterol; 341 g water

Banana Melon Smoothies

I like smoothies for a quick breakfast, but I find that I'm often hungry before noon. Adding some extra protein with the tofu seems to help fill me up longer.

6 ounces (170 g) soft tofu

1 banana

1 cup (155 g) cantaloupe

½ cup (120 ml) skim milk

½ cup (120 ml) apple juice

Place all ingredients in a blender and process until smooth.

—Yield: 2 servings

NUTRITIONAL ANALYSIS

PER SERVING: 230 calories (11% from fat, 14% from protein, 75% from carbohydrate); 9 g protein; 3 g total fat; 1 g saturated fat; 1 g monounsaturated fat; 1 g polyunsaturated fat; 46 g carbohydrate; 4 g fiber; 28 g sugar; 164 mg phosphorus; 131 mg calcium; 1 mg iron; 60 mg sodium; 979 mg potassium; 3190 IU vitamin A; 38 mg ATE vitamin E; 43 mg vitamin C; 1 mg cholesterol; 347 g water

CHAPTER 2

Snacks and Nibbles

Ah, snacks. This chapter contains recipes that range from traditional appetizers like chicken wings and meatballs though a wide selection of finger food, healthy crispy dippers like crackers and low fat, low sodium versions of tortilla and potato chips to a wide variety of nut and snack mixes. So nibble away and don't feel guilty about it.

Boneless Buffalo Wings

Chicken wings tend to be fairly high in saturated fat, since it isn't easy to avoid eating the skin, where most of it is. But that doesn't mean you have to do without that Buffalo wing taste at your party. Make boneless wings from chicken breasts, cooking them in the oven instead of frying them.

6 boneless, skinless chicken breasts

3 tablespoons (45 ml) hot pepper sauce

2 tablespoons (30 ml) white vinegar

Preheat oven to 350°F (180°C, or gas mark 4). Cut the breasts into strips, about eight per breast. Place in roasting pan sprayed with nonstick vegetable oil spray and roast for 20 minutes, or until done. Mix hot pepper sauce and white vinegar. Place chicken pieces in a large bowl with a tight-sealing cover. Pour vinegar mixture over the pieces and shake to coat. Remove, allowing extra sauce to drain.

—Yield: 16 servings

NUTRITIONAL ANALYSIS

PER SERVING: 30 calories (11% from fat, 88% from protein, 1% from carbohydrate); 6 g protein; 0 g total fat; 0 g saturated fat; 0 g monounsaturated fat; 0 g polyunsaturated fat; 0 g carbohydrate; 0 g fiber; 0 g sugar; 53 mg phosphorus; 3 mg calcium; 0 mg iron; 34 mg sodium; 73 mg potassium; 49 IU vitamin A; 2 mg ATE vitamin E; 0 mg vitamin C; 15 mg cholesterol; 24 g water

Chicken Wings Nibblers

These can be used as an appetizer or the basis of a meal.

20 chicken wings

2 eggs

2 tablespoons (30 ml) skim milk

1½ cups (190 g) Reduced-Fat Whole Wheat Biscuit Mix (see recipe page 139)

½ cup (60 g) sesame seeds

2 teaspoons (5 g) paprika

1½ teaspoons (4.5 g) dry mustard

Preheat oven to 425°F (220°C, or gas mark 7). Separate chicken wings at joints; discard tips. Spray two rectangular 9 × 13-inch (23 × 33-cm) pans with nonstick vegetable oil spray. Beat eggs and milk with fork in bowl. Mix biscuit mix, sesame seeds, paprika, and mustard in a second bowl. Soak chicken in egg mixture and then coat with sesame seed mixture. Arrange close together in baking pans. Bake uncovered for 35 to 40 minutes, or until brown and crisp.

—Yield: 10 servings

NUTRITIONAL ANALYSIS

PER SERVING: 139 calories (23% from fat, 33% from protein, 44% from carbohydrate); 11 g protein; 4 g total fat; 1 g saturated fat; 1 g monounsaturated fat; 1 g polyunsaturated fat; 15 g carbohydrate; 1 g fiber; 0 g sugar; 171 mg phosphorus; 70 mg calcium; 2 mg iron; 69 mg sodium; 75 mg potassium; 395 IU vitamin A; 2 mg ATE vitamin E; 1 mg vitamin C; 60 mg cholesterol; 41 g water

Taco Chicken Wings

You can use these taco-flavored wings either as appetizers or the main dish. This particular dish seems to be very popular with young people.

12 chicken wings

½ cup (62 g) flour

2 tablespoons (15 g) chili powder

1 teaspoon (2.5 g) cumin

1 teaspoon (1 g) dried oregano

½ teaspoon (1.5 g) onion powder

¼ teaspoon (0.8 g) garlic powder

⅛ teaspoon (0.3 g) cayenne pepper

1 egg

1 cup (28 g) corn chips, crushed

Preheat oven to 350°F (180°C, or gas mark 4). Cut wings into sections, discarding the tips. Combine flour and next 6 ingredients (through cayenne pepper) in a plastic bag. Pour egg into a shallow dish. Spread crushed corn chips in another shallow dish. Shake a few wing sections at a time in the flour mixture, then roll in the egg, then the corn chips. Place in a 9 × 13-inch (23 × 33-cm) pan. Bake for 45 minutes, or until done.

—Yield: 6 servings

NUTRITIONAL ANALYSIS

PER SERVING: 198 calories (34% from fat, 23% from protein, 43% from carbohydrate); 11 g protein; 8 g total fat; 1 g saturated fat; 2 g monounsaturated fat; 3 g polyunsaturated fat; 22 g carbohydrate; 2 g fiber; 1 g sugar; 117 mg phosphorus; 56 mg calcium; 2 mg iron; 189 mg sodium; 75 mg potassium; 830 IU vitamin A; 6 mg ATE vitamin E; 2 mg vitamin C; 49 mg cholesterol; 36 g water

Steak Bites

These little steak bites will please the toughest one in your party crowd.

½ cup (120 ml) Reduced Sodium Soy Sauce (see recipe page 133)

6 tablespoons (78 g) sugar

3 tablespoons (45 ml) sesame oil

2 pounds (1 kg) round steak, cubed

½ cup (50 g) chopped scallions

2 tablespoons (30 ml) white wine

Combine soy sauce, sugar, and sesame oil in a shallow dish. Add steak, and refrigerate for 4 hours. Remove steak from marinade, reserving marinade. Place a large skillet over medium-high heat, and cook steak to desired doneness. Pour the reserved marinade into a medium saucepan and place over medium-high heat. Bring to a boil and cook for 5 minutes. Add cooked steak, scallions, and wine to the boiling marinade. Transfer the entire contents of the saucepan to a large bowl, and serve hot.

—Yield: 16 servings

NUTRITIONAL ANALYSIS

PER SERVING: 141 calories (14% from fat, 20% from protein, 66% from carbohydrate); 16 g protein; 5 g total fat; 1 g saturated fat; 2 g monounsaturated fat; 2 g polyunsaturated fat; 54 g carbohydrate; 0 g fiber; 6 g sugar; 111 mg phosphorus; 10 mg calcium; 1 mg iron; 74 mg sodium; 163 mg potassium; 34 IU vitamin A; 0 mg ATE vitamin E; 1 mg vitamin C; 33 mg cholesterol, 52 g water

Turkey Cocktail Meatballs

These tasty little meatballs can also be used as the basis of a dinner, served over rice with a vegetable. When we've made them for a get-together, they are always one of the first items to disappear.

1 pound (455 g) ground turkey breast

1 egg

¾ cup (50 g) saltine crackers, crushed

4 ounces part-skim shredded mozzarella

¼ cup (40 g) chopped onion

½ teaspoon (0.9 g) ground ginger

6 tablespoons (90 g) Dijon mustard, divided

1¼ cups (295 ml) unsweetened pineapple juice

¼ cup (37 g) chopped green bell pepper

2 tablespoons (30 ml) honey

1 tablespoon (8 g) cornstarch

¼ teaspoon (0.7 g) onion powder

Preheat oven to 350°F (180°C, or gas mark 4). In a bowl, combine turkey, egg, cracker crumbs, mozzarella, onion, ginger, and 3 tablespoons (45 g) mustard. Form into 30 balls, 1 inch (2.5 cm) each. Spray a 9 × 13-inch (23 × 33-cm) baking dish with nonstick vegetable oil spray. Place meatballs in dish. Bake, uncovered, for 20 to 25 minutes, or until cooked through. In a saucepan, combine pineapple juice, green pepper, honey, cornstarch, onion powder, and remaining mustard. Bring to a boil, stirring constantly. Cook and stir until thickened. Brush meatballs with about ¼ cup (60 ml) sauce and return to the oven for 10 minutes. Serve remaining sauce as a dip for meatballs.

—Yield: 15 servings

NUTRITIONAL ANALYSIS

PER SERVING: 100 calories (23% from fat, 41% from protein, 36% from carbohydrate); 10 g protein; 2 g total fat; 1 g saturated fat; 1 g monounsaturated fat; 0 g polyunsaturated fat; 9 g carbohydrate; 0 g fiber; 5 g sugar; 116 mg phosphorus; 75 mg calcium; 1 mg iron; 181 mg sodium; 67 mg potassium; 66 IU vitamin A; 9 mg ATE vitamin E; 4 mg vitamin C; 64 mg cholesterol; 58 g water

Asian Tuna Bites

Tasty little tuna bites are sure to be a hit with everyone.

1 pound tuna steaks, cut in 1" cubes

¼ cup sesame seeds

¼ teaspoon black pepper

Spray tuna with non-stick cooking spray. Sprinkle with sesame seeds and pepper. In a large non-stick skillet brown on all sides until slightly pink in the center. Thread on cocktail toothpicks to serve.

—Yield: 10 servings

NUTRITIONAL ANALYSIS

PER SERVING: 86 calories (43% from fat, 53% from protein , 4% from carb); 11 g protein ; 4 g total fat; 1 g saturated fat; 1 g monounsaturated fat; 1 g polyun-saturated fat; 1 g carb; 0 g fiber; 0 g sugar; 138 mg phosphorus; 39 mg calcium; 18 mg sodium; 132 mg potassium; 991 IU vitamin A; 297 mg ATE vitamin E; 0 mg vitamin C; 17 mg cholesterol

Quiche Nibblers

Low fat, crustless quiche bites that are sure to be a hit, whether they're just for your family or for guests. No one will ever know that we've taken out the fat, the cholesterol, and the calories.

1 tablespoon (15 ml) olive oil

½ cup (75 g) red bell pepper, finely chopped

¼ cup (25 g) scallions, finely chopped

3 eggs

2 tablespoons (30 ml) skim milk

2 ounces (55 g) low fat Cheddar cheese, shredded

⅛ teaspoon (0.3 g) ground black pepper

Preheat oven to 425°F (220°C, or gas mark 7). Grease 24 mini-muffin cups with nonstick vegetable oil spray. In a small saucepan, heat olive oil over moderate heat. Add red bell pepper and scallions; sauté for 5 minutes, or until soft. Remove the pan from the heat and let the mixture cool slightly. In a medium bowl, combine eggs, milk, cheese, and pepper. Stir in the bell pepper mixture. Spoon about 1 tablespoon of the mixture into each muffin cup. Bake for 8 to 10 minutes, or until the centers are set. Let cool for 1 minute. Using a knife, loosen the quiches around the edges and remove.

—Yield: 12 servings

NUTRITIONAL ANALYSIS

PER SERVING: 35 calories (52% from fat, 38% from protein, 10% from carbohydrate); 3 g protein; 2 g total fat; 0 g saturated fat; 1 g monounsaturated fat; 0 g polyunsaturated fat; 1 g carbohydrate; 0 g fiber; 0 g sugar; 47 mg phosphorus; 34 mg calcium; 0 mg iron; 59 mg sodium; 29 mg potassium; 287 IU vitamin A; 4 mg ATE vitamin E; 8 mg vitamin C; 1 mg cholesterol; 76 g water

Antipasto on a Skewer

This is handy finger food for your next outdoor meal, much easier to carry around than a plate from a typical antipasto tray.

½ teaspoon minced garlic

1 teaspoon black pepper

1 teaspoon Italian seasoning

1 teaspoon dry mustard

½ teaspoon crushed oregano

⅓ cup (78 ml) red wine vinegar

1 cup (235 ml) olive oil

8 ounces (225 g) mozzarella cheese, cut in ½ × ¼ × 2-inch (1 × .5 × 5-cm) sticks

12 slices salami

24 cherry tomatoes

24 black olives

12 mushrooms

10 ounces (283 g) artichoke hearts, cooked

In a tight-sealing container, combine seasonings and vinegar; shake well. Add oil and shake again for about 30 seconds. Pour marinade in a 13 × 9 × 2-inch (33 × 23 × 5-cm) baking dish. Wrap each cheese stick in one slice of salami. On each of 12 skewers, thread tomato, olive, mushroom, salami and cheese, artichoke heart, olive, and tomato. Place skewers in marinade. Marinate in refrigerator at least 24 hours, turning several times to coat all sides.

—Yield: 12 servings

NUTRITIONAL ANALYSIS

PER SERVING: 72 g water; 341 calories (78% from fat, 15% from protein, 7% from carb); 13 g protein; 30 g total fat; 8 g saturated fat; 19 g monounsaturated fat; 3 g polyunsaturated fat; 6 g carbohydrate; 2 g fiber; 1 g sugar; 168 mg phosphorus; 169 mg calcium; 1 mg iron; 742 mg sodium; 317 mg potassium; 403 IU vitamin A; 24 mg vitamin E; 9 mg vitamin C; 38 mg cholesterol

Mexican Pinwheels

These make a great snack or lunch. You can also slice them about ¾ inch (2 cm) thick and serve as an appetizer.

1 avocado, chopped

3 ounces (85 g) cream cheese, softened

6 whole wheat tortillas, 6 inch (15 cm)

4 ounces (113 g) shredded Monterey Jack cheese

1 ounce (28 g) leaf lettuce

½ cup (17 g) alfalfa sprouts

½ cup (130 g) salsa

Combine avocado and cream cheese; blend dip. Spread each tortilla evenly with avocado mixture to within ½ inch (1 cm) of edge. Arrange cheese, lettuce, and sprouts over avocado mixture. Spoon on salsa. Roll up each tortilla; cut in half; secure with toothpicks. Serve immediately or wrap in plastic wrap and refrigerate.

—Yield: 6 servings

NUTRITIONAL ANALYSIS

PER SERVING: 67 g water; 259 calories (57% from fat, 14% from protein, 30% from carb); 9 g protein; 17 g total fat; 8 g saturated fat; 6 g monounsaturated fat; 1 g polyunsaturated fat; 19 g carbohydrate; 3 g fiber; 1 g sugar; 158 mg phosphorus; 203 mg calcium; 2 mg iron; 388 mg sodium; 269 mg potassium; 787 IU vitamin A; 87 mg vitamin E; 3 mg vitamin C; 32 mg cholesterol

Tortilla Roll-Ups

Tasty little tortilla snacks, with just enough heat to be interesting.

8 whole wheat tortillas

8 ounces (225 g) cream cheese, softened

4 ounces (115 g) black olives, chopped

4 ounces (115 g) diced green chiles

¼ teaspoon Tabasco sauce

Cream together cream cheese, olives, chiles, and Tabasco sauce. Spread approximately 2 tablespoons onto a tortilla, roll jelly-roll fashion, roll in plastic wrap, and chill. Before serving cut into ⅜-inch-wide (1-cm) pieces.

—Yield: 16 servings

NUTRITIONAL ANALYSIS

PER SERVING: 25 g water; 105 calories (59% from fat, 9% from protein, 32% from carb); 2 g protein; 7 g total fat; 3 g saturated fat; 3 g monounsaturated fat; 0 g polyunsaturated fat; 9 g carbohydrate; 2 g fiber; 0 g sugar; 34 mg phosphorus; 37 mg calcium; 1 mg iron; 200 mg sodium; 41 mg potassium; 221 IU vitamin A; 51 mg vitamin E; 0 mg vitamin C; 16 mg cholesterol

Black Bean Tortilla Pinwheels

While intended as an appetizer, you could make a meal of this by not cutting it into slices.

8 ounces (225 g) cream cheese, softened

1 cup (230 g) sour cream

1 cup (115 g) shredded Monterey Jack cheese

¼ cup (25 g) pimento-stuffed olives

¼ cup (40 g) chopped red onion

⅛ teaspoon garlic powder

2 cups (344 g) cooked black beans, drained

6 whole wheat tortillas

Combine cream cheese and sour cream; mix until well blended. Stir in Monterey Jack cheese, olives, onion, and garlic powder. Chill 2 hours. Spread thin layer of cream cheese mixture on each tortilla. Puree beans in food processor or blender. Starting in middle of tortilla, spread a layer covering half of tortilla with beans. Roll up tortilla tightly, starting with end that has the beans. Chill. Cut into ¾-inch (2-cm) slices. Serve with salsa.

—Yield: 20 servings

NUTRITIONAL ANALYSIS

PER SERVING: 36 g water; 134 calories (56% from fat, 15% from protein, 29% from carb); 5 g protein; 8 g total fat; 5 g saturated fat; 3 g monounsaturated fat; 0 g polyunsaturated fat; 10 g carbohydrate; 2 g fiber; 0 g sugar; 89 mg phosphorus; 89 mg calcium; 1 mg iron; 146 mg sodium; 113 mg potassium; 256 IU vitamin A; 65 mg vitamin E; 0 mg vitamin C; 23 mg cholesterol

New York Goodwich Roll-Ups

Wherever you are and whatever you call it, it's tasty and filling.

½ cup (80 g) sliced onion

2 teaspoons (10 ml) olive oil

1 teaspoon (5 ml) barbecue sauce

2 whole wheat tortillas

1 tablespoon mayonnaise

1 cup (71 g) broccoli, cut in florets and steamed

½ cup (50 g) cauliflower, crumbled and steamed

2 slices dill pickle

2 tablespoons grated carrot

2 tablespoons grated red cabbage

2 tablespoons grated yellow squash

½ cup (28 g) shredded lettuce

½ cup (17 g) alfalfa sprouts

2 slices avocado

Sauté onion in oil until it begins to soften. Add barbecue sauce and sauté until tender. In hot dry skillet, heat tortillas, turning from one side to the other until soft but not crisp. Place on large sheet of plastic wrap. Spread tortillas with mayonnaise. Add broccoli in a line down center. Add cauliflower, then pickle, grated vegetables and a line of barbecued onions. Top with lettuce, sprouts, and avocado. Roll, crepe style, around vegetables. Wrap tightly until ready to serve.

—Yield: 2 servings

NUTRITIONAL ANALYSIS

PER SERVING: 258 g water; 462 calories (62% from fat, 7% from protein, 31% from carb); 8 g protein; 34 g total fat; 5 g saturated fat; 19 g monounsaturated fat; 7 g polyunsaturated fat; 38 g carbohydrate; 14 g fiber; 6 g sugar; 181 mg phosphorus; 106 mg calcium; 3 mg iron; 294 mg sodium; 1076 mg potassium; 2036 IU vitamin A; 6 mg vitamin E; 75 mg vitamin C; 3 mg cholesterol

Skillet Nachos

Great as an appetizer, served right from the skillet. But also good as a meal, wrapped up in a tortilla.

1 pound (455 g) ground beef

1 cup (160 g) chopped onion

2 cups (520 g) salsa

2 cups (344 g) cooked black beans, drained

1 teaspoon chili powder

1 cup (180 g) chopped tomato

1 avocado, seeded and diced

½ cup (50 g) sliced black olives

1 cup (115 g) shredded Cheddar cheese

1 cup (230 g) sour cream

In 12-inch (30-cm) skillet, brown beef with onion; drain. Add salsa, beans, and chili powder; bring to a boil. Reduce heat and simmer uncovered 5 minutes. Stir in tomato, avocado, and olives; remove from heat. Sprinkle with cheese. Spoon sour cream onto center of meat mixture. Serve with tortilla chips and/or flour tortillas.

—Yield: 6 servings

NUTRITIONAL ANALYSIS

PER SERVING: 276 g water; 486 calories (41% from fat, 30% from protein, 29% from carb); 28 g protein; 17 g total fat; 7 g saturated fat; 7 g monounsaturated fat; 1 g polyunsaturated fat; 27 g carbohydrate; 9 g fiber; 5 g sugar; 392 mg phosphorus; 267 mg calcium; 4 mg iron; 360 mg sodium; 970 mg potassium; 1035 IU vitamin A; 97 mg vitamin E; 9 mg vitamin C; 91 mg cholesterol

Veggie Pizza Bites

Like miniature pieces of pizza, these small wedges are sure to be a hit with nibblers of all ages.

2 teaspoons chopped garlic

1 cup (180 g) sliced tomato

2 tablespoons (28 ml) olive oil

⅛ teaspoon black pepper

6 ounces (170 g) mozzarella cheese, sliced

2 whole wheat tortillas

2 tablespoons minced fresh basil

½ cup (50 g) grated Parmesan cheese

Preheat the oven to 350°F (180°C, gas mark 4). In a small bowl place the garlic, tomato, olive oil, and pepper. Thoroughly coat the tomatoes. Place the cheese slices over the tortillas. Place the soaked tomatoes on top. Sprinkle on the basil and Parmesan. Place the tortillas on a baking sheet and bake them for 8 minutes or until the cheese is melted. Cut the pizza into wedges.

—Yield: 6 servings

NUTRITIONAL ANALYSIS

PER SERVING: 43 g water; 201 calories (63% from fat, 21% from protein, 16% from carb); 11 g protein; 14 g total fat; 6 g saturated fat; 6 g monounsaturated fat; 1 g polyunsaturated fat; 8 g carbohydrate; 1 g fiber; 1 g sugar; 184 mg phosphorus; 267 mg calcium; 1 mg iron; 372 mg sodium; 131 mg potassium; 449 IU vitamin A; 59 mg vitamin E; 7 mg vitamin C; 30 mg cholesterol

Pizza Pitas

Pizza snacks are always a hit. And you don't have to tell anyone that these are actually good for them.

1 whole wheat pita

2 tablespoons pizza sauce

⅛ teaspoon crushed dried oregano

½ cup (75 g) sliced red bell pepper

½ cup (80 g) sliced onion

2 ounces (56 g) shredded mozzarella cheese

Split pita bread round in half, forming 2 thin circles. Spread each circle with half of the sauce. Sprinkle half of the oregano over each. Top each circle with half of the veggies and half of the cheese. Place pita bread halves on a baking sheet. Bake in a 375°F (190°C, gas mark 5) oven for 8 to 10 minutes or until cheese is bubbly and edges of pita bread are crisp. Remove from baking sheet; cool slightly.

—Yield: 2 servings

NUTRITIONAL ANALYSIS

PER SERVING: 109 g water; 189 calories (26% from fat, 22% from protein, 52% from carb); 11 g protein; 6 g total fat; 3 g saturated fat; 1 g monounsaturated fat; 1 g polyunsaturated fat; 26 g carbohydrate; 4 g fiber; 5 g sugar; 216 mg phosphorus; 241 mg calcium; 1 mg iron; 434 mg sodium; 278 mg potassium; 1434 IU vitamin A; 35 mg vitamin E; 53 mg vitamin C; 18 mg cholesterol

Crostini with Mushrooms

Another appetizer that's fancy enough to serve to company, but still easy to make.

2 cups (140 g) mushrooms, whole

1 tablespoon (15 ml) olive oil

¼ teaspoon (0.8 g) crushed garlic

1 tablespoon (4 g) fresh parsley, chopped

12 slices Italian bread, sliced ¼-inch (0.64 cm) thick

Clean and cut the mushrooms into very thin little pieces. In a large saucepan, heat oil with crushed garlic. Cook over medium heat until the garlic turns light brown, and then add the mushrooms. Cook the mushrooms for 10 minutes, or until the liquid from the mushrooms dries. Turn off the heat and allow to cool. Add parsley and stir. Toast the bread and spread the mushroom mixture on top. Serve at once.

—Yield: 6 servings

NUTRITIONAL ANALYSIS

PER SERVING: 188 calories (21% from fat, 13% from protein, 66% from carbohydrate); 6 g protein; 4 g total fat; 1 g saturated fat; 2 g monounsaturated fat; 1 g polyunsaturated fat; 31 g carbohydrate; 2 g fiber; 1 g sugar; 82 mg phosphorus; 49 mg calcium; 2 mg iron; 352 mg sodium; 144 mg potassium; 53 IU vitamin A; 0 mg ATE vitamin E; 1 mg vitamin C; 0 mg cholesterol; 44 g water

Tuscan Bruschetta

The simplest form of bruschetta, with just enough garlic to taste and a little olive oil.

4 slices low sodium Italian bread, sliced no more than ½-inch (1.3 cm) thick

1 small clove garlic

2 tablespoons (30 ml) extra-virgin olive oil

Toast bread until light brown. Take off the garlic skin and rub garlic firmly across the face of the toast. Drizzle with just enough olive oil to cover the entire surface of the bread.

—Yield: 4 servings

NUTRITIONAL ANALYSIS

PER SERVING: 143 calories (49% from fat, 8% from protein, 43% from carbohydrate); 3 g protein; 8 g total fat; 1 g saturated fat; 5 g monounsaturated fat; 1 g polyunsaturated fat; 15 g carbohydrate; 1 g fiber; 0 g sugar; 26 mg calcium; 1 mg iron; 16 mg sodium; 39 mg potassium; 0 IU vitamin A; 0 mg vitamin C; 0 mg cholesterol; exchanges = 1 starch—1½ fat; 12 g water

Chicken and Mushroom Quesadillas

If you have an indoor grill like the George Foreman models, it is perfect for making these quesadillas. Otherwise, place them on a baking sheet and bake at 350°F (180°C, or gas mark 4) until crisp.

1 tablespoon (15 ml) olive oil

2½ teaspoons (6.5 g) chili powder

½ teaspoon (1.5 g) minced garlic

1 teaspoon (1 g) dried oregano

8 ounces (225 g) mushrooms, sliced

1 cup (110 g) chicken breast, cooked and shredded

⅔ cup (110 g) onion, finely chopped

½ cup (30 g) fresh cilantro, chopped

1½ cups (170 g) shredded low fat Monterey Jack cheese

16 5½-inch (13.75-cm) corn tortillas

Heat olive oil in a large skillet over medium-high heat. Add chili powder, garlic, and oregano and sauté for 1 minute. Add mushrooms and sauté for 10 minutes, or until tender. Remove from heat and stir in the chicken, onion, and cilantro. Cool for 10 minutes, then mix in the cheese. Spray olive oil spray on one side of 8 of the tortillas and place them oiled-side down on a baking sheet. Divide chicken mixture among tortillas, spreading to an even thickness. Top with the remaining tortillas and spray the tops with olive oil spray. Grill quesadillas for 3 minutes per side, or until heated through and golden brown. Cut into wedges to serve.

—Yield: 12 servings

NUTRITIONAL ANALYSIS

PER SERVING: 122 calories (26% from fat, 32% from protein, 43% from carbohydrate); 10 g protein; 4 g total fat; 1 g saturated fat; 2 g monounsaturated fat; 1 g polyunsaturated fat; 13 g carbohydrate; 2 g fiber; 1 g sugar; 206 mg phosphorus; 97 mg calcium; 1 mg iron; 128 mg sodium; 181 mg potassium; 315 IU vitamin A; 11 mg ATE vitamin E; 2 mg vitamin C; 13 mg cholesterol; 57 g water

TIP

Serve with salsa and fat-free sour cream.

Fat-Free Potato Skins

Because they're baked instead of fried, these tasty potato skins contain no fat.

4 potatoes

1½ teaspoons (3 g) ground coriander

½ teaspoon (1 g) black pepper

1½ teaspoons (4 g) chili powder

1½ teaspoons (3 g) curry powder

Preheat the oven to 400°F (200°C, or gas mark 6). Bake the potatoes for 1 hour. Remove the potatoes from the oven, but keep the oven on. Slice the potatoes in half lengthwise, and let them cool for 10 minutes. Scoop out most of the potato flesh, leaving about ¼ inch (0.6 cm) of flesh against the potato skin (you can save the potato flesh for another use, like mashed potatoes). Cut each potato half crosswise into 3 pieces. Spray with olive oil spray. Combine the spices and sprinkle the mixture over the potatoes. Bake the potato skins for 15 minutes or until they are crispy and brown.

—Yield: 24 servings

NUTRITIONAL ANALYSIS

PER SERVING: 44 calories (3% from fat, 11% from protein, 87% from carbohydrate); 1 g protein; 0 g total fat; 0 g saturated fat; 0 g monounsaturated fat; 0 g polyunsaturated fat; 10 g carbohydrate; 1 g fiber; 1 g sugar; 39 mg phosphorus; 8 mg calcium; 1 mg iron; 5 mg sodium; 287 mg potassium; 54 IU vitamin A; 0 mg ATE vitamin E; 6 mg vitamin C; 0 mg cholesterol; 50 g water

Potstickers

A fairly traditional recipe for Chinese dumplings.

FOR FILLING:

4 ounces (115 g) napa cabbage, shredded

½ pound (225 g) ground pork loin

2 tablespoons (12 g) scallions, chopped

½ tablespoon (7.5 ml) white wine

½ teaspoon (1.3 g) cornstarch

½ teaspoon (2.5 ml) sesame oil

Dash white pepper

FOR DOUGH:

1 cup (125 g) flour

½ cup (120 ml) boiling water

1 tablespoon (15 ml) olive oil

To make the filling: In a large bowl, mix the cabbage, pork, scallions, wine, cornstarch, sesame oil, and pepper. Set aside.

To make the dough: In a bowl, mix the flour and boiling water until a soft dough forms. Knead the dough on a lightly floured surface for 5 minutes, or until smooth. Shape into a roll 12 inches (30 cm) long and cut into ½-inch (1.3-cm) slices.

To assemble, roll 1 slice of dough into a 3-inch (7.5-cm) circle and place 1 tablespoon (13 g) pork mixture in the center of the circle. Lift up the edges of the circle and pinch 5 pleats to create a sealed pouch to encase the mixture. Repeat with the remaining dough and filling. Heat a wok or nonstick skillet until very hot. Add 1 tablespoon (15 ml) olive oil, tilting the wok to coat the sides. Place 12 dumplings in a single layer in the wok and fry 2 minutes, or until the bottoms are golden brown. Add ½ cup (120 ml) water. Cover and cook 6 to 7 minutes, or until the water is absorbed. Repeat with the remaining dumplings.

—Yield: 24 servings

Chickpea-Stuffed Eggs

A healthier alternative to the usual deviled eggs, these have no cholesterol, but 2 grams of fiber.

7 eggs, hard boiled, peeled

1 cup (164 g) cooked chickpeas, drained

2 tablespoons (30 g) plain fat-free yogurt

1 teaspoon Dijon mustard

½ teaspoon minced garlic

Slice eggs in half and discard yolks. In food processor, combine all other ingredients. Spoon mixture into egg cavities.

—Yield: 7 servings

NUTRITIONAL ANALYSIS

PER SERVING: 58 g water; 61 calories (7% from fat, 37% from protein, 56% from carb); 6 g protein; 0 g total fat; 0 g saturated fat; 0 g monounsaturated fat; 0 g polyunsaturated fat; 8 g carbohydrate; 2 g fiber; 1 g sugar; 44 mg phosphorus; 23 mg calcium; 1 mg iron; 169 mg sodium; 126 mg potassium; 9 IU vitamin A; 0 mg vitamin E; 1 mg vitamin C; 0 mg cholesterol

Broccoli Bites

A tasty little snack or a nice side dish.

10 ounces (280 g) frozen broccoli

1 cup (72 g) stuffing mix

½ cup (50 g) grated Parmesan cheese

3 eggs, beaten

4 tablespoons (55 g) unsalted butter, softened

¼ teaspoon black pepper

Cook broccoli according to package directions; drain well. In a medium bowl, combine cooked broccoli, stuffing mix, cheese, eggs, butter, and pepper. Shape mixture into small balls, about 1 inch (2.5 cm). Freeze, well covered, for at least 3 hours. Preheat oven to 350°F (180°C, gas mark 4). Place frozen balls on baking sheet coated with nonstick vegetable oil spray. Bake until brown, about 15 minutes.

—Yield: 15 servings

NUTRITIONAL ANALYSIS

PER SERVING: 27 g water; 63 calories (72% from fat, 20% from protein, 8% from carb); 3 g protein; 5 g total fat; 3 g saturated fat; 2 g monounsaturated fat; 0 g polyunsaturated fat; 1 g carbohydrate; 1 g fiber; 0 g sugar; 56 mg phosphorus; 50 mg calcium; 0 mg iron; 116 mg sodium; 47 mg potassium; 377 IU vitamin A; 45 mg vitamin E; 8 mg vitamin C; 58 mg cholesterol

Banana Bites

A quick way to add crunch and flavor.

3 cups (450 g) sliced banana

6 ounces (213 g) orange juice concentrate

2 cups (164 g) granola

Cut bananas into bite-size pieces. Pour orange juice concentrate into mixing bowl. Spread granola on baking sheet. Dip banana bits into the orange juice. Roll in granola.

—Yield: 6 servings

NUTRITIONAL ANALYSIS

PER SERVING: 103 g water; 251 calories (6% from fat, 6% from protein, 88% from carb); 4 g protein; 2 g total fat; 0 g saturated fat; 1 g monounsaturated fat; 0 g polyunsaturated fat; 59 g carbohydrate; 5 g fiber; 34 g sugar; 116 mg phosphorus; 25 mg calcium; 1 mg iron; 105 mg sodium; 671 mg potassium; 179 IU vitamin A; 0 mg vitamin E; 49 mg vitamin C; 0 mg cholesterol

Date Chews

Sweet little treats to nibble on.

1 cup (145 g) cut-up dates

3 teaspoons flour

1 cup (110 g) finely chopped pecans

½ cup (100 g) sugar

2 eggs

1 teaspoon vanilla extract

Combine dates with flour and stir to coat. Stir all ingredients enough to blend. Place 1 teaspoon each in mini muffin pans that have been sprayed with nonstick vegetable oil spray. Bake at 375°F (190°C, gas mark 5) for 12 to 15 minutes.

—Yield: 32 servings

NUTRITIONAL ANALYSIS

PER SERVING: 4 g water; 58 calories (42% from fat, 6% from protein, 52% from carb); 1 g protein; 3 g total fat; 0 g saturated fat; 2 g monounsaturated fat; 1 g polyunsaturated fat; 8 g carbohydrate; 1 g fiber; 7 g sugar; 20 mg phosphorus; 7 mg calcium; 0 mg iron; 5 mg sodium; 56 mg potassium; 20 IU vitamin A; 5 mg vitamin E; 0 mg vitamin C; 15 mg cholesterol

Apricot Chews

Treats that are perfect when you just want a little something sweet.

2 ounces (57 g) cream cheese, softened

1 tablespoon confectioners' sugar

¼ teaspoon vanilla extract

8 ounces (225 g) dried apricots

1 tablespoon wheat germ

3 tablespoons (27 g) slivered almonds

Blend cream cheese, confectioners' sugar, and vanilla until softened. Place small amount of mixture between two halves of apricots. Sprinkle wheat germ and almonds on top. Chill for 15 minutes.

—Yield: 15 servings

NUTRITIONAL ANALYSIS

PER SERVING: 15 g water; 35 calories (57% from fat, 10% from protein, 33% from carb); 1 g protein; 2 g total fat; 1 g saturated fat; 1 g monounsaturated fat; 0 g polyunsaturated fat; 3 g carbohydrate; 1 g fiber; 2 g sugar; 21 mg phosphorus; 10 mg calcium; 0 mg iron; 12 mg sodium; 47 mg potassium; 307 IU vitamin A; 14 mg vitamin E; 1 mg vitamin C; 4 mg cholesterol

Cheese Crisps

These little snacks taste great either warm from the oven or cold. There usually aren't any left to eat cold, however, when we make them.

1 cup (120 g) grated Cheddar cheese

¼ cup (55 g) unsalted butter

½ cup (60 g) whole wheat flour

In large bowl, combine the cheese and butter. Add the flour and mix thoroughly. Roll into small balls. Place the balls on an baking sheet sprayed with nonstick vegetable oil spray and flatten. Bake at 400°F (200°C, gas mark 6) for 5 to 8 minutes. Do not let the edges get browned.

—Yield: 12 servings

NUTRITIONAL ANALYSIS

PER SERVING: 5 g water; 95 calories (70% from fat, 14% from protein, 16% from carb); 3 g protein; 8 g total fat; 5 g saturated fat; 2 g monounsaturated fat; 0 g polyunsaturated fat; 4 g carbohydrate; 1 g fiber; 0 g sugar; 75 mg phosphorus; 82 mg calcium; 0 mg iron; 69 mg sodium; 32 mg potassium; 229 IU vitamin A, 60 mg vitamin E, 0 mg vitamin C; 22 mg cholesterol

Wheat Germ Crackers

Tasty little crackers, these are good without anything, but also make a healthy dipper for any of the dips and spreads in this book.

3 cups (240 g) quick-cooking oats

2 cups (240 g) whole wheat pastry flour

1 cup (112 g) wheat germ

3 tablespoons (39 g) sugar

1 cup (235 ml) water

¾ cup (175 ml) canola oil

Mix dry ingredients together. Add water and oil; stir until all is wet. Roll out thin on upside-down baking sheet. Score and prick with fork. Bake at 325°F (170°C, gas mark 3) for 30 minutes or more, until brown. This is enough for 2 baking sheets, approximately 10 × 15 inches (25 × 37 cm) or 11 × 16 inches (27 × 40 cm).

—Yield: 60 servings

NUTRITIONAL ANALYSIS

PER SERVING: 5 g water; 63 calories (46% from fat, 11% from protein, 44% from carb); 2 g protein; 3 g total fat; 0 g saturated fat; 2 g monounsaturated fat; 1 g polyunsaturated fat; 7 g carbohydrate; 1 g fiber; 1 g sugar; 55 mg phosphorus; 4 mg calcium; 0 mg iron; 1 mg sodium; 48 mg potassium; 2 IU vitamin A; 0 mg vitamin E; 0 mg vitamin C; 0 mg cholesterol

Pita Chips

Simple and easy. Make your own low-fat, high-fiber chips for snacking or dipping in about 5 minutes.

2 whole wheat pitas

Cut pita into triangles, then separate. Place on foil-covered baking sheet. Spray with nonstick vegetable oil spray; season if desired. Bake in 375°F (190°C, gas mark 5) oven until crisp, about 5 minutes. Remove and cool.

—Yield: 4 servings

NUTRITIONAL ANALYSIS

PER SERVING: 10 g water; 85 calories (8% from fat, 14% from protein, 78% from carb); 3 g protein; 1 g total fat; 0 g saturated fat; 0 g monounsaturated fat; 0 g polyunsaturated fat; 18 g carbohydrate; 2 g fiber; 0 g sugar; 58 mg phosphorus; 5 mg calcium; 1 mg iron; 170 mg sodium; 54 mg potassium; 0 IU vitamin A; 0 mg vitamin E; 0 mg vitamin C; 0 mg cholesterol

Parmesan-Garlic Pita Toasts

Use these flavorful pita crisps for any of the spreads or dips in the book. Or just nibble on them for a healthier-than-usual snack option.

2 whole wheat pitas, cut into 8 triangles each

3 tablespoons (42 g) unsalted butter

1 teaspoon minced garlic

½ teaspoon black pepper, fresh ground

¼ cup (25 g) grated Parmesan cheese

Melt butter; cook garlic in butter over low heat, stirring occasionally, for 5 minutes. Brush mixture lightly on rough side of pita triangles. Arrange butter side up in 1 layer on baking sheet. Sprinkle pepper and Parmesan cheese on top. Bake in oven preheated to 350°F (180°C, gas mark 4) for 12 to 15 minutes, until crisp and light brown. Cool on racks and store in airtight container in dry place.

—Yield: 8 servings

NUTRITIONAL ANALYSIS

PER SERVING: 7 g water; 95 calories (51% from fat, 12% from protein, 37% from carb); 3 g protein; 6 g total fat; 3 g saturated fat; 1 g monounsaturated fat; 0 g polyunsaturated fat; 9 g carbohydrate; 1 g fiber; 0 g sugar; 54 mg phosphorus; 40 mg calcium; 1 mg iron; 134 mg sodium; 35 mg potassium; 147 IU vitamin A; 39 mg vitamin E; 0 mg vitamin C; 14 mg cholesterol

Spicy Pita Dippers

Pepper and cumin give these pita triangles a southwestern flavor that goes particularly well with bean dips.

½ cup (112 g) unsalted butter, melted

2 teaspoons lemon pepper

2 teaspoons ground cumin

6 whole wheat pitas, cut into triangles

To make dippers, preheat the broiler. Combine the melted butter, lemon pepper, and cumin in a bowl. Dip the pita pieces quickly in the mixture, then place on a baking sheet. Broil 2 to 4 minutes, until crisp. Cool on a rack.

—Yield: 12 servings

NUTRITIONAL ANALYSIS

PER SERVING: 12 g water; 155 calories (48% from fat, 8% from protein, 44% from carb); 3 g protein; 9 g total fat; 5 g saturated fat; 2 g monounsaturated fat; 1 g polyunsaturated fat; 18 g carbohydrate; 2 g fiber; 0 g sugar; 62 mg phosphorus; 12 mg calcium; 1 mg iron; 172 mg sodium; 67 mg potassium; 242 IU vitamin A; 63 mg vitamin E; 0 mg vitamin C; 20 mg cholesterol

CHAPTER 3

Main Dishes: Poultry

*Poultry is a great healthy meat choice. It tends to be signifi-
cantly lower in saturated fat then red meats. There are poultry
dishes here that range from down home Sunday dinner
comfort food like roast or fried chicken to a variety of dishes
with flavors from around the world. A number of them use
boneless skinless chicken breasts to lower the fat content even
more. But you won't miss the fat with the great taste.*

Grilled Roaster

If you cook a large chicken on the weekend, you can have a great meal and lots of leftovers to use during the week. This one has a smoky flavor, but not so much as to overpower other ingredients.

1 large roasting chicken, 5 to 6 pounds (2.3 to 2.7 kg)

2 tablespoons (30 ml) olive oil

1 teaspoon (2.5 g) paprika

1 teaspoon (3 g) onion powder

½ teaspoon (1 g) black pepper

½ teaspoon (0.5 g) dried thyme

¼ teaspoon (0.8 g) garlic powder

1 teaspoon (5 ml) liquid smoke

Split chicken in half along the backbone and breastbone. Mix together remaining ingredients and rub into both sides of chicken halves. Grill over indirect heat, turning occasionally, for 1½ to 2 hours, or until done. Place over low heat the last 15 minutes to brown skin.

—Yield: 12 servings

NUTRITIONAL ANALYSIS

PER SERVING: 289 calories (69% from fat, 30% from protein, 1% from carbohydrate); 22 g protein; 22 g total fat; 6 g saturated fat; 9 g monounsaturated fat; 4 g polyunsaturated fat; 1 g carbohydrate; 0 g fiber; 0 g sugar; 2 mg phosphorus; 15 mg calcium; 2 mg iron; 0 mg sodium; 255 mg potassium; 209 IU vitamin A; 0 mg ATE vitamin E; 3 mg vitamin C; 113 mg cholesterol; 0 g water

Rotisserie-Flavored Chicken Breasts

This recipe gives you a flavor reminiscent of carryout rotisserie chicken, but with lower-fat chicken breasts as the basis.

¼ cup (60 ml) honey

1 teaspoon (2.5 g) paprika

1 teaspoon (3 g) onion powder

½ teaspoon (1 g) black pepper

½ teaspoon (0.5 g) dried thyme

¼ teaspoon (0.8 g) garlic powder

4 boneless chicken breasts

Preheat oven to 325°F (170°C, or gas mark 3). Mix honey, paprika, onion powder, black pepper, thyme, and garlic powder. Rub onto chicken. Roast for 45 minutes, or until done, basting occasionally with pan juices.

—Yield: 4 servings

NUTRITIONAL ANALYSIS

PER SERVING: 148 calories (6% from fat, 44% from protein, 50% from carbohydrate); 17 g protein; 1 g total fat; 0 g saturated fat; 0 g monounsaturated fat; 0 g polyunsaturated fat; 19 g carbohydrate; 0 g fiber; 18 g sugar; 145 mg phosphorus; 16 mg calcium; 1 mg iron; 48 mg sodium; 217 mg potassium; 324 IU vitamin A; 4 mg ATE vitamin E; 2 mg vitamin C; 41 mg cholesterol; 57 g water

Grilled Marinated Chicken Breasts

These thin grilled chicken breasts make great sandwiches. They are also good sliced on top of a salad or stirred into a pasta salad.

¼ cup (60 ml) olive oil

¼ cup (60 ml) red wine vinegar

¼ teaspoon (0.8 g) minced garlic

1 teaspoon (3 g) onion powder

1½ teaspoons (1 g) Italian seasoning

½ teaspoon (0.5 g) dried thyme

2 boneless chicken breasts

Combine all ingredients except chicken in a resealable plastic bag and mix well. Slice breasts in half crosswise, making two thin fillets from each. Add the chicken to the bag, seal, and marinate for at least 2 hours, turning occasionally. Remove chicken from marinade and grill over medium heat until done, turning once.

—Yield: 4 servings

NUTRITIONAL ANALYSIS

PER SERVING: 165 calories (77% from fat, 20% from protein, 2% from carbohydrate); 8 g protein; 14 g total fat; 2 g saturated fat; 10 g monounsaturated fat; 2 g polyunsaturated fat; 1 g carbohydrate; 0 g fiber; 0 g sugar; 74 mg phosphorus; 16 mg calcium; 1 mg iron; 25 mg sodium; 110 mg potassium; 38 IU vitamin A; 2 mg ATE vitamin E; 1 mg vitamin C; 21 mg cholesterol; 41 g water

Grilled Chicken and Vegetables

Chicken and vegetables grilled with a lemon and herb marinade.

1½ teaspoons basil

1½ teaspoon garlic powder

¼ teaspoon black pepper

1 teaspoon lemon peel, gated

1 tablespoon lemon juice

1 tablespoon olive oil

4 boneless skinless chicken breasts

1 small eggplant, sliced

1 zucchini, sliced lengthwise

1 red bell peppers, sliced crosswise

Combine first six ingredients. Heat grill to medium heat. Brush chicken and vegetables with herb mixture. Grill chicken until no longer pink in the center, about 5–10 minutes per side. Grill vegetables until crisp tender, about 5 minutes per side.

—Yield: 4 servings

NUTRITIONAL ANALYSIS

TOTAL RECIPE: 543 calories (30% from fat, 52% from protein, 19% from carb); 71 g protein; 18 g total fat; 3 g saturated fat; 11 g monounsaturated fat; 3 g polyunsaturated fat; 26 g carb; 9 g fiber; 13 g sugar; 711 mg phosphorus; 109 mg calcium; 210 mg sodium; 1826 mg potassium; 5220 IU vitamin A; 17 mg ATE vitamin E; 331 mg vitamin C; 165 mg cholesterol

Italian Chicken Kabobs

Sort of like pizza on a stick, these tasty kabobs are sure to please young and old alike.

1 pound boneless skinless chicken breast, cut in 1" cubes

1 cup green bell peppers, cut in 1" pieces

1 cup red bell peppers, cut in 1" pieces

8 ounces mushrooms

¼ cup reduced fat Italian dressing

1 teaspoon Italian seasoning

¼ cup parmesan cheese, grated

Heat grill to medium. Thread chicken and vegetables on skewers. Brush with dressing and sprinkle with Italian seasoning. Grill until chicken is no longer pink in center, about 10 minutes. Remove from skewers and sprinkle with cheese.

—Yield: 4 servings

NUTRITIONAL ANALYSIS

PER SERVING: 193 calories (21% from fat, 65% from protein , 14% from carb); 31 g protein ; 5 g total fat; 2 g saturated fat; 1 g monounsaturated fat; 1 g polyunsaturated fat; 7 g carb; 2 g fiber; 4 g sugar; 335 mg phosphorus; 95 mg calcium; 178 mg sodium; 636 mg potassium; 1373 IU vitamin A; 14 mg ATE vitamin E; 104 mg vitamin C; 72 mg cholesterol

TIP

Serve with spaghetti sauce for dipping.

Lemon Thyme Chicken

Lemon and honey add a sort of sweet and sour flavor to these grilled chicken breasts.

¼ cup honey

1 tablespoon lemon peel, grated

1 tablespoon lemon juice

½ teaspoon thyme

¼ teaspoon black pepper

4 boneless skinless chicken breasts

Heat grill to medium heat. Combine honey, lemon peel, lemon juice, thyme, and pepper. Grill chicken until no longer pink in the center, about 15–20 minutes. Brush with sauce during the last 10 minutes.

—Yield: 4 servings

NUTRITIONAL ANALYSIS

PER SERVING: 145 calories (6% from fat, 45% from protein , 50% from carb); 17 g protein ; 1 g total fat; 0 g saturated fat; 0 g monounsaturated fat; 0 g polyunsaturated fat; 18 g carb; 0 g fiber; 18 g sugar; 141 mg phosphorus; 14 mg calcium; 47 mg sodium; 202 mg potassium; 21 IU vitamin A; 4 mg ATE vitamin E; 5 mg vitamin C; 41 mg cholesterol

Oven-Fried Chicken

Fried chicken doesn't have to be as unhealthy as it usually is. Get rid of the skin and "fry" the chicken in the oven, and it's a perfectly acceptable food. Not to mention that it tastes good.

¼ cup (55 g) unsalted butter, melted

¼ teaspoon (0.5 g) black pepper

3 pounds (1.4 kg) chicken, cut into pieces, skin removed

1 cup (56 g) corn flake crumbs

Preheat oven to 350°F (180°C, or gas mark 4). Combine butter and pepper. Roll chicken in butter mixture , then corn flake crumbs. Place in an ungreased baking pan and bake about 1 hour, or until done.

—Yield: 8 servings

NUTRITIONAL ANALYSIS

PER SERVING: 267 calories (38% from fat, 57% from protein, 5% from carbohydrate); 37 g protein; 12 g total fat; 7 g saturated fat; 3 g monounsaturated fat; 1 g polyunsaturated fat; 3 g carbohydrate; 0 g fiber; 0 g sugar; 297 mg phosphorus; 22 mg calcium; 3 mg iron; 159 mg sodium; 395 mg potassium; 423 IU vitamin A; 104 mg ATE vitamin E; 6 mg vitamin C; 129 mg cholesterol; 130 g water

Potato-Coated Oven-Fried Chicken

This is my favorite recipe for oven-fried chicken.

1 egg

2 tablespoons (30 ml) water

¼ cup (25 g) Parmesan cheese, grated

3 pounds (1.4 kg) chicken, cut into pieces, skin removed

1 cup (60 g) instant mashed potato flakes

Preheat oven to 375°F (190°C, or gas mark 5). Combine egg, water, and cheese. Dip chicken in egg mixture, then roll in potato flakes. Place in ungreased baking pan. Bake for 1 hour, or until done.

—Yield: 8 servings

NUTRITIONAL ANALYSIS

PER SERVING: 249 calories (24% from fat, 65% from protein, 10% from carbohydrate); 39 g protein; 6 g total fat; 2 g saturated fat; 2 g monounsaturated fat; 1 g polyunsaturated fat; 6 g carbohydrate; 0 g fiber; 0 g sugar; 338 mg phosphorus; 61 mg calcium; 2 mg iron; 201 mg sodium; 402 mg potassium; 131 IU vitamin A; 31 mg ATE vitamin E; 10 mg vitamin C; 152 mg cholesterol; 140 g water

Baked Chicken Nuggets

You can greatly reduce the amount of fat in chicken nuggets by baking them instead of frying them. The flavor is just as good, and they are a lot better for you.

½ cup (14 g) crushed corn flakes

2 tablespoons (15 g) nonfat dry milk

1 tablespoon (0.4 g) dried parsley

1 tablespoon (7 g) paprika

1 teaspoon (3 g) onion powder

¼ teaspoon (0.8 g) garlic powder

½ teaspoon (0.4 g) poultry seasoning

1 pound (455 g) boneless chicken breasts, cut in strips

1 egg, beaten

Preheat oven to 350°F (180°C, or gas mark 4). Mix together crushed corn flakes and next 6 ingredients (through poultry seasoning) in a resealable plastic bag. Dip chicken pieces in egg, then place in bag. Shake to coat evenly. Place on baking sheet coated with nonstick vegetable oil spray. Bake for 20 minutes, or until chicken is done and coating is crispy.

—Yield: 4 servings

NUTRITIONAL ANALYSIS

PER SERVING: 167 calories (12% from fat, 73% from protein, 14% from carbohydrate); 29 g protein; 2 g total fat; 1 g saturated fat; 1 g monounsaturated fat; 1 g polyunsaturated fat; 6 g carbohydrate; 1 g fiber; 2 g sugar; 274 mg phosphorus; 61 mg calcium; 2 mg iron; 116 mg sodium; 342 mg potassium; 1088 IU vitamin A; 22 mg ATE vitamin E; 3 mg vitamin C; 136 mg cholesterol; 98 g water

Honey Mustard Fruit Sauced Chicken

What can I say? I was looking for something a little different, and this just came to me. It is a true original. I actually used tropical fruit cocktail, but the regular kind should work just as well.

6 boneless chicken breasts

1 cup (240 g) fruit cocktail, in juice

2 tablespoons (30 ml) red wine vinegar

2 tablespoons (30 ml) honey

2 tablespoons (30 ml) honey mustard

Preheat oven to 350°F (180°C, or gas mark 4). Place chicken breasts in a roasting pan. Purée fruit cocktail, vinegar, honey, and mustard in a blender. Pour over chicken. Bake for 50 to 60 minutes, or until done.

—Yield: 6 servings

NUTRITIONAL ANALYSIS

PER SERVING: 122 calories (8% from fat, 56% from protein, 36% from carbohydrate); 17 g protein; 1 g total fat; 0 g saturated fat; 0 g monounsaturated fat; 0 g polyunsaturated fat; 11 g carbohydrate; 1 g fiber; 10 g sugar; 151 mg phosphorus; 15 mg calcium; 1 mg iron; 105 mg sodium; 231 mg potassium; 139 IU vitamin A; 4 mg ATE vitamin E; 2 mg vitamin C; 41 mg cholesterol; 98 g water

Maple Glazed Chicken

Maple sweetness and mustard tanginess is a winning combination for these grilled chicken breasts.

¾ cup maple syrup

¼ cup Dijon mustard

2 tablespoons chives

4 boneless skinless chicken breasts

¼ teaspoon salt free seasoning blend such as Mrs. Dash

¼ teaspoon black pepper

Heat grill to medium. Combine syrup, mustard, and chives. Sprinkle chicken with seasoning blend and pepper. Grill until no longer pink in center, about 15–20 minutes, brushing with sauce occasionally. Heat remaining sauce to boiling and boil for one minute. Serve with chicken.

—Yield: 4 servings

NUTRITIONAL ANALYSIS

PER SERVING: 247 calories (5% from fat, 27% from protein , 67% from carb); 17 g protein ; 1 g total fat; 0 g saturated fat; 1 g monounsaturated fat; 0 g polyunsaturated fat; 42 g carb; 1 g fiber; 36 g sugar; 155 mg phosphorus; 62 mg calcium; 227 mg sodium; 333 mg potassium; 104 IU vitamin A; 4 mg ATE vitamin E; 2 mg vitamin C; 41 mg cholesterol

Chicken and Snow Peas

The stir-frying and ingredients give this an Asian feel, although it doesn't use the typical seasonings. It's good over rice, and I would think it would go well with pasta too.

2 tablespoons (30 ml) olive oil, divided

1 pound (455 g) boneless chicken breasts, sliced

1 egg, beaten

⅓ cup (43 g) cornstarch

1½ cups (240 g) onions, sliced

½ cup (75 g) green bell pepper, sliced

6 ounces (170 g) snow peas

¼ cup (60 ml) honey

2 tablespoons (16 g) almonds, slivered

Heat 1 tablespoon (15 ml) of the oil in a wok. Dip half the chicken in the egg and dust with cornstarch. Stir-fry for 4 to 5 minutes, or until just cooked. Remove cooked chicken from pan and repeat with remaining chicken. Remove chicken from pan; add the rest of the oil to the wok. Stir-fry the onion until it begins to soften. Add the green bell pepper and snow peas and stir-fry for 4 minutes, or until crisp-tender. Add the honey and toss the vegetables in it until well coated. Add the chicken and toss until coated and heated through. Sprinkle the almonds over the top.

—Yield: 4 servings

NUTRITIONAL ANALYSIS

PER SERVING: 375 calories (27% from fat, 33% from protein, 40% from carbohydrate); 31 g protein; 11 g total fat; 2 g saturated fat; 7 g monounsaturated fat; 2 g polyunsaturated fat; 38 g carbohydrate; 3 g fiber; 22 g sugar; 309 mg phosphorus; 66 mg calcium; 3 mg iron; 109 mg sodium; 489 mg potassium; 613 IU vitamin A; 7 mg ATE vitamin E; 46 mg vitamin C; 136 mg cholesterol; 211 g water

Chicken Polynesian

A kind of variation on sweet-and-sour chicken, made different by the citrus fruit sections in the sauce.

2 chicken breasts, halved

4 chicken thighs

1 grapefruit

3 oranges

½ cup (120 ml) light corn syrup

¼ cup (60 ml) mustard

¼ cup (60 ml) cider vinegar

¼ teaspoon Tabasco sauce

⅛ teaspoon ginger

2 teaspoons cornstarch

1 tablespoon (15 ml) water

9 ounces (255 g) crushed pineapple

⅓ cup (36 g) slivered toasted almonds

Place chicken skin side down in shallow baking dish. Section grapefruit, holding over bowl to catch juice. Measure juice. Section oranges, adding enough orange juice to grapefruit juice to make ½ cup (120 ml). In saucepan, blend corn syrup, mustard, vinegar, Tabasco, ginger, and fruit juices. Add cornstarch mixed with water; bring to boil. Boil 5 minutes, stirring constantly. Brush chicken with this mixture. Bake at 350°F (180°C, gas mark 4) for 1 hour, basting with sauce occasionally and turning once. Add crushed pineapple, orange and grapefruit sections, and almonds to remaining sauce. Heat; pour over chicken for last 5 minutes of baking time.

—Yield: 8 servings

NUTRITIONAL ANALYSIS

PER SERVING: 159 g water; 223 calories (22% from fat, 19% from protein, 59% from carb); 11 g protein; 6 g total fat; 1 g saturated fat; 3 g monounsaturated fat; 1 g polyunsaturated fat; 34 g carbohydrate; 3 g fiber; 19 g sugar; 97 mg phosphorus; 62 mg calcium; 1 mg iron; 39 mg sodium; 341 mg potassium; 573 IU vitamin A; 4 mg vitamin E; 54 mg vitamin C; 26 mg cholesterol

TIP

Serve over brown rice.

Lemon Rosemary Chicken

This technique has become my new favorite way of grilling chicken. It allows it to cook relatively quickly, stay juicy, and not get too blackened. Plus, you usually have some left over for sandwiches or salads the next day. Whole chickens can be very low in saturated fat as long as you don't eat the skin.

1 whole chicken, 3 to 4 pounds (1.4 to 1.8 kg)

½ cup (120 ml) lemon juice

1 teaspoon (1.2 g) dried rosemary

Split chicken in half, cutting along backbone and breast bone. Place in resealable plastic bag with lemon juice and rosemary. Marinate at least two hours, turning frequently. Preheat grill, making one side hot and the other low heat. Cook over the low side, turning several times, for about 1 hour or until done. Discard the skin.

—Yield: 8 servings

NUTRITIONAL ANALYSIS

PER SERVING: 33 calories (20% from fat, 64% from protein, 16% from carbohydrate); 5 g protein; 1 g total fat; 0 g saturated fat; 0 g monounsaturated fat; 0 g polyunsaturated fat; 1 g carbohydrate; 0 g fiber; 0 g sugar; 44 mg phosphorus; 4 mg calcium; 0 mg iron; 19 mg sodium; 76 mg potassium; 18 IU vitamin A; 4 mg ATE vitamin E; 8 mg vitamin C; 17 mg cholesterol; 32 g water

Pulled Chicken

Here's a good use for leftover smoked or grilled chicken.

8 ounces (225 g) no-salt-added tomato sauce

¼ cup (60 ml) vinegar

¼ cup (60 ml) molasses

½ teaspoon (1.5 g) onion powder

½ teaspoon (1.3 g) chili powder

½ teaspoon (1.5 g) dry mustard

¼ teaspoon (0.5 g) cayenne pepper

¼ teaspoon (0.8 g) garlic powder

2 cups (220 g) smoked chicken, shredded

Mix the first 8 ingredients (through garlic powder). Add chicken and stir to combine or place chicken on rolls and spoon sauce over chicken.

—Yield: 6 servings

NUTRITIONAL ANALYSIS

PER SERVING: 146 calories (23% from fat, 39% from protein, 38% from carbohydrate); 14 g protein; 4 g total fat; 1 g saturated fat; 1 g monounsaturated fat; 1 g polyunsaturated fat; 14 g carbohydrate; 1 g fiber; 8 g sugar; 116 mg phosphorus; 45 mg calcium; 3 mg iron; 227 mg sodium; 475 mg potassium; 490 IU vitamin A; 7 mg ATE vitamin E; 3 mg vitamin C; 42 mg cholesterol; 76 g water

Moroccan Chicken

Sweet spices contrast with olives and tomatoes in this chicken dish that invokes the flavors of North Africa.

1 tablespoon olive oil

4 boneless skinless chicken breasts

14 ounces no salt added tomatoes

¼ cup ripe olives

2 cups zucchini, sliced

1 cup red bell peppers, sliced

1½ teaspoon cumin

½ teaspoon cinnamon

1 teaspoon lemon peel, grated

Heat oil over medium heat in a large non-stick skillet. Add chicken and cook until browned on each side, about 5 minutes. Combine remaining ingredients and pour over chicken. Cover and simmer until chicken is no longer pink in the center, about 20 minutes.

—Yield: 4 servings

NUTRITIONAL ANALYSIS

PER SERVING: 160 calories (31% from fat, 45% from protein , 24% from carb); 19 g protein ; 6 g total fat; 1 g saturated fat; 4 g monounsaturated fat; 1 g polyunsaturated fat; 10 g carb; 3 g fiber; 6 g sugar; 195 mg phosphorus; 68 mg calcium; 138 mg sodium; 664 mg potassium; 1479 IU vitamin A; 4 mg ATE vitamin E; 97 mg vitamin C; 41 mg cholesterol

Chicken with Asparagus

My wife came home with some asparagus recently, and this recipe came up while searching our recipe file.

4 boneless chicken breasts

1 tablespoon (4 g) cilantro, chopped

2 tablespoons (30 ml) olive oil

½ pound (225 g) asparagus, cut in 3-inch (7.5-cm) lengths

1½ cups (355 ml) low sodium chicken broth

1 tablespoon (8 g) cornstarch

1 tablespoon (15 ml) lemon juice

½ teaspoon (1 g) black pepper

Slice the chicken breasts into strips about ¼-inch (62-mm) thick. Sprinkle with cilantro and toss to coat. Heat the oil in a large frying pan and fry the chicken quickly in small batches, 1 to 2 minutes per side. Remove from pan when no longer pink. Add asparagus and chicken broth to pan and bring to a boil. Cook for 4 to 5 minutes, or until asparagus is tender. Mix the cornstarch with a little water and stir into the broth. Cook until thickened. Add the chicken. Stir in the lemon juice and pepper. Cook until chicken is heated through.

—Yield: 4 servings

NUTRITIONAL ANALYSIS

PER SERVING: 170 calories (49% from fat, 43% from protein, 8% from carbohydrate); 18 g protein; 9 g total fat; 2 g saturated fat; 6 g monounsaturated fat; 1 g polyunsaturated fat; 3 g carbohydrate; 0 g fiber; 0 g sugar; 148 mg phosphorus; 14 mg calcium; 1 mg iron; 66 mg sodium; 225 mg potassium; 67 IU vitamin A; 3 mg ATE vitamin E; 2 mg vitamin C; 44 mg cholesterol; 126 g water

Chicken and Bean Skillet

This is a great, quick dinner for those nights when you don't have something planned and everyone is hungry. Simple and fast, but loaded with flavor and nutrition.

1 cup (160 g) chopped onion

⅓ cup (50 g) chopped red bell pepper

¾ teaspoon crushed garlic

2 teaspoons (10 ml) olive oil

½ pound (225 g) boneless chicken breast, cut in 1-inch (2.5-cm) cubes

¾ teaspoon cumin

½ teaspoon cinnamon

10 ounces (280 g) navy beans, drained

10 ounces (280 g) kidney beans, drained

2 cups (510 g) no-salt-added stewed tomatoes, undrained

Sauté onion, pepper, and garlic in oil in medium saucepan 2 to 3 minutes. Add chicken, cumin, and cinnamon; cook over medium-high heat until chicken is lightly browned, about 3 to 4 minutes. Add beans and tomatoes; heat to boiling. Reduce heat and simmer, uncovered, until slightly thickened, 5 to 8 minutes. Season to taste with salt and pepper.

—Yield: 4 servings

NUTRITIONAL ANALYSIS

PER SERVING: 299 g water; 325 calories (10% from fat, 33% from protein, 57% from carb); 27 g protein; 4 g total fat; 1 g saturated fat; 2 g monounsaturated fat; 1 g polyunsaturated fat; 47 g carbohydrate; 16 g fiber; 8 g sugar; 353 mg phosphorus; 163 mg calcium; 6 mg iron; 53 mg sodium; 1076 mg potassium; 631 IU vitamin A; 3 mg vitamin E; 31 mg vitamin C; 33 mg cholesterol

TIP

This dish is delicious served over cooked rice, couscous, or pasta.

Chicken and Black Beans

A Mexican-flavored skillet meal featuring marinated chicken and black beans.

½ cup (120 ml) Italian dressing

½ teaspoon crushed garlic

¼ teaspoon red pepper flakes

12 ounces (340 g) boneless chicken breast, cut in 1-inch (2.5-cm) cubes

2 teaspoons (10 ml) olive oil

1 cup (150 g) chopped green bell pepper

¾ cup (120 g) chopped onion

¾ teaspoon oregano

¼ teaspoon black pepper, fresh ground

¼ teaspoon cumin

2 cups (344 g) cooked black beans, drained and rinsed

2 cups (480 g) no-salt-added canned tomatoes

¼ cup chopped fresh cilantro

Combine dressing, garlic, and red pepper. Place chicken in large glass bowl, pour dressing over chicken, cover, and refrigerate 30 to 60 minutes (or overnight). Remove chicken from marinade, drain well, and discard marinade. Heat oil in large skillet over medium-high heat until hot. Add chicken, cook 5 to 7 minutes, stirring until chicken is slightly brown, spooning off any excess liquid. Add bell pepper, onion, oregano, pepper, and cumin. Cook, stirring 4 to 5 minutes or until vegetables are tender. Add black beans and tomatoes. Cook 2 to 3 minutes more, or until thoroughly heated. Garnish with cilantro; serve immediately.

—Yield: 4 servings

NUTRITIONAL ANALYSIS

PER SERVING: 314 g water; 355 calories (31% from fat, 32% from protein, 37% from carb); 29 g protein; 12 g total fat; 2 g saturated fat; 4 g monounsaturated fat; 5 g polyunsaturated fat; 33 g carbohydrate; 10 g fiber; 7 g sugar; 332 mg phosphorus; 90 mg calcium; 4 mg iron; 562 mg sodium; 896 mg potassium; 550 IU vitamin A; 5 mg vitamin E; 46 mg vitamin C; 49 mg cholesterol

TIP

Serve over rice.

Indian-Flavored Chicken

This is similar to the recipe for country captain soup, a curried chicken dish that supposedly came to England from India originally. The curry powder I use most often is a Blue Mountain brand from Jamaica that I get at a local Hispanic market. It's milder than most Asian curries, so if you can't find something similar, you may want to reduce the amount.

6 chicken thighs

2 cups (480 g) no-salt-added canned tomatoes

1 cup (160 g) chopped onion

½ teaspoon garlic powder

1 cup (130 g) frozen peas

1½ tablespoons curry powder

Place chicken in a 9 x 13-inch (23 x 33-cm) baking dish. Mix other ingredients together and pour over chicken. Bake at 350°F (180°C, gas mark 4) until chicken is done, about 45 minutes

—Yield: 6 servings

NUTRITIONAL ANALYSIS

PER SERVING: 152 g water; 100 calories (18% from fat, 41% from protein, 41% from carb); 11 g protein; 2 g total fat; 0 g saturated fat; 1 g monounsaturated fat; 1 g polyunsaturated fat; 11 g carbohydrate; 3 g fiber; 4 g sugar; 119 mg phosphorus; 49 mg calcium; 2 mg iron; 67 mg sodium; 340 mg potassium; 696 IU vitamin A; 8 mg vitamin E; 12 mg vitamin C; 34 mg cholesterol

Reduced Fat Chicken and Dumplings

This is classic comfort food any time of year, but especially as the weather gets colder. You can also make the dumplings using 2 cups (250 g) of Reduced Fat Whole Wheat Biscuit Mix (see recipe page 139) rather than the flour, baking powder, and butter called for here.

FOR CHICKEN:

1½ cups (165 g) chicken breast, cooked and cubed

3 cups (710 ml) low sodium chicken broth

3 cups (710 ml) water

1½ cups (195 g) carrot, sliced

6 potatoes, peeled and cubed

1 cup (160 g) onion, chopped

FOR DUMPLINGS:

2 cups (250 g) flour

1 tablespoon (14 g) baking powder

2 tablespoons (28 g) butter

⅔ cup (160 g) skim milk

To make the chicken: Place chicken, broth, water, carrots, potatoes, and onion in a large pan. Bring to a boil.

To make the dumplings: Stir together the flour and baking powder. Cut in butter until mixture resembles coarse crumbs. Stir in milk until dough holds together in a ball. Drop dumplings on top of boiling chicken mixture by spoonfuls. Reduce heat and simmer uncovered for 10 minutes. Cover and simmer 10 minutes more.

—Yield: 6 servings

NUTRITIONAL ANALYSIS

PER SERVING: 556 calories (11% from fat, 19% from protein, 71% from carbohydrate); 26 g protein; 7 g total fat; 6 g saturated fat; 1 g monounsaturated fat; 0 g polyunsaturated fat; 100 g carbohydrate; 9 g fiber; 7 g sugar; 488 mg phosphorus; 251 mg calcium; 6 mg iron; 413 mg sodium; 2113 mg potassium; 5668 IU vitamin A; 65 mg ATE vitamin E; 36 mg vitamin C; 30 mg cholesterol; 637 g water

Chicken-Pasta Stir-Fry

An Asian-flavored use for leftover chicken, quick and easy to make.

2 tablespoons (28 ml) olive oil

1 cup (160 g) coarsely chopped onion

1 cup (150 g) coarsely chopped bell pepper

2 cups (142 g) broccoli florets

1 teaspoon minced garlic

2 cups (280 g) cubed cooked chicken

8 ounces (225 g) whole wheat pasta, cooked

¼ cup (60 ml) Reduced Sodium Soy Sauce (see recipe page 133)

3 tablespoons (45 ml) rice wine

1½ tablespoons (19 g) sugar

1½ tablespoons (25 ml) Worcestershire sauce

½ teaspoon ginger

Heat oil in wok or skillet. Sauté garlic and vegetables in hot oil until just tender. Stir in chicken and pasta. Mix together remaining ingredients and stir in until meat, pasta, and vegetables are well coated.

—Yield: 4 servings

NUTRITIONAL ANALYSIS

PER SERVING: 128 g water; 343 calories (20% from fat, 13% from protein, 67% from carb); 11 g protein; 8 g total fat; 1 g saturated fat; 2 g monounsaturated fat; 4 g polyunsaturated fat; 59 g carbohydrate; 6 g fiber; 8 g sugar; 219 mg phosphorus; 57 mg calcium; 3 mg iron; 172 mg sodium; 470 mg potassium; 2238 IU vitamin A; 0 mg vitamin E; 94 mg vitamin C; 0 mg cholesterol

Chicken Pot Pie

A chicken and dumplings variation that is topped with mashed potatoes. This makes a large amount and is good for a family meal or leftovers for lunch.

2 pounds (905 g) boneless chicken breasts

2 cups (470 ml) low sodium chicken broth

1 cup (160 g) onion, coarsely chopped

1 cup (130 g) carrot, sliced

1⅓ cups (170 g) frozen peas, thawed

⅔ cup (84 g) flour

1 cup (235 g) water

1 tablespoon (0.4 g) dried parsley

1 teaspoon (1 g) dried thyme

6 potatoes, peeled and diced

1 cup (235 ml) skim milk

Preheat broiler. Place chicken and broth in a slow cooker or Dutch oven and cook until chicken is done. Remove chicken from broth, chop coarsely. Strain any fat from broth and add enough water to make 5 cups (1.2 L). Return broth to Dutch oven. Add onions, carrots, and peas and cook for 15 minutes, or until carrots are tender. Add flour to water in a jar with a tight-fitting lid. Shake until dissolved. Add to broth and cook until thickened. Stir in chicken, parsley, and thyme. While chicken mixture is cooking boil potatoes until done. Mash with milk. Drop mashed potatoes by spoonful onto top of chicken mixture. Broil until potatoes start to brown.

—Yield: 8 servings

NUTRITIONAL ANALYSIS

PER SERVING: 411 calories (5% from fat, 35% from protein, 59% from carbohydrate); 36 g protein; 2 g total fat; 1 g saturated fat; 1 g monounsaturated fat; 1 g polyunsaturated fat; 61 g carbohydrate; 7 g fiber; 5 g sugar; 486 mg phosphorus; 109 mg calcium; 4 mg iron; 209 mg sodium; 1791 mg potassium; 3265 IU vitamin A; 26 mg ATE vitamin E; 30 mg vitamin C; 66 mg cholesterol; 474 g water

Stir-Fried Chicken and Brown Rice

Asian-style chicken stir-fry.

2 tablespoons (28 ml) olive oil, divided

8 ounces (225 g) boneless chicken breast sliced into strips

½ cup (75 g) chopped red bell pepper

½ cup (50 g) chopped scallions

3 cups (660 g) cooked, cooled brown rice

2 tablespoons (28 ml) Reduced Sodium Soy Sauce (see recipe page 133)

1 tablespoon (15 ml) rice wine vinegar

1 cup (130 g) frozen peas, thawed

Heat large nonstick skillet over medium heat. Add 1 tablespoon oil. Add chicken, bell pepper, and scallions. Cook 5 minutes until chicken is cooked through. Remove to plate. Heat remaining oil in skillet. Add rice and cook 1 minute. Stir in soy sauce, vinegar, and peas; cook 1 minute. Stir in chicken and vegetable mixture.

—Yield: 4 servings

NUTRITIONAL ANALYSIS

PER SERVING: 213 g water; 349 calories (26% from fat, 25% from protein, 49% from carb); 21 g protein; 10 g total fat; 2 g saturated fat; 6 g monounsaturated fat; 2 g polyunsaturated fat; 43 g carbohydrate; 6 g fiber; 3 g sugar; 313 mg phosphorus; 49 mg calcium; 2 mg iron; 77 mg sodium; 425 mg potassium; 1560 IU vitamin A; 3 mg vitamin E; 31 mg vitamin C; 33 mg cholesterol

Turkey Vegetable Sauté

Turkey and vegetable sauce with just a hint of Mexican flavor. I particularly like this one over whole wheat spaghetti, but it's also good over brown rice.

1 pound (455 g) ground turkey

1 cup (160 g) onion, cut in rings

1 cup (130 g) sliced carrot

½ cup (50 g) sliced celery

½ cup (75 g) chunked green bell pepper

4 ounces (115 g) mushrooms, sliced

½ teaspoon cumin

½ teaspoon garlic salt

1 cup (180 g) chopped tomato

15 black olives, halved

3 slices low-sodium bacon, cooked and broken into pieces (optional)

Brown turkey. Add onion, carrot, celery, bell pepper, and mushrooms; add cumin and garlic salt and cook over medium heat until vegetables are crisp-tender. Add tomatoes, olives, and bacon and heat through.

—Yield: 6 servings

NUTRITIONAL ANALYSIS

PER SERVING: 161 g water; 197 calories (32% from fat, 52% from protein, 17% from carb); 25 g protein; 7 g total fat; 2 g saturated fat; 2 g monounsaturated fat; 1 g polyunsaturated fat; 8 g carbohydrate; 2 g fiber; 3 g sugar; 226 mg phosphorus; 50 mg calcium; 2 mg iron; 217 mg sodium; 521 mg potassium; 3873 IU vitamin A; 0 mg vitamin E; 20 mg vitamin C; 62 mg cholesterol

Turkey Skillet Pie

This is a great dish to make with leftover holiday turkey and stuffing.

1 tablespoon (15 ml) olive oil

⅓ cup (35 g) celery, chopped

2 tablespoons (20 g) onion, finely chopped

⅔ cup (160 ml) fat-free evaporated milk

2 cups (400 g) prepared stuffing

3 cups (525 g) cooked turkey, chopped

1 cup (110 g) low fat Swiss cheese, shredded

Heat olive oil in a small skillet; cook celery and onion until soft. In a large bowl, combine milk, stuffing, and onion mixture. Stir in turkey. Pour into a large skillet and sprinkle with cheese. Cook until heated through, about 10 minutes.

—Yield: 6 servings

NUTRITIONAL ANALYSIS

PER SERVING: 305 calories (33% from fat, 42% from protein, 25% from carbohydrate); 31 g protein; 11 g total fat; 3 g saturated fat; 5 g monounsaturated fat; 3 g polyunsaturated fat; 19 g carbohydrate; 2 g fiber; 5 g sugar; 359 mg phosphorus; 325 mg calcium; 2 mg iron; 501 mg sodium; 364 mg potassium; 370 IU vitamin A; 113 mg ATE vitamin E; 1 mg vitamin C; 77 mg cholesterol; 133 g water

Turkey-Stuffed Zucchini

This is perfect for those times when you don't get back to check the garden as often as you should and find a couple of zucchini that would make great softball bats. Discard the seeds and any center part of the squash that has gotten hard or stringy, and put the rest of what you scoop out into the filling.

3 large zucchini

1¼ pounds (570 g) ground turkey

1 cup (160 g) onion, chopped

2 cloves garlic, crushed

2 cups (360 g) canned no-salt-added tomatoes

1½ cups (250 g) cooked rice, or small pasta

1 teaspoon (0.7 g) dried basil

12 ounces (340 g) Swiss cheese, sliced

Preheat broiler. Cut the zucchini in half lengthwise. Scrape out the center, leaving a thickness of about ½ inch (1.2 cm). Discard the seeds and chop the remainder of the flesh; set aside. In a large skillet, cook the turkey, onion, and garlic until turkey is done. Stir in tomatoes, rice, basil, and chopped zucchini flesh. Cook the zucchini halves in boiling water until it begins to soften. Drain and place in baking pan. Divide the filling between the zucchini halves. Place a slice of cheese on top of each. Place under broiler until cheese is melted and bubbly.

—Yield: 6 servings

NUTRITIONAL ANALYSIS

PER SERVING: 309 calories (15% from fat, 54% from protein, 32% from carbohydrate); 42 g protein; 5 g total fat; 2 g saturated fat; 1 g monounsaturated fat; 1 g polyunsaturated fat; 24 g carbohydrate; 4 g fiber; 7 g sugar; 633 mg phosphorus; 625 mg calcium; 4 mg iron; 236 mg sodium; 1012 mg potassium; 563 IU vitamin A; 22 mg ATE vitamin E; 41 mg vitamin C; 89 mg cholesterol; 408 g water

Shepherd's Pie with Cornbread Crust

A meal in a pan. The cornbread on the bottom adds some substance to this while adding minimal fat and sodium.

1 pound (455 g) ground turkey

1 cup (160 g) chopped onion

12 ounces (340 g) mixed vegetables

3 cups (675 g) mashed potatoes

4 ounces (113 g) shredded Cheddar cheese

Cornbread Crust

1 cup (120 g) whole wheat pastry flour

½ cup (70 g) cornmeal

1 tablespoon sugar

2 teaspoons baking powder

1 cup (235 ml) skim milk

1 egg

2 tablespoons (28 ml) canola oil

Sauté turkey and onion. Drain. Cook vegetables until almost done. Drain. To make crust, stir together flour, cornmeal, sugar, and baking powder. Combine milk, egg, and oil. Stir into dry ingredients until just mixed. Spread cornbread in the bottom of a 9 x 13-inch (23 x 33-cm) baking dish sprayed with nonstick vegetable oil spray. On top of cornbread, layer meat mixture, veggies, and potatoes. Sprinkle with cheese. Bake at 425°F (220°C, gas mark 7) for 20 minutes.

—Yield: 8 servings

NUTRITIONAL ANALYSIS

PER SERVING: 131 g water; 417 calories (27% from fat, 27% from protein, 46% from carb); 28 g protein; 13 g total fat; 5 g saturated fat; 3 g monounsaturated fat; 3 g polyunsaturated fat; 48 g carbohydrate; 6 g fiber; 5 g sugar; 390 mg phosphorus; 258 mg calcium; 3 mg iron; 320 mg sodium; 672 mg potassium; 2091 IU vitamin A; 66 mg vitamin E; 21 mg vitamin C; 85 mg cholesterol

CHAPTER 4

Main Dishes: Beef

Beef has gotten a reputation for being bad for you. And it can be. The key to heart healthy beef lies in the selection of the cut used and the preparation. Most of the dishes here use low fat cuts like round steak or extra lean ground beef. The preparation is careful to keep it tender and flavorful without adding fat or sodium. We still eat beef more often than is recommended, but recipes like these make it tasty as well as good for you. Many contain the nutrition and fiber boost of whole grains and legumes.

Tex-Mex Meat Loaf

We love meat loaf and we love food with a Mexican flavor, so it's no surprise that this turned out to be a big hit around our house.

1½ pounds (675 g) ground beef

2 cups (200 g) cooked kidney beans, rinsed and drained

1½ cups (390 g) salsa, divided

1 cup (160 g) chopped onion

½ teaspoon minced garlic

½ cup (60 g) bread crumbs

2 eggs

1½ teaspoons ground cumin

2 tablespoons (30 g) brown sugar

Combine beef, beans, 1 cup (260 g) salsa, onion, garlic, bread crumbs, eggs, and cumin. Mix well. Press into a loaf shape on a broiler pan or roasting pan. Bake 1 hour at 350°F (180°C, gas mark 4). Carefully pour off any drippings. Combine remaining salsa and brown sugar; mix well. Spread over top of meat loaf. Continue baking 15 minutes; remove and let stand 10 minutes.

—Yield: 6 servings

NUTRITIONAL ANALYSIS

PER SERVING: 176 g water; 579 calories (20% from fat, 34% from protein, 46% from carb); 41 g protein; 10 g total fat; 4 g saturated fat; 4 g monounsaturated fat; 1 g polyunsaturated fat; 55 g carbohydrate; 17 g fiber; 10 g sugar; 492 mg phosphorus; 155 mg calcium; 9 mg iron; 223 mg sodium; 1484 mg potassium; 287 IU vitamin A; 26 mg vitamin E; 6 mg vitamin C; 157 mg cholesterol

German Meatballs

These German-flavored meatballs would traditionally be served over spaetzle, but they are also good with noodles, rice, or mashed potatoes.

1 egg

¼ cup (60 ml) skim milk

¼ cup (29 g) bread crumbs

¼ teaspoon (0.2 g) poultry seasoning

1 pound (455 g) extra-lean ground beef (93% lean)

2 cups (470 ml) low sodium beef broth

½ cup (35 g) mushrooms, sliced

½ cup (80 g) onion, chopped

1 cup (230 g) fat free sour cream

1 tablespoon (8 g) flour

1 teaspoon (2.1 g) caraway seed

Combine egg and milk. Stir in bread crumbs and poultry seasoning. Add beef and mix well. Form into 24 meatballs, each about 1½ inches (3.8-cm). Brown meatballs in skillet. Drain. Add broth, mushrooms, and onion to the skillet. Cover and simmer for 30 minutes. Stir together sour cream, flour, and caraway seed. Add to skillet. Cook and stir until thickened.

—Yield: 6 servings

NUTRITIONAL ANALYSIS

PER SERVING: 281 calories (32% from fat, 47% from protein, 21% from carbohydrate); 19 g protein; 6 g total fat; 2 g saturated fat; 2 g monounsaturated fat; 1 g polyunsaturated fat; 8 g carbohydrate; 1 g fiber; 1 g sugar; 199 mg phosphorus; 87 mg calcium; 2 mg iron; 172 mg sodium; 317 mg potassium; 212 IU vitamin A; 47 mg ATE vitamin E; 2 mg vitamin C; 105 mg cholesterol; 194 g water

Reduced-Fat Meatballs

This meatball recipe has been in the family for years, long before we were concerned with heart-healthy cooking. It's been modified a number of times as our diets changed, first to reduce the sodium, and later to make it lower in fat. The meatballs are good by themselves, but they're better if allowed to simmer in the sauce in a slow cooker for a few hours.

1½ pounds (680 g) extra-lean ground beef (93% lean)

3 eggs

½ cup Parmesan cheese, shredded

½ teaspoon (1.5 g) garlic powder

1 tablespoon (0.4 g) dried parsley

½ tablespoon (1.5 g) dried oregano

4 slices bread, crumbled

2 cups (320 g) onion, chopped

6 ounces (170 g) no-salt-added tomato paste

1½ cups (355 ml) water

½ cup (120 ml) red wine vinegar

3 tablespoons (45 g) brown sugar

Preheat oven to 375°F (190°C, or gas mark 5). Combine beef, eggs, cheese, garlic powder, parsley, oregano, and bread. Form into 1-inch (2.5-cm) balls. Bake for 30 to 40 minutes, turning once. Pour a few tablespoons (45 ml) of meat drippings into a skillet; sauté onion. Combine onions, tomato paste, water, vinegar, and brown sugar and place in slow cooker. Add meatballs. Stir to mix and cook on low for several hours.

—Yield: 6 servings

NUTRITIONAL ANALYSIS

PER SERVING: 457 calories (31% from fat, 37% from protein, 32% from carbohydrate); 32 g protein; 12 g total fat; 5 g saturated fat; 4 g monounsaturated fat; 1 g polyunsaturated fat; 28 g carbohydrate; 4 g fiber; 15 g sugar; 340 mg phosphorus; 173 mg calcium; 5 mg iron; 398 mg sodium; 787 mg potassium; 653 IU vitamin A; 10 mg ATE vitamin E; 11 mg vitamin C; 186 mg cholesterol; 254 g water

Stuffed Banana Peppers

Another recipe that uses some excess peppers. The original recipe I used to develop this one called for frying, but I decided to make them in the oven instead to reduce the amount of fat, since the meat and cheese already have a significant amount.

12 banana peppers, hot or sweet

1 pound (455 g) extra-lean ground beef (93% lean)

½ cup (80 g) onion, finely chopped

½ cup (55 g) Swiss cheese, shredded

1 egg

¼ teaspoon (0.5 g) black pepper

¼ cup (30 g) flour

Preheat oven to 350°F (180°C, or gas mark 4). Wash and clean peppers, then cut off the top and a small part of the bottom of peppers. In a large skillet, sauté ground beef and onions until meat is browned. Stir in cheese. Stuff mixture into peppers. Whisk egg and black pepper in a bowl. Dip peppers in egg mixture. Roll in flour, dip in egg again, and roll in flour again. Place in 9 x 13-inch (23 x 33-cm) baking dish and coat surface with nonstick vegetable oil spray until flour is moistened. Bake for 20 minutes, or until cheese is melted and coating begins to brown.

—Yield: 4 servings

Beef Barley Skillet

A tasty and healthy family meal that cooks in one pan.

¾ pound (338 g) ground beef

½ cup (80 g) chopped onion

¼ cup (38 g) chopped green bell pepper

¼ cup (25 g) chopped celery

¼ teaspoon black pepper

½ teaspoon marjoram

1 teaspoon sugar

1 teaspoon Worcestershire sauce

2 cups (480 g) no-salt-added canned tomatoes, broken up

1½ cups (355 ml) water

¾ cup (150 g) pearl barley

Sauté meat, onion, green pepper, and celery in nonstick fry pan. Drain off excess fat; stir in remaining ingredients. Bring to a boil. Reduce heat to simmer; cover and cook about 1 hour.

—Yield: 3 servings

NUTRITIONAL ANALYSIS

PER SERVING: 389 g water; 477 calories (21% from fat, 31% from protein, 48% from carb); 29 g protein; 9 g total fat; 3 g saturated fat; 3 g monounsaturated fat; 1 g polyunsaturated fat; 45 g carbohydrate; 10 g fiber; 7 g sugar; 326 mg phosphorus; 90 mg calcium; 6 mg iron; 129 mg sodium; 932 mg potassium; 292 IU vitamin A; 0 mg vitamin E; 30 mg vitamin C; 78 mg cholesterol

Brisket of Beef with Beans

Kind of like baked beans with the addition of the beef. The cooking liquid gives the beef a nice flavor, and the beans go well with it.

1 pound (455 g) navy beans

2 pound (900 g) beef brisket

2 slices bacon

½ teaspoon black pepper, freshly ground

2 cups (475 ml) water

¼ cup (60 ml) maple syrup

½ cup (115 g) packed brown sugar

½ teaspoon dry mustard

Soak beans in water overnight. Drain the beans. Brown the fat side of the brisket in a Dutch oven or heavy skillet over medium-high heat. Add the bacon and brown the other side. Add the pepper, water, and beans. Reduce heat to medium and cook, covered, for 2 hours or until the beef and beans are tender, stirring occasionally to prevent sticking. Remove the beef and keep warm. Add the maple syrup, brown sugar, and mustard to the beans. Mix thoroughly, and simmer over medium heat for another 10 minutes. Slice the brisket thinly and serve with the beans.

—Yield: 6 servings

NUTRITIONAL ANALYSIS

PER SERVING: 221 g water; 644 calories (49% from fat, 22% from protein, 29% from carb); 35 g protein; 35 g total fat; 14 g saturated fat; 15 g monounsaturated fat; 2 g polyunsaturated fat; 47 g carbohydrate; 8 g fiber; 26 g sugar; 379 mg phosphorus; 103 mg calcium; 5 mg iron; 165 mg sodium; 829 mg potassium; 2 IU vitamin A; 0 mg vitamin E; 0 mg vitamin C; 125 mg cholesterol

TIP

The beef also makes great sandwiches.

Ground Beef Stroganoff

Fiber up your stroganoff by using whole wheat noodles.

½ pound (225 g) ground beef, extra lean

½ cup (35 g) sliced mushrooms

1 packet onion soup mix

1 tablespoon whole wheat flour

1¾ cups (414 ml) water

8 ounces (225 g) whole wheat noodles, cooked and drained

8 tablespoons (120 g) plain fat-free yogurt

Brown beef and drain. Add mushrooms. Whisk dry soup mix and flour into water and heat. Stir until thickened. Combine thickened onion soup and cooked beef. Serve over whole wheat noodles. Garnish with a dollop of yogurt.

—Yield: 4 servings

NUTRITIONAL ANALYSIS

PER SERVING: 178 g water; 360 calories (26% from fat, 23% from protein, 51% from carb); 21 g protein; 11 g total fat; 4 g saturated fat; 4 g monounsaturated fat; 1 g polyunsaturated fat; 48 g carbohydrate; 2 g fiber; 3 g sugar; 288 mg phosphorus; 95 mg calcium; 3 mg iron; 222 mg sodium; 397 mg potassium; 2 IU vitamin A; 1 mg vitamin E; 1 mg vitamin C; 40 mg cholesterol

Beef Stroganoff

Serve this creamy beef dish over noodles. Lima beans always seem to go well as an accompaniment to me.

1 pound (455 g) beef round steak

2 tablespoons (30 ml) olive oil

1½ cups (105 g) mushrooms, sliced

½ cup (120 ml) dry sherry

¼ cup (60 ml) low sodium beef broth

1 cup (230 g) fat-free sour cream

Cut beef into ¼-inch (63-mm) strips. Heat oil in skillet. Cook beef quickly, 2 to 4 minutes. Remove beef from skillet. Add mushrooms to skillet and cook for 2 to 3 minutes. Remove mushrooms. Add sherry and broth to skillet and cook until liquid is reduced to about ⅓ cup (80 ml). Stir in sour cream. Stir in beef and mushrooms. Heat through, but do not boil.

—Yield: 4 servings

NUTRITIONAL ANALYSIS

PER SERVING: 419 calories (36% from fat, 55% from protein, 9% from carbohydrate); 44 g protein; 13 g total fat; 3 g saturated fat; 7 g monounsaturated fat; 1 g polyunsaturated fat; 7 g carbohydrate; 0 g fiber; 1 g sugar; 341 mg phosphorus; 72 mg calcium; 4 mg iron; 89 mg sodium; 576 mg potassium; 225 IU vitamin A; 61 mg ATE vitamin E; 1 mg vitamin C; 126 mg cholesterol; 175 g water

Cholent

Cholent is a European delicacy that enabled Jews to prepare a warm Sabbath meal without violating the prohibition against cooking, since the dish is prepared on Friday and slow cooks until Sabbath lunch. If you are not preparing it in the traditional manner, it will be done in 10 to 12 hours, but the longer cooking time makes the meat even more tender and the flavors more developed.

1 cup (250 g) dried kidney beans

1 cup (208 g) dried navy beans

1 cup (225 g) dried split peas

3 pound (1¼ kg) beef brisket, cut into large chunks

1½ cups (240 g) sliced onion

1 cup (200 g) pearl barley

4 potatoes, peeled and sliced

½ cup (120 ml) water

¼ teaspoon black pepper

Boil all beans in a separate pot for 5 minutes, then drain and rinse beans. Arrange in a slow cooker layers of meat, onion, beans, barley, and potatoes. Add pepper, then water. Cover tightly. Set slow cooker on lowest setting; it will be done within 24 hours.

—Yield: 10 servings

NUTRITIONAL ANALYSIS

PER SERVING: 253 g water; 710 calories (40% from fat, 22% from protein, 38% from carb); 40 g protein; 31 g total fat; 12 g saturated fat; 13 g monounsaturated fat; 2 g polyunsaturated fat; 68 g carbohydrate; 16 g fiber; 4 g sugar; 551 mg phosphorus; 107 mg calcium; 7 mg iron; 101 mg sodium; 1749 mg potassium; 16 IU vitamin A; 0 mg vitamin E; 16 mg vitamin C; 110 mg cholesterol

Cornbread-Topped Bean Casserole

A meal in a pan. Preparation is made easier by using canned pork and beans, but the flavor definitely says homemade.

1 pound (455 g) ground beef

½ cup (80 g) chopped onion

2 cups (506 g) pork and beans

4 ounces (115 g) chopped green chiles, drained

2 tablespoons taco seasoning mix

¼ cup (60 ml) water

1¼ cups (175 g) cornmeal

¼ cup (31 g) flour

1 tablespoon baking powder

1 tablespoon sugar

1 cup (115 g) shredded Cheddar cheese

1 cup (235 ml) skim milk

1 egg

3 tablespoons (45 ml) canola oil

Brown ground beef and onion; drain. Stir in pork and beans, chiles, seasoning mix, and water. Spread in 8-inch (20-cm) glass baking dish. Heat oven to 350°F (180°C, gas mark 4). Combine dry ingredients. Add cheese, tossing to coat. Add remaining ingredients, stirring just until dry ingredients are moistened. Spread topping evenly over ground beef mixture. Bake 30 to 35 minutes or until wooden pick comes out clean. Let stand 5 minutes before cutting to serve.

—Yield: 9 servings

NUTRITIONAL ANALYSIS

PER SERVING: 136 g water; 402 calories (37% from fat, 22% from protein, 41% from carb); 20 g protein; 15 g total fat; 5 g saturated fat; 6 g monounsaturated fat; 2 g polyunsaturated fat; 36 g carbohydrate; 4 g fiber; 5 g sugar; 317 mg phosphorus; 281 mg calcium; 4 mg iron; 669 mg sodium; 445 mg potassium; 440 IU vitamin A; 64 mg vitamin E; 7 mg vitamin C; 78 mg cholesterol

Three Bean Casserole

If you like baked beans, but you are one of those people who want meat with their meal, this one-dish bean and beef dinner should be just the thing for you.

15 ounces (420 g) kidney beans, rinsed and drained

15 ounces (420 g) chickpeas, rinsed and drained

15 ounces (420 g) lima beans, rinsed and drained

1 pound (455 g) ground beef, extra lean

1 cup (160 g) chopped onion

½ teaspoon minced garlic

¼ cup (60 g) brown sugar

½ teaspoon black pepper

2 tablespoons (28 ml) mustard

½ cup (120 ml) low-sodium ketchup

1 teaspoon cumin

¼ cup (60 ml) water

1 tablespoon (15 ml) cider vinegar

In 2½-quart (2.5-L) casserole dish combine beans; set aside. In skillet cook beef, onion, and garlic. Remove from heat and drain. Add remaining ingredients. Mix well. Stir beef mix into beans. Bake 350°F (180°C, gas mark 4) for 45 minutes.

—Yield: 6 servings

NUTRITIONAL ANALYSIS

PER SERVING: 246 g water; 495 calories (26% from fat, 24% from protein, 50% from carb); 30 g protein; 14 g total fat; 5 g saturated fat; 6 g monounsaturated fat; 1 g polyunsaturated fat; 63 g carbohydrate; 15 g fiber; 15 g sugar; 366 mg phosphorus; 120 mg calcium; 7 mg iron; 295 mg sodium; 1092 mg potassium; 333 IU vitamin A; 0 mg vitamin E; 13 mg vitamin C; 52 mg cholesterol

Western Casserole

A simple beef-and-noodle casserole, updated to give you more fiber without sacrificing taste.

1 pound (455 g) beef stew meat, cut in cubes

¼ cup (30 g) whole wheat flour

¼ cup (60 ml) olive oil

6 ounces (170 g) no-salt-added tomato paste

½ cup (120 ml) dry red wine

1 cup (235 ml) water

1 teaspoon thyme

1 teaspoon oregano

1 cup (70 g) sliced mushrooms

1 cup (180 g) chopped tomato

4 ounces (115 g) whole wheat noodles, cooked and drained

1 cup (115 g) shredded Cheddar cheese

Coat meat with flour; brown in oil. Add all ingredients except noodles and cheese. Cover and simmer for 1 hour. Add noodles and cheese. Simmer 5 minutes more and serve.

—Yield: 4 servings

NUTRITIONAL ANALYSIS

PER SERVING: 264 g water; 607 calories (47% from fat, 27% from protein, 26% from carb); 41 g protein; 31 g total fat; 11 g saturated fat; 15 g monounsaturated fat; 2 g polyunsaturated fat; 39 g carbohydrate; 3 g fiber; 6 g sugar; 563 mg phosphorus; 299 mg calcium; 6 mg iron; 341 mg sodium; 1114 mg potassium; 1239 IU vitamin A; 85 mg vitamin E; 20 mg vitamin C; 96 mg cholesterol

Sauerbraten

Round roasts are not the tenderest cut of beef. But marinating followed by slow, moist cooking makes this one a treat to eat, not to mention the great flavor. Serve with egg noodles.

FOR MARINADE:

2½ cups (590 ml) water

1½ cups (355 ml) red wine vinegar

1 tablespoon (13 g) sugar

¼ teaspoon (0.5 g) ground ginger

12 whole cloves

6 bay leaves

2 cups (320 g) onion, sliced

FOR MEAT:

4 pounds (1.8 kg) beef round roast

2 tablespoons (30 ml) olive oil

½ cup (65 g) carrot, finely chopped

½ cup (50 g) celery, finely chopped

½ cup (80 g) onion, finely chopped

1 cup (100 g) gingersnaps, crushed

⅔ cup (160 ml) water

In a large bowl combine the marinade ingredients. Add roast. Cover and refrigerate for 1½ to 2 days, turning occasionally. Remove meat and wipe dry. Strain and reserve marinade liquid.

In a Dutch oven, brown meat in oil on all sides. Add reserved marinade, carrots, celery, and onion. Cover and simmer until meat is tender, 2 to 2½ hours. Remove meat to platter and slice thinly. Reserve 2 cups of cooking liquid in pot. Add gingersnaps and water. Cook and stir until thickened. Serve sauce with meat.

—Yield: 10 servings

NUTRITIONAL ANALYSIS

PER SERVING: 323 calories (30% from fat, 54% from protein, 16% from carbohydrate); 41 g protein; 10 g total fat; 3 g saturated fat; 5 g monounsaturated fat; 1 g polyunsaturated fat; 12 g carbohydrate; 1 g fiber; 5 g sugar; 419 mg phosphorus; 62 mg calcium; 4 mg iron; 183 mg sodium; 792 mg potassium; 1100 IU vitamin A; 0 mg ATE vitamin E; 4 mg vitamin C; 91 mg cholesterol; 288 g water

Beef Paprikash

The origin of this meal is Hungarian. It's the kind of slow-cooker meal that greets you with a wonderful aroma when you return home from work. Stick a loaf of bread in the bread machine on timed bake and you have an instant dinner.

2 pounds (900 g) round steak, cubed

6 potatoes, cut in ¾-inch (2-cm) pieces

1 cup frozen pearl onions

¼ cup (31 g) flour

1 tablespoon paprika

½ teaspoon black pepper

¼ teaspoon caraway seed

2 cups (475 ml) low-sodium beef broth

1 cup (130 g) no-salt-added frozen peas

½ cup (115 g) sour cream

Add beef, potatoes, onions, flour, and spices to slow cooker. Pour beef broth over. Cover and cook on low 7 to 8 hours. Stir in peas and sour cream. Cover and cook on low about 15 minutes longer, until peas are tender.

—Yield: 6 servings

NUTRITIONAL ANALYSIS

PER SERVING: 472 g water; 590 calories (15% from fat, 36% from protein, 49% from carb); 52 g protein; 10 g total fat; 4 g saturated fat; 4 g monounsaturated fat; 1 g polyunsaturated fat; 72 g carbohydrate; 8 g fiber; 5 g sugar; 463 mg phosphorus; 76 mg calcium; 6 mg iron; 148 mg sodium; 1513 mg potassium; 1252 IU vitamin A; 20 mg vitamin E; 28 mg vitamin C; 96 mg cholesterol

Pot Roast with Root Vegetables

This is a simple fall pot roast, featuring root vegetables and not containing a lot of added ingredients. Cooking it in a covered roasting pan will ensure that the meat is very tender.

2 pound (900 g) beef bottom round roast

4 potatoes, quartered

4 turnips, peeled and cut into quarters

6 carrots, sliced

1 onion, peeled and quartered

1 parsnip, peeled and sliced

2 cups (475 ml) low-sodium beef broth

2 cups (480 g) no-salt-added canned tomatoes

Place all ingredients in large roasting pan. Cover and roast at 350°F (180°C, gas mark 4) until vegetables are done and meat is tender, about 2 hours.

—Yield: 8 servings

NUTRITIONAL ANALYSIS

PER SERVING: 383 g water; 527 calories (38% from fat, 31% from protein, 31% from carb); 40 g protein; 22 g total fat; 9 g saturated fat; 9 g monounsaturated fat; 1 g polyunsaturated fat; 41 g carbohydrate; 6 g fiber; 6 g sugar; 370 mg phosphorus; 72 mg calcium; 5 mg iron; 209 mg sodium; 1492 mg potassium; 4280 IU vitamin A; 0 mg vitamin E; 35 mg vitamin C; 108 mg cholesterol

Country Beef Stew

A hearty stew of beef and beans, perfect for a winter day.

2 tablespoons (28 ml) olive oil

2 pound (900 g) boneless beef chuck, cut into 1-inch (2.5-cm) cubes

2 cups (480 g) canned no-salt-added tomatoes

1 cup (160 g) coarsely chopped onion

1½ cups (355 ml) water

1 tablespoon (15 ml) Worcestershire sauce

¾ teaspoon tarragon

½ teaspoon black pepper

½ teaspoon garlic powder

2 cups (260 g) sliced carrot

5 cups (885 g) cooked great northern beans, drained

In large kettle or Dutch oven, heat oil until hot. Add half of the beef and brown on all sides. Remove with slotted spoon and repeat with remaining beef. Return meat to kettle. Add tomatoes, onion, water, Worcestershire sauce, tarragon, black pepper, and garlic powder. Bring to a boil. Reduce heat and simmer, covered, until meat is almost tender, about 1 hour. Add carrot. Simmer, covered, until carrot and meat are tender, about 20 minutes. Stir in beans and cook until beans are heated through, about 5 minutes.

—Yield: 8 servings

NUTRITIONAL ANALYSIS

PER SERVING: 321 g water; 587 calories (40% from fat, 31% from protein, 29% from carb); 46 g protein; 26 g total fat; 9 g saturated fat; 10 g monounsaturated fat; 3 g polyunsaturated fat; 42 g carbohydrate; 10 g fiber; 4 g sugar; 452 mg phosphorus; 141 mg calcium; 6 mg iron; 110 mg sodium; 1102 mg potassium; 5455 IU vitamin A; 0 mg vitamin E; 15 mg vitamin C; 108 mg cholesterol

Beef and Barley Stew

A hearty stew that makes a meal in a bowl (although I prefer it with a slice of fresh hot bread).

1½ pounds (675 g) beef round steak

¼ cup (31 g) flour

2 tablespoons (28 ml) olive oil

1 cup (160 g) chopped onion

½ teaspoon crushed garlic

3 cups (710 ml) low-sodium beef broth

2 cups (260 g) sliced carrot

¼ cup (50 g) pearl barley

1 tablespoon (15 ml) Reduced Sodium Soy Sauce (see recipe page 133)

½ teaspoon oregano

½ cup (50 g) chopped celery

½ teaspoon black pepper

Trim fat from meat and cut into bite-size cubes. Dust beef with flour. Using a heavy pot, brown beef in hot oil, browning all sides. Remove meat and set aside. Add onion and garlic to drippings and cook until onion is transparent. Return the meat to pot. Add broth, barley, soy sauce, and oregano. Cover and simmer for 45 minutes. Add carrot and celery and simmer until meat is tender, about 40 minutes. Add water as needed. Season with pepper.

—Yield: 6 servings

NUTRITIONAL ANALYSIS

PER SERVING: 257 g water; 352 calories (28% from fat, 52% from protein, 20% from carb); 45 g protein; 11 g total fat; 3 g saturated fat; 6 g monounsaturated fat; 1 g polyunsaturated fat; 17 g carbohydrate; 3 g fiber; 3 g sugar; 327 mg phosphorus; 42 mg calcium; 5 mg iron; 210 mg sodium; 693 mg potassium; 7222 IU vitamin A; 0 mg vitamin E; 5 mg vitamin C; 102 mg cholesterol

CHAPTER 5

Main Dishes: Pork

Like beef, pork doesn't have to be as bad for you as it is often portrayed. Most of these recipes use lean cuts of pork from the loin, either as chops or roasts. This lets you get the great taste of pork done up in a variety of ways, from Southern to Indian, without worrying about eating heart healthy.

Skillet Pork Chops

This is a great skillet meal. Not exactly typical Hamburger Helper fare, but the kind of thing that you would want to serve on the patio after a summer day of working in the yard.

6 pork loin chops

1 tablespoon (15 ml) olive oil

1 cup (160 g) onion, chopped

½ teaspoon (1.5 g) minced garlic

½ cup (120 ml) low sodium chicken broth

½ cup (120 ml) barbecue sauce

4 cups (900 g) no-salt-added canned pinto beans, drained

2 jalapeno peppers, chopped

In a large skillet, sear pork chops in oil for 5 minutes, or until brown. Remove pork chops and place on a plate. Add onion and garlic to skillet; cook 10 minutes. Stir in broth, barbecue sauce, beans, and jalapenos. Heat mixture to a boil. Return pork to skillet. Reduce heat; cover and simmer 50 to 60 minutes, stirring sauce and turning chops occasionally until meat is fork-tender.

—Yield: 6 servings

NUTRITIONAL ANALYSIS

PER SERVING: 370 calories (18% from fat, 35% from protein, 47% from carbohydrate); 33 g protein; 7 g total fat; 2 g saturated fat; 4 g monounsaturated fat; 1 g polyunsaturated fat; 43 g carbohydrate; 11 g fiber; 9 g sugar; 403 mg phosphorus; 73 mg calcium; 3 mg iron; 261 mg sodium; 938 mg potassium; 45 IU vitamin A; 2 mg ATE vitamin E; 6 mg vitamin C; 64 mg cholesterol; 206 g water

Grilled Pork Chops

A quick and easy grill recipe for a summer evening. You could make a little extra of the marinade and put it on zucchini slices to grill as a side dish.

2 tablespoons (30 ml) honey

¼ cup (60 ml) Worcestershire sauce

¼ teaspoon (0.5 g) black pepper

¼ teaspoon (0.8 g) garlic powder

4 boneless pork loin chops

In a shallow glass dish or bowl, mix together honey, Worcestershire sauce, pepper, and garlic powder. Add pork chops and toss to coat. Cover and refrigerate for no more than 4 hours. Lightly oil grill and preheat to medium. Remove pork chops from marinade. Grill 20 to 30 minutes, or until cooked through, turning often.

—Yield: 4 servings

NUTRITIONAL ANALYSIS

PER SERVING: 174 calories (22% from fat, 50% from protein, 27% from carbohydrate); 22 g protein; 4 g total fat; 1 g saturated fat; 2 g monounsaturated fat; 0 g polyunsaturated fat; 12 g carbohydrate; 0 g fiber; 9 g sugar; 238 mg phosphorus; 14 mg calcium; 2 mg iron; 199 mg sodium; 503 mg potassium; 24 IU vitamin A; 2 mg ATE vitamin E; 28 mg vitamin C; 64 mg cholesterol; 80 g water

Barbecue Pork Chops

A nice sweet-and-sour sort of barbecue sauce gives these chops great flavor.

4 pork loin chops, 1 inch (2.5 cm) thick

1 cup (160 g) onion, finely chopped

2 tablespoons (30 ml) vinegar

1 tablespoon (15 ml) canola oil

½ teaspoon (1.5 g) dry mustard

1 tablespoon (15 ml) Worcestershire sauce

1 teaspoon (2 g) black pepper

1 tablespoon (13 g) sugar

½ teaspoon (1.3 g) paprika

Score the edges of the chops to prevent curling. Place into a large baking pan; set aside. Combine remaining ingredients and mix well. Pour over the chops to coat well. Cover and chill for 2 to 4 hours. Grill chops to desired doneness, basting often.

—Yield: 4 servings

NUTRITIONAL ANALYSIS

PER SERVING: 196 calories (37% from fat, 46% from protein, 17% from carbohydrate); 22 g protein; 8 g total fat; 2 g saturated fat; 4 g monounsaturated fat; 2 g polyunsaturated fat; 8 g carbohydrate; 1 g fiber; 5 g sugar; 238 mg phosphorus; 26 mg calcium; 1 mg iron; 91 mg sodium; 482 mg potassium; 166 IU vitamin A; 2 mg ATE vitamin E; 11 mg vitamin C; 64 mg cholesterol; 118 g water

Southern Pork Chops

Slow-cooked stuffed pork chops. Great with greens and cornbread.

4 pork loin chops, 1 inch (2.5 cm) thick

2 cups (215 g) cornbread stuffing mix

2 tablespoons (30 ml) low sodium chicken broth

⅓ cup (80 ml) orange juice

1 tablespoon (8 g) pecans, finely chopped

¼ cup (60 ml) light corn syrup

½ teaspoon (0.9 g) grated orange peel

With a sharp knife, cut a horizontal slit in side of each chop forming a pocket for stuffing. Combine stuffing with remaining ingredients. Fill pockets with stuffing mixture. Place chops on a metal rack in a slow cooker. Cover and cook on low for 6 to 8 hours. Uncover; turn to high and brush with sauce again. Cook on high for 15 to 20 minutes.

—Yield: 4 servings

NUTRITIONAL ANALYSIS

PER SERVING: 322 calories (19% from fat, 31% from protein, 50% from carbohydrate); 25 g protein; 7 g total fat; 2 g saturated fat; 3 g monounsaturated fat; 1 g polyunsaturated fat; 41 g carbohydrate; 4 g fiber; 7 g sugar; 262 mg phosphorus; 42 mg calcium; 2 mg iron; 431 mg sodium; 485 mg potassium; 70 IU vitamin A; 2 mg ATE vitamin E; 9 mg vitamin C; 64 mg cholesterol; 106 g water

Stuffed Pork Chops

These make an elegant meal. If possible, get the meat cutter at the store to cut the slit in the chops. The idea is to open it up inside, but not cut the whole way around the chop, so it's easier to close back up.

6 pork loin chops, cut 1½ inches (3.8 cm) thick

1 tablespoon (15 ml) olive oil

¼ cup (37 g) green bell peppers, chopped

¼ cup (40 g) onion, chopped

1 egg

1½ cups (120 g) bread cubes

¼ teaspoon (0.6 g) cumin

Make a slit in each chop to allow for stuffing. Heat oil in a small skillet over medium heat. Cook green bell pepper and onion until soft. Combine egg, bread, and cumin in a bowl. Pour pepper and onion mixture over bread mixture and toss to combine. Spoon an equal amount of the stuffing into the pocket of each chop. Secure with a wooden toothpick or skewer. Grill over medium heat about 20 minutes. Turn and grill 15 minutes more, or until done.

—Yield: 6 servings

NUTRITIONAL ANALYSIS

PER SERVING: 193 calories (36% from fat, 50% from protein, 14% from carbohydrate); 24 g protein; 7 g total fat; 2 g saturated fat; 4 g monounsaturated fat; 1 g polyunsaturated fat; 7 g carbohydrate; 1 g fiber; 1 g sugar; 245 mg phosphorus; 27 mg calcium; 2 mg iron; 123 mg sodium; 340 mg potassium; 69 IU vitamin A; 2 mg ATE vitamin E; 6 mg vitamin C; 99 mg cholesterol; 95 g water

TIP

If you have some raisin bread on hand, it's great in this recipe.

Pineapple-Stuffed Pork Chops

Feel like you need a trip to the islands? Let these pineapple-stuffed chops ferry you away.

4 pork loin chops, 1 inch (2.5-cm) thick

8 ounces (225 g) pineapple slices canned in juice, undrained

¼ cup (60 g) low sodium ketchup

1 tablespoon (6 g) scallions, chopped

½ teaspoon (1.5 g) dry mustard

Cut a pocket in each chop to make room for pineapple. Drain pineapple, reserving liquid. Cut two pineapple slices in half; cut up remaining pineapple and set aside. Place a half pineapple slice in the pocket of each chop. Heat grill to medium and grill about 20 minutes, turning once. Meanwhile, in a small saucepan combine ketchup, scallions, mustard, and the reserved pineapple juice and pieces. Heat to boiling, reduce heat and simmer 10 minutes. Grill chops 5 minutes more, brushing with sauce and turning several times.

—Yield: 4 servings

NUTRITIONAL ANALYSIS

PER SERVING: 189 calories (21% from fat, 46% from protein, 33% from carbohydrate); 22 g protein; 4 g total fat; 1 g saturated fat; 2 g monounsaturated fat; 0 g polyunsaturated fat; 15 g carbohydrate; 1 g fiber; 13 g sugar; 230 mg phosphorus; 25 mg calcium; 1 mg iron; 55 mg sodium; 495 mg potassium; 171 IU vitamin A; 2 mg ATE vitamin E; 8 mg vitamin C; 64 mg cholesterol; 131 g water

Hawaiian Kabobs

Serve these with rice for an island treat.

½ cup (120 ml) Reduced Sodium Soy Sauce
(see recipe page 133)

2 tablespoons (30 ml) olive oil

1 tablespoon (15 g) brown sugar

½ teaspoon (1.5 g) minced garlic

1 teaspoon (3 g) dry mustard

1 teaspoon (1.8 g) ground ginger

2 pounds (905 g) pork tenderloin,
cut in 1-inch (2.5-cm) cubes

2 cups (300 g) green bell peppers,
cut in 1-inch (2.5-cm) pieces

20 cherry tomatoes

6 ounces (170 g) pineapple chunks

In a large bowl combine soy sauce, oil, brown sugar, garlic, mustard, and ginger. Add pork cubes; cover and refrigerate overnight. Drain meat, reserving marinade. Thread meat, green bell pepper, tomatoes, and pineapple on skewers. Grill over medium-hot fire for 15 minutes, or until pork is done. Baste with marinade with cooking.

—Yield: 6 servings

NUTRITIONAL ANALYSIS

PER SERVING: 279 calories (11% from fat, 17% from protein, 72% from carbohydrate); 33 g protein; 10 g total fat; 2 g saturated fat; 6 g monounsaturated fat; 4 g polyunsaturated fat; 140 g carbohydrate; 2 g fiber; 8 g sugar; 370 mg phosphorus; 34 mg calcium; 2 mg iron; 217 mg sodium; 867 mg potassium; 566 IU vitamin A; 3 mg ATE vitamin E; 54 mg vitamin C; 98 mg cholesterol; 213 g water

Pork Chop and Bean Skillet

This makes a good dinner with fried potatoes.

6 center-cut pork chops

1 tablespoon (15 ml) olive oil

1 cup (160 g) chopped onion

½ teaspoon minced garlic

½ cup (120 ml) low-sodium chicken broth

½ cup (125 g) barbecue sauce

2 jalapeño peppers, chopped

4 cups (684 g) no-salt-added pinto beans, drained

In a large skillet, sear pork chops in oil until brown, about 5 minutes. Remove pork chops and place on plate. Add onion and garlic to skillet; cook 10 minutes. Stir in broth, barbecue sauce, jalapeños, and beans. Heat mixture to a boil. Return pork to skillet. Reduce heat. Cover and simmer 50 to 60 minutes, stirring sauce and turning chops occasionally until meat is fork-tender.

—Yield: 6 servings

NUTRITIONAL ANALYSIS

PER SERVING: 171 g water; 401 calories (23% from fat, 33% from protein, 43% from carb); 34 g protein; 10 g total fat; 3 g saturated fat; 5 g monounsaturated fat; 1 g polyunsaturated fat; 43 g carbohydrate; 11 g fiber; 9 g sugar; 370 mg phosphorus; 76 mg calcium; 3 mg iron; 269 mg sodium; 874 mg potassium; 43 IU vitamin A; 1 mg vitamin E; 6 mg vitamin C; 63 mg cholesterol

TIP

You can either use canned no-salt-added beans or cook your own dried ones.

Apple and Pork Chop Skillet

A newsletter subscriber originally sent in this recipe. It's just spicy enough to satisfy even those people who aren't on a diet.

1 tablespoon (15 ml) olive oil

½ cup (80 g) onion, chopped

3 pork loin chops

2 tablespoons (13 g) fresh ginger, peeled and thinly sliced

1 apple, peeled and thinly sliced

½ cup (120 ml) water

Heat oil in a nonstick skillet over medium heat. Sauté the chopped onion for 2 to 4 minutes, or until lightly browned. Push the onion pieces to one side of the skillet and place the chops in the center of the skillet. Brown the chops on each side. Spoon the onion pieces on top of each chop, dividing evenly. Layer each chop with sliced ginger and apple. Add the water to the skillet and cover tightly. Cook over low heat for 30 to 40 minutes depending on the thickness of the pork chops.

—Yield: 3 servings

NUTRITIONAL ANALYSIS

PER SERVING: 213 calories (39% from fat, 42% from protein, 20% from carbohydrate); 22 g protein; 9 g total fat; 2 g saturated fat; 5 g monounsaturated fat; 1 g polyunsaturated fat; 10 g carbohydrate; 1 g fiber; 6 g sugar; 238 mg phosphorus; 27 mg calcium; 1 mg iron; 55 mg sodium; 500 mg potassium; 29 IU vitamin A; 2 mg ATE vitamin E; 5 mg vitamin C; 64 mg cholesterol; 175 g water

Pork and Chickpea Stir-Fry

Another quick, tasty, nutritious dinner.

½ pound (225 g) boneless pork loin chops, cut into 1½-inch-thick (4-cm) strips

¼ cup (25 g) sliced scallions, with tops

½ teaspoon crushed garlic

2 teaspoons (10 ml) olive oil

1½ cups (106 g) broccoli florets

10 ounces (280 g) chickpeas, drained and rinsed

¼ cup (60 ml) low-sodium beef broth

¼ cup (60 ml) Reduced Sodium Soy Sauce (see recipe page 133)

2 teaspoons cornstarch

1 cup (220 g) cooked brown rice

Stir-fry pork, scallions, and garlic in oil in wok or large skillet over high heat until pork is browned, 3 to 5 minutes. Add broccoli and stir-fry 2 to 3 minutes. Add chickpeas and cook, covered, over medium heat until broccoli is crisp-tender, 3 to 4 minutes. Combine broth, soy sauce, and cornstarch. Stir into mixture. Cook and stir until thickened. Serve over rice.

—Yield: 4 servings

NUTRITIONAL ANALYSIS

PER SERVING: 176 g water; 287 calories (22% from fat, 30% from protein, 49% from carb); 21 g protein; 7 g total fat; 1 g saturated fat; 3 g monounsaturated fat; 2 g polyunsaturated fat; 35 g carbohydrate; 7 g fiber; 4 g sugar; 323 mg phosphorus; 69 mg calcium; 3 mg iron; 185 mg sodium; 579 mg potassium; 884 IU vitamin A; 1 mg vitamin E; 28 mg vitamin C; 36 mg cholesterol

Pork and Apple Curry

Curry flavor creates a new kind of pork dish.

2 tablespoons (30 ml) olive oil

4 pork loin chops

½ cup (80 g) onion, thinly sliced

¼ teaspoon (0.8 g) minced garlic

1 apple, peeled and sliced

½ cup (75 g) red bell pepper, cut in strips

½ cup (120 ml) low sodium chicken broth

1 teaspoon (2 g) cornstarch

1 teaspoon (2 g) curry powder

½ teaspoon (1.3 g) ground cumin

½ teaspoon (1.2 g) cinnamon

¼ teaspoon (0.5 g) freshly ground black pepper

In a heavy frying pan, heat oil over medium-high heat. Cook pork chops until browned on both sides and almost cooked through; remove from pan and set aside. Over medium heat, cook the onion, garlic, apple, and red bell pepper strips for 2 minutes or until softened. Blend chicken broth with cornstarch; add to pan along with curry powder, cumin, and cinnamon; cook for 1 or 2 minutes, or until slightly reduced and thickened. Return pork chops to frying pan. Cook for 1 or 2 minutes or until heated through. Serve pork chops with sauce and sprinkle with pepper.

—Yield: 4 servings

NUTRITIONAL ANALYSIS

PER SERVING: 228 calories (45% from fat, 39% from protein, 15% from carbohydrate); 23 g protein; 11 g total fat; 3 g saturated fat; 7 g monounsaturated fat; 1 g polyunsaturated fat; 9 g carbohydrate; 2 g fiber; 5 g sugar; 247 mg phosphorus; 31 mg calcium; 2 mg iron; 63 mg sodium; 513 mg potassium; 612 IU vitamin A; 2 mg ATE vitamin E; 28 mg vitamin C; 64 mg cholesterol; 166 g water

Pork Loin Roast

This pork roast has a Latin flavor. The sauce is good over rice or noodles.

3 pounds (1.4 kg) pork loin roast

1 tablespoon (7.5 g) chili powder

½ cup (120 ml) lime juice

1 teaspoon (2.5 g) cumin

1 teaspoon (1 g) dried oregano

½ teaspoon (1 g) black pepper

½ teaspoon (1.5 g) minced garlic

6 ounces (170 g) orange juice concentrate, thawed, divided

¼ cup (60 ml) dry white wine

½ cup (115 g) fat free sour cream

Place pork roast in a shallow glass dish. Mix chili powder, lime juice, cumin, oregano, pepper, garlic, and ¼ cup (60 ml) of orange juice concentrate and brush mixture onto the pork roast. Cover and refrigerate at least 8 hours. Preheat oven to 325°F (170°C, or gas mark 3). Place pork on a rack in a shallow roasting pan. Roast uncovered for 1½ to 2 hours, or until thermometer registers 170°F (77°C). Remove pork and rack from the pan. Strain the drippings from the pan and set aside. Add enough water to remaining orange juice concentrate to measure ¾ cup (180 ml); stir juice and wine into the drippings, then stir in the sour cream. Serve with the pork roast.

—Yield: 9 servings

NUTRITIONAL ANALYSIS

PER SERVING: 255 calories (26% from fat, 57% from protein, 17% from carbohydrate); 33 g protein; 7 g total fat; 2 g saturated fat; 3 g monounsaturated fat; 1 g polyunsaturated fat; 10 g carbohydrate; 1 g fiber; 7 g sugar; 361 mg phosphorus; 49 mg calcium; 2 mg iron; 93 mg sodium; 748 mg potassium; 397 IU vitamin A; 16 mg ATE vitamin E; 32 mg vitamin C; 100 mg cholesterol; 151 g water

Stuffed Pork Roast

This pork loin is filled with a traditional cornbread stuffing. If you put a drip pan under the roast during the indirect cooking phase and add some water to it, you will end up with the makings of a delicious gravy. Remember not to let the drip pan dry out.

2 tablespoons (30 ml) olive oil

½ cup (160 g) onion, chopped

1 teaspoon (3 g) minced garlic

1 tablespoon (2 g) dried sage, chopped

4 cups (600 g) Lower-Fat Cornbread, cubed (see recipe page 112)

1 egg

1 cup (235 ml) low sodium chicken broth

2 pounds (905 g) pork loin roast

In a skillet, heat oil over medium-high heat. Add onions and garlic and cook until tender. Add sage and cook for about 30 seconds. Remove from heat and add cornbread, onion mixture, and egg. Stir, adding the chicken broth slowly until it becomes spreadable (it should look like stuffing). Butterfly the pork loin. Spread stuffing over the pork loin and roll up. Secure with kitchen twine at 1-inch (2.5-cm) intervals. Preheat grill and prepare for indirect grilling. Place pork loin on grill over direct heat. Turn every two minutes until the surface of the pork loin is seared. Move to indirect portion of grill and continue cooking for about 30 minutes or until the meat reaches an internal temperature of 155°F (68°C). Remove from grill and let rest for 5 minutes. Slice and serve.

—Yield: 8 servings

NUTRITIONAL ANALYSIS

PER SERVING: 371 calories (31% from fat, 38% from protein, 31% from carbohydrate); 28 g protein; 10 g total fat; 3 g saturated fat; 6 g monounsaturated fat; 2 g polyunsaturated fat; 24 g carbohydrate; 3 g fiber; 4 g sugar; 303 mg phosphorus; 53 mg calcium; 2 mg iron; 222 mg sodium; 452 mg potassium; 391 IU vitamin A; 75 mg ATE vitamin E; 3 mg vitamin C; 102 mg cholesterol; 193 g water

Glazed Pork Roast

I actually grill this when it's warm enough. If you want to do that, it's best to grill using indirect heat. Place a pan of water under the roast and mound the charcoal around it. Close the grill to hold in the heat and smoke. This makes excellent sandwiches when sliced thinly and served cold.

¼ cup (60 ml) honey

1 tablespoon (9 g) dry mustard

¼ cup (60 ml) white wine vinegar

1 teaspoon (2.6 g) chili powder

2 pounds (905 g) pork tenderloin

Preheat oven to 350°F (180°C, or gas mark 4). Mix together the first 4 ingredients. Trim excess fat from pork roast. Brush with honey glaze. Roast for 1 to 1½ hours, or until done, brushing with additional glaze occasionally.

—Yield: 8 servings

NUTRITIONAL ANALYSIS

PER SERVING: 173 calories (22% from fat, 57% from protein, 21% from carbohydrate); 24 g protein; 4 g total fat; 1 g saturated fat; 2 g monounsaturated fat; 0 g polyunsaturated fat; 9 g carbohydrate; 0 g fiber; 9 g sugar; 258 mg phosphorus; 9 mg calcium; 2 mg iron; 61 mg sodium; 436 mg potassium; 101 IU vitamin A; 2 mg ATE vitamin E; 1 mg vitamin C; 74 mg cholesterol; 94 g water

Pork Loin Roast with Asian Vegetables

Serve this Asian-style pork roast with rice for a complete meal.

1 teaspoon (1.8 g) ground ginger

2 tablespoons (30 ml) olive oil

2 pounds (905 g) pork loin roast

1¼ cups (295 ml) water, divided

1 cup (160 g) onion, coarsely chopped

¼ cup (60 ml) Reduced Sodium Soy Sauce (see recipe page 133)

¼ cup (60 ml) red wine vinegar

2 tablespoons (30 g) brown sugar

½ teaspoon (1.5 g) garlic powder

¼ teaspoon (0.5 g) black pepper

4 cups (250 g) snow pea pods

2 cups (360 g) canned no-salt-added tomatoes, undrained

8 ounces (225 g) water chestnuts

1 cup mushrooms (70 g), sliced

2 tablespoons (16 g) cornstarch

In a large Dutch oven, sauté ginger in oil for 30 seconds. Add pork roast and brown meat on all sides. Add 1 cup (235 ml) water, onion, soy sauce, vinegar, brown sugar, garlic powder, and pepper. Cover and simmer for 1½ hours, or until tender. Add pea pods, tomatoes and liquid, water chestnuts, and mushrooms. Cover and simmer for 3 to 5 minutes, or until crisp-tender. Remove vegetables and meat. Skim any fat from pan juices. Blend the remaining ¼ cup (60 ml) water with the cornstarch and stir into the pot. Cook and stir until bubbly. Serve sauce with vegetables and meat.

—Yield: 8 servings

NUTRITIONAL ANALYSIS

PER SERVING: 273 calories (16% from fat, 23% from protein, 60% from carbohydrate); 27 g protein; 8 g total fat; 2 g saturated fat; 5 g monounsaturated fat; 2 g polyunsaturated fat; 70 g carbohydrate; 3 g fiber; 10 g sugar; 325 mg phosphorus; 72 mg calcium; 3 mg iron; 128 mg sodium; 893 mg potassium; 615 IU vitamin A; 2 mg ATE vitamin E; 39 mg vitamin C; 71 mg cholesterol; 285 g water

Apple Cranberry Stuffed Pork Roast

When I said I was going to make this, my wife wondered about going to the trouble of butterflying the roast, but the results were worth what turned out to be not a lot of effort. This is the kind of meal you could serve to anyone without worrying that it seems like a special "diet" food.

⅔ cup (160 ml) apple cider

¼ cup (60 ml) cider vinegar

½ cup (115 g) light brown sugar, packed

1 tablespoon (0.9 g) dried shallots

1 cup (86 g) dried apples

½ cup (75 g) dried cranberries

1 teaspoon (1.8 g) ground ginger

½ teaspoon (1.9 g) mustard seed

½ teaspoon (0.8 g) ground allspice

⅛ teaspoon (0.3 g) cayenne pepper

2 pounds (905 g) boneless pork loin roast

Combine all ingredients except pork in medium saucepan and bring to a simmer over medium-high heat. Cover; reduce heat to low, and cook until apples are very soft, about 20 minutes. Strain through a fine-mesh sieve, using a rubber spatula to press against the apple mixture in the sieve to extract as much liquid as possible; reserve the liquid. Return liquid to saucepan and simmer over medium-high heat until reduced to ½ cup (120 ml), about 5 minutes. Remove from heat, set aside, and reserve for use as a glaze.

Preheat oven to 350°F (180°C, or gas mark 4) or prepare your grill for indirect heat. Lay the roast down, fat side up. Insert a knife into the roast ½ inch (1.3 cm) horizontally from the bottom of the roast, along the long side of the roast. Make a long cut along the bottom of the roast, stopping ½ inch (1.3 cm) before the edge of the roast. You might find it easier to handle by starting at a corner of the roast. Open up the roast and continue to cut through the thicker half of the roast, again keeping ½ inch (1.3 cm) from the bottom. Repeat until the roast is an even ½-inch (1.3-cm) thickness all over when laid out. Spread out the filling on the roast, leaving a ½-inch (1.3-cm) border from the edges. Starting with the short side of the roast, roll it up very tightly. Secure with kitchen twine at 1-inch (2.5-cm) intervals. If baking, place the roast on a rack in a roasting pan and cook on the middle rack of the oven. If you are grilling using indirect heat, preheat the grill and wipe the grates with olive oil. Place roast, fat side up, on the side of the grill that has no coals underneath. Cover the grill with the lid. Cook for 45 to 60 minutes (if you are grilling, turn roast halfway through the cooking). Brush the roast with half of the glaze and cook for 5 minutes longer. Remove the roast from the oven or grill. Place it on a cutting board. Cover with foil to rest and keep warm for 15 minutes before slicing. Slice into ½-inch (1.3-cm) pieces, removing the cooking twine as you cut the roast. Serve with remaining glaze.

—Yield: 8 servings

NUTRITIONAL ANALYSIS

PER SERVING: 269 calories (26% from fat, 38% from protein, 37% from carbohydrate); 25 g protein; 8 g total fat; 3 g saturated fat; 3 g monounsaturated fat; 1 g polyunsaturated fat; 24 g carbohydrate; 1 g fiber; 22 g sugar; 245 mg phosphorus; 24 mg calcium; 1 mg iron; 58 mg sodium; 581 mg potassium; 41 IU vitamin A; 2 mg ATE vitamin E; 1 mg vitamin C; 62 mg cholesterol; 121 g water

CHAPTER 6

Main Dishes:
Fish and Seafood

Fish is one thing we should all eat more of. Not only is it low in fat, but cold water varieties like salmon and tuna also contain significant quantities of omerga-3 fatty acids, which have been shown to reduce cholesterol and promote heart health. You wouldn't go wrong eating fish two or three times a week. And with the variety of recipes here you could. They use a number of different kinds of fish and different preparations like grilling, baking, oven frying, and casseroles, so you have lots of fish options to choose from.

Tuna Steaks

If you get them on sale, tuna steaks are a good bargain, as well as containing lots of omega-3 fatty acids. The key to cooking them is not to overcook them and dry them out. It's fine for them to be medium or even medium-rare. Soaking them in a simple marinade also helps to keep them moist and flavorful.

2 tablespoons (30 ml) olive oil

2 tablespoons (30 ml) lemon juice

6 ounces (170 g) tuna steaks

½ teaspoon (1 g) freshly ground black pepper

Combine the olive oil and lemon juice. Marinate the steaks in the mixture for at least 30 minutes, turning occasionally. Heat a skillet over high heat. Add the steaks and cook 2 minutes. Sprinkle with pepper, turn over, and cook 2 minutes longer.

—Yield: 2 servings

NUTRITIONAL ANALYSIS

PER SERVING: 247 calories (65% from fat, 32% from protein, 3% from carbohydrate); 20 g protein; 18 g total fat; 3 g saturated fat; 11 g monounsaturated fat; 3 g polyunsaturated fat; 2 g carbohydrate; 0 g fiber; 0 g sugar; 218 mg phosphorus; 10 mg calcium; 1 mg iron; 34 mg sodium; 240 mg potassium; 1861 IU vitamin A; 557 mg ATE vitamin E; 7 mg vitamin C; 32 mg cholesterol; 72 g water

Grilled Tuna Steaks

Tuna steaks tend to get tough if you cook them too long, so take them off the grill while they are still pink in the center to keep them juicy.

½ cup (120 ml) balsamic vinegar

2 tablespoons (26 g) sugar

1 tablespoon (2.1 g) Italian seasoning

½ teaspoon (1.5 g) garlic powder

1 tablespoon (15 ml) olive oil

1 pound (455 g) tuna steaks

1 tablespoon (15 ml) lemon juice

Combine all ingredients except tuna and lemon juice and pour in a 9 × 9-inch (23 × 23-cm) glass baking dish. Add tuna and marinate 15 minutes, turning frequently. Heat grill to high. Place fish on grill and grill until medium doneness, about 3 minutes per side. Place on serving plates and drizzle lemon juice over.

—Yield: 4 servings

NUTRITIONAL ANALYSIS

PER SERVING: 228 calories (37% from fat, 49% from protein, 14% from carbohydrate); 27 g protein; 9 g total fat; 2 g saturated fat; 4 g monounsaturated fat; 2 g polyunsaturated fat; 8 g carbohydrate; 0 g fiber; 7 g sugar; 294 mg phosphorus; 24 mg calcium; 2 mg iron; 46 mg sodium; 329 mg potassium; 2528 IU vitamin A; 743 mg ATE vitamin E; 2 mg vitamin C; 43 mg cholesterol; 109 g water

Grilled Tuna with Honey Mustard Marinade

These tuna steaks can be grilled or broiled. If it's not good weather for outdoor grilling, they also work well on a contact grill like the George Foreman models.

⅓ cup (80 ml) red wine vinegar

1 tablespoon (15 g) spicy brown mustard

1 tablespoon (15 ml) honey

3 tablespoons (45 ml) extra-virgin olive oil

1 pound (455 g) tuna steaks

Combine the vinegar, mustard, honey, and olive oil in a jar or covered container; shake to mix well. Put tuna in a resealable plastic bag; add the mustard mixture. Seal the bag and let marinate for about 20 minutes. Heat the grill. Remove the tuna from the marinade and pour the marinade in a small saucepan. Bring marinade to a boil; remove from heat and set aside. Grill the tuna over high heat for about 2 minutes on each side, or to desired doneness. Drizzle with the hot marinade.

—Yield: 4 servings

NUTRITIONAL ANALYSIS

PER SERVING: 275 calories (53% from fat, 40% from protein, 7% from carbohydrate); 27 g protein; 16 g total fat; 3 g saturated fat; 9 g monounsaturated fat; 3 g polyunsaturated fat; 5 g carbohydrate; 0 g fiber; 4 g sugar; 294 mg phosphorus; 13 mg calcium; 1 mg iron; 89 mg sodium; 302 mg potassium; 2478 IU vitamin A; 743 mg ATE vitamin E; 0 mg vitamin C; 43 mg cholesterol; 100 g water

Marinated Tuna Steaks

Marinated in a southwestern-flavored sauce, these tuna steaks go well with Spanish rice and corn.

2 tablespoons (30 ml) olive oil

2 teaspoons (5 g) cumin

2 tablespoons (30 ml) lime juice

2 teaspoons (2.6 g) cilantro

1 pound (455 g) tuna steaks

Combine first 4 ingredients in a shallow dish; add fish and turn to coat. Marinate for 20 minutes, turning occasionally. Heat the grill. Remove the tuna from the marinade and grill the tuna over high heat for 2 minutes on each side, or until desired doneness.

—Yield: 4 servings

NUTRITIONAL ANALYSIS

PER SERVING: 229 calories (50% from fat, 48% from protein, 2% from carb); 27 g protein; 13 g total fat; 2 g saturated fat; 7 g monounsaturated fat; 2 g polyunsaturated fat; 1 g carbohydrate; 0 g fiber; 0 g sugar; 294 mg phosphorus; 20 mg calcium; 2 mg iron; 46 mg sodium; 315 mg potassium; 2521 IU vitamin A; 743 mg ATE vitamin E; 3 mg vitamin C; 43 mg cholesterol; 85 g water

Poached Salmon

Poaching fish is a healthy way to cook it, as well as making sure it stays moist and adding a little extra flavor.

4 cups (946 ml) water

2 tablespoons (30 ml) lemon juice

¼ cup (30 g) carrot, thinly sliced

½ cup (80 g) onion, thinly sliced

1 bay leaf

1 tablespoon (4 g) fresh dill, chopped

½ pound (225 g) salmon fillets

Preheat oven to 350°F (180°C, or gas mark 4). Combine all ingredients except salmon in a saucepan and heat to boiling. Reduce heat and simmer 5 minutes. Place salmon in a glass baking dish large enough to hold salmon in a single layer; pour poaching liquid over. Cover and bake for 20 minutes, or until salmon flakes easily.

—Yield: 2 servings

NUTRITIONAL ANALYSIS

PER SERVING: 238 calories (47% from fat, 40% from protein, 13% from carbohydrate); 24 g protein; 12 g total fat; 3 g saturated fat; 4 g monounsaturated fat; 4 g polyunsaturated fat; 7 g carbohydrate; 1 g fiber; 3 g sugar; 291 mg phosphorus; 71 mg calcium; 1 mg iron; 97 mg sodium; 595 mg potassium; 2841 IU vitamin A; 17 mg ATE vitamin E; 16 mg vitamin C; 67 mg cholesterol; 614 g water

Maple Salmon

The sweetness of the maple syrup and the flavor of the balsamic vinegar go well with salmon.

¼ cup (60 ml) balsamic vinegar

¼ cup (60 ml) water

2 tablespoons (30 ml) olive oil

2 tablespoons (30 ml) maple syrup

¼ teaspoon (0.8 g) garlic powder

½ pound (225 g) salmon fillets

Heat all ingredients except salmon in a large skillet, stirring to combine. Add salmon fillets. Cover and cook for 10 minutes, or until salmon is done, turning once.

—Yield: 2 servings

NUTRITIONAL ANALYSIS

PER SERVING: 387 calories (61% from fat, 24% from protein, 15% from carbohydrate); 23 g protein; 26 g total fat; 4 g saturated fat; 14 g monounsaturated fat; 6 g polyunsaturated fat; 14 g carbohydrate; 0 g fiber; 12 g sugar; 268 mg phosphorus; 31 mg calcium; 1 mg iron; 71 mg sodium; 478 mg potassium; 57 IU vitamin A; 17 mg ATE vitamin E; 4 mg vitamin C; 67 mg cholesterol; 142 g water

Grilled Salmon and Vegetables

On hot days, it's sometimes a good idea to not use the stove at all. This recipe gives you protein, vegetables, and starch in one easy grilled packet.

1 cup (195 g) instant rice, uncooked

1 cup (235 ml) low sodium chicken broth

½ cup (56 g) zucchini, sliced

½ cup (60 g) carrot, shredded

½ pound (225 g) salmon fillets

¼ teaspoon (0.5 g) black pepper

½ lemon, sliced

Heat grill to medium. Spray two large pieces of heavy-duty aluminum foil with nonstick vegetable oil spray. In a small bowl, mix together rice and broth. Let stand for 5 minutes, or until most of broth is absorbed. Stir in zucchini and carrots, and set aside. Place a salmon fillet in the center of each piece of foil. Sprinkle with pepper and place lemon slices on top. Place rice mixture around each fillet. Fold up foil and bring edges together. Fold over several times to seal. Fold in ends, allowing some room for the rice to expand during cooking. Place on the grill and cook for 10 to 15 minutes, or until salmon is done.

—Yield: 2 servings

NUTRITIONAL ANALYSIS

PER SERVING: 347 calories (35% from fat, 33% from protein, 32% from carbohydrate); 28 g protein; 14 g total fat; 3 g saturated fat; 5 g monounsaturated fat; 5 g polyunsaturated fat; 28 g carbohydrate; 2 g fiber; 3 g sugar; 369 mg phosphorus; 54 mg calcium; 2 mg iron; 130 mg sodium; 765 mg potassium; 5502 IU vitamin A; 17 mg ATE vitamin E; 19 mg vitamin C; 67 mg cholesterol; 320 g water

Grilled Salmon Fillets

You can use a whole salmon fillet for this recipe. It makes an impressive display, but it can be difficult to turn. I usually cut the fillet into serving-sized pieces, but then you need to be careful not to overcook them and dry them out. The sweetness of the sauce goes well with the salmon.

¼ cup (60 g) brown sugar

2 tablespoons (30 ml) cider vinegar

2 tablespoons (30 ml) honey

¼ teaspoon (1 ml) liquid smoke

¼ teaspoon (0.5 g) black pepper

¼ teaspoon (0.8 g) crushed garlic

2 pounds (905 g) salmon fillets

Preheat grill. In a small mixing bowl, combine the first 6 ingredients (through garlic). Mix well. Brush one side of the salmon with the basting sauce, then place the salmon (basted side down) on the grill. When the salmon is half finished cooking, baste the top portion of the salmon and flip the fillet so the fresh basting sauce is on the grill. When the fish is almost finished cooking, apply the basting sauce and flip the salmon again. Baste and flip the salmon once more and serve.

—Yield: 6 servings

NUTRITIONAL ANALYSIS

PER SERVING: 110 g water ; 334 calories (45% from fat, 37% from protein, 18% from carbohydrate); 30 g protein; 16 g total fat; 3 g saturated fat; 6 g monounsaturated fat; 6 g polyunsaturated fat; 15 g carbohydrate; 0 g fiber; 15 g sugar; 355 mg phosphorus; 27 mg calcium; 1 mg iron; 93 mg sodium; 587 mg potassium; 76 IU vitamin A; 23 mg ATE vitamin E; 6 mg vitamin C; 89 mg cholesterol

Cedar Planked Salmon

Grilling salmon on a cedar plank gives it a marvelous smoky flavor. You can grill it plain, but we like this honey mustard sauce on it.

¼ cup (60 g) Dijon mustard

1 tablespoon (15 ml) honey

1 teaspoon (1 g) dried dill

1 pound (455 g) salmon fillets

Mix mustard, honey, and dill. Pour over salmon in a glass baking dish and marinate while you prepare the grill. Preheat grill to medium and soak planks according to package directions. Place the plank on the heated grill and allow to preheat for 3 minutes. Turn the plank over and place salmon on plank. Close grill and cook for 12 minutes, or until fish flakes easily.

—Yield: 4 servings

NUTRITIONAL ANALYSIS

PER SERVING: 234 calories (50% from fat, 40% from protein, 9% from carbohydrate); 23 g protein; 13 g total fat; 3 g saturated fat; 5 g monounsaturated fat; 5 g polyunsaturated fat; 5 g carbohydrate; 1 g fiber; 4 g sugar; 282 mg phosphorus; 27 mg calcium; 1 mg iron; 238 mg sodium; 443 mg potassium; 82 IU vitamin A; 17 mg ATE vitamin E; 5 mg vitamin C; 67 mg cholesterol; 91 g water

TIP

You can find cedar planks at stores with a large selection of grills and grilling equipment, such as Lowe's or The Home Depot.

Thyme Roasted Salmon

Simple in its preparation, with just three ingredients, this salmon doesn't lack for flavor.

1 pound salmon fillets

1 teaspoon dried thyme

¼ teaspoon black pepper

Spray a baking sheet with non-stick cooking spray. Place the fillets on the sheet. Sprinkle with thyme and pepper. Cook at 350°F until fish flakes easily, about 20 minutes.

—Yield: 4 servings

NUTRITIONAL ANALYSIS

PER SERVING: 182 calories (55% from fat, 45% from protein , 1% from carb); 20 g protein ; 11 g total fat; 2 g saturated fat; 4 g monounsaturated fat; 4 g polyunsaturated fat; 0 g carb; 0 g fiber; 0 g sugar; 231 mg phosphorus; 17 mg calcium; 59 mg sodium; 362 mg potassium; 59 IU vitamin A; 15 mg ATE vitamin E; 4 mg vitamin C; 58 mg cholesterol

Salmon with Honey Mustard Glaze

Salmon is naturally sweet, making this honey mustard glaze especially appropriate.

1 pound salmon fillets

2 tablespoons honey

2 tablespoons Dijon mustard

½ teaspoon thyme

1 tablespoon olive oil

Heat oil over medium heat in a large non-stick skillet. Combine honey, mustard, and thyme. Brush on both sides of fish. Cook in oil until fish flakes easily, about 5 minutes per side.

—Yield: 4 servings

NUTRITIONAL ANALYSIS

PER SERVING: 249 calories (52% from fat, 32% from protein , 15% from carb); 20 g protein ; 14 g total fat; 3 g saturated fat; 6 g monounsaturated fat; 4 g polyunsaturated fat; 9 g carb; 0 g fiber; 9 g sugar; 238 mg phosphorus; 21 mg calcium; 147 mg sodium; 377 mg potassium; 65 IU vitamin A; 15 mg ATE vitamin E; 4 mg vitamin C; 58 mg cholesterol

Mediterranean Salmon

This complete meal makes a great presentation, not to mention that it tastes delicious.

1 pound (455 g) salmon fillets

1 cup (175 g) couscous

1 cup (113 g) zucchini, sliced

1 cup (160 g) red onion, peeled and sliced

4 ounces (115 g) mushrooms, sliced

½ cup (75 g) red bell pepper, cut in strips

2 tablespoons (30 ml) olive oil, divided

1 tablespoon (2.5 g) fresh basil

Prepare couscous according to package instructions. Meanwhile, preheat a skillet or griddle pan. Toss the zucchini, onion, mushrooms, and red bell pepper in 1 tablespoon (15 ml) oil. Sauté vegetables for 8 to 10 minutes, turning once. Remove from pan. Brush the salmon with the remaining 1 tablespoon (15 ml) oil and cook for 6 to 8 minutes, turning once. Add the vegetables and basil to the couscous and toss well. Serve the vegetable couscous topped with the salmon.

—Yield: 4 servings

NUTRITIONAL ANALYSIS

PER SERVING: 460 calories (39% from fat, 26% from protein, 35% from carbohydrate); 30 g protein; 20 g total fat; 4 g saturated fat; 9 g monounsaturated fat; 5 g polyunsaturated fat; 40 g carbohydrate; 4 g fiber; 3 g sugar; 392 mg phosphorus; 51 mg calcium; 2 mg iron; 78 mg sodium; 768 mg potassium; 752 IU vitamin A; 17 mg ATE vitamin E; 37 mg vitamin C; 67 mg cholesterol; 190 g water

Lemon Baked Salmon

This method will give you a little more intense lemon flavor than most. You can use this same preparation for a number of kinds of fish.

1 lemon

1 pound (455 g) salmon fillets

¼ cup (60 ml) lemon juice

2 tablespoons (6 g) dill

2 teaspoons (10 ml) olive oil

Preheat oven to 350°F (180°C, or gas mark 4). Spray a 9 × 13-inch (23 × 33-cm) glass baking dish with nonstick vegetable oil spray. Slice lemon into ¼-inch (0.6-cm) slices and place in bottom of pan. Lay fillets over slices. Combine lemon juice, dill, and oil and pour over fillets. Bake for 12 to 15 minutes, or until fish flakes easily.

—**Yield: 4 servings**

NUTRITIONAL ANALYSIS

PER SERVING: 213 calories (55% from fat, 38% from protein, 7% from carbohydrate); 20 g protein; 13 g total fat; 2 g saturated fat; 5 g monounsaturated fat; 4 g polyunsaturated fat; 4 g carbohydrate; 1 g fiber; 1 g sugar; 242 mg phosphorus; 44 mg calcium; 1 mg iron; 62 mg sodium; 449 mg potassium; 146 IU vitamin A; 15 mg ATE vitamin E; 19 mg vitamin C; 58 mg cholesterol; 95 g water

Salmon with Dill

This is a simple stick-it-in-the-oven-and-wait type of dish. It goes well with boiled potatoes (you could make a little extra of the sauce to put on them).

2 tablespoons (30 ml) olive oil

1 teaspoon (1 g) dried dill

1 teaspoon (3 g) onion powder

½ teaspoon (1 g) black pepper

1 pound (455 g) salmon fillets

Preheat oven to 400°F (200°C, or gas mark 6). Mix together oil, dill, onion powder, and pepper. Place salmon in a 9 × 13-inch (23 × 33-cm) baking dish that has been coated with nonstick vegetable oil spray. Brush all of the olive oil mixture on the fish. Bake for 20 minutes, or until fish flakes easily.

—**Yield: 4 servings**

NUTRITIONAL ANALYSIS

PER SERVING: 271 calories (65% from fat, 34% from protein, 1% from carbohydrate); 23 g protein; 19 g total fat; 3 g saturated fat; 9 g monounsaturated fat; 5 g polyunsaturated fat; 1 g carbohydrate; 0 g fiber; 0 g sugar; 268 mg phosphorus; 22 mg calcium; 1 mg iron; 68 mg sodium; 428 mg potassium; 73 IU vitamin A; 17 mg ATE vitamin E; 5 mg vitamin C; 67 mg cholesterol; 78 g water

Oven-Steamed Salmon and Vegetables

I've also cooked this on a gas grill.

8 ounces (225 g) salmon fillets

2 medium potatoes, diced

½ cup (56 g) yellow squash, thinly sliced

½ cup (65 g) carrot, thinly sliced

¼ cup (25 g) scallions, thinly sliced

½ cup (35 g) mushrooms, sliced

2 teaspoons (10 ml) white wine

½ teaspoon (0.5 g) dried dill

½ teaspoon (1.5 g) minced garlic

¼ teaspoon (0.5 g) black pepper, fresh ground

Preheat oven to 425°F (220°C, or gas mark 7). Place a baking sheet in the oven to preheat as well. Meanwhile, spray the center of two 12-inch (30-cm) squares of aluminum foil with nonstick vegetable oil spray. Combine salmon, potatoes, squash, carrots, scallions, and mushrooms and divide evenly among the prepared foil sheets. Sprinkle with wine, dill, garlic, and pepper; fold diagonally to form a triangle; tightly seal edges. Place foil package on preheated baking sheet, then return to oven and bake 10 to 15 minutes, or until salmon is opaque and vegetables are tender.

—**Yield: 2 servings**

NUTRITIONAL ANALYSIS

PER SERVING: 498 calories (23% from fat, 25% from protein, 52% from carbohydrate); 31 g protein; 13 g total fat; 3 g saturated fat; 4 g monounsaturated fat; 5 g polyunsaturated fat; 65 g carbohydrate; 8 g fiber; 6 g sugar; 535 mg phosphorus; 82 mg calcium; 4 mg iron; 116 mg sodium; 2374 mg potassium; 5659 IU vitamin A; 17 mg ATE vitamin E; 46 mg vitamin C; 67 mg cholesterol; 464 g water

Mediterranean Tilapia

A tasty topping featuring sun-dried tomatoes and olives gives these simple fillets exceptional flavor.

¼ cup sun dried tomatoes, oil packed, chopped

8 ripe olives, chopped

2 tablespoons pimento, diced

2 tablespoons fresh parsley

1 tablespoon fresh basil

1 tablespoon olive oil

4 tilapia fillets

¼ teaspoon paprika

⅛ teaspoon cayenne

Spray a baking sheet with non-stick cooking spray. Combine tomatoes, olives, pimento, parsley, basil, and oil. Set aside. Place fillets on baking sheet. Sprinkle with paprika and cayenne. Bake at 400°F until fish flakes easily, about 15 minutes. Transfer to serving plates and spoon tomato mixture over top.

—Yield: 4 servings

NUTRITIONAL ANALYSIS

PER SERVING: 273 calories (58% from fat, 38% from protein , 4% from carb); 25 g protein ; 17 g total fat; 4 g saturated fat; 9 g monounsaturated fat; 3 g polyunsaturated fat; 3 g carb; 1 g fiber; 0 g sugar; 336 mg phosphorus; 40 mg calcium; 182 mg sodium; 626 mg potassium; 669 IU vitamin A; 24 mg ATE vitamin E; 16 mg vitamin C; 75 mg cholesterol

Greek Islands Fish

The flavor of this fish will whisk you away to a Mediterranean island. Serve with couscous.

6 tilapia fillets

1 cup no salt added tomatoes, diced

½ cup artichoke hearts, chopped

½ cup ripe olives, chopped

½ cup feta cheese, crumbled

Place fillets in a 9 × 13-inch baking pan coated with non-stick cooking spray. Top with remaining ingredients. Bake at 400°F for 15 to 20 minutes or until fish flakes easily.

—Yield: 6 servings

NUTRITIONAL ANALYSIS

PER SERVING: 274 calories (53% from fat, 40% from protein, 6% from carb); 27 g protein ; 16 g total fat; 5 g saturated fat; 7 g monounsaturated fat; 3 g polyunsaturated fat; 4 g carb; 1 g fiber; 2 g sugar; 380 mg phosphorus; 101 mg calcium; 333 mg sodium; 612 mg potassium; 253 IU vitamin A; 39 mg ATE vitamin E; 7 mg vitamin C; 86 mg cholesterol

Grilled Swordfish

We don't have swordfish all that often, but occasionally I'll find it on sale and buy some. It works well for this simple barbecue recipe because it's dense enough to hold together.

¼ cup (60 ml) barbecue sauce

1 tablespoon (15 ml) Worcestershire sauce

2 tablespoons (30 ml) fresh lime juice

2 tablespoons (20 g) chopped onion

½ teaspoon (1.5 g) minced garlic

2 swordfish steaks

Combine all ingredients except swordfish to make marinade. Marinate swordfish steaks for 6 hours or overnight, turning occasionally. When ready to grill, reserve marinade. Grill or cook as desired (do not overcook). Heat reserved marinade to boiling and pour over fish to serve.

—Yield: 2 servings

NUTRITIONAL ANALYSIS

PER SERVING: 242 calories (21% from fat, 47% from protein, 32% from carbohydrate); 28 g protein; 6 g total fat; 1 g saturated fat; 2 g monounsaturated fat; 1 g polyunsaturated fat; 19 g carbohydrate; 0 g fiber; 12 g sugar; 372 mg phosphorus; 11 mg calcium; 2 mg iron; 498 mg sodium; 487 mg potassium; 179 IU vitamin A; 49 mg ATE vitamin E; 20 mg vitamin C; 53 mg cholesterol; 147 g water

Baked Swordfish with Vegetables

This is a fairly simple recipe, with the flavor coming from the vegetables. It's good with pasta or plain brown rice.

4 ounces (115 g) mushrooms, sliced

1 cup (160 g) onion, sliced

2 tablespoons (19 g) green bell pepper, chopped

2 tablespoons (30 ml) lemon juice

¼ teaspoon (0.3 g) dried dill

1 pound (455 g) swordfish steaks

4 small bay leaves

2 tomatoes, sliced

Preheat oven to 400°F (200°C, or gas mark 6). In a bowl, combine mushrooms, onions, green bell pepper, lemon juice, and dill. Line a shallow baking pan with foil. Spread vegetable mixture in bottom then arrange swordfish steaks on top. Place a bay leaf and 2 tomato slices on each swordfish steak. Cover pan with foil and bake for 45 to 55 minutes or until fish flakes easily with a fork.

—Yield: 4 servings

NUTRITIONAL ANALYSIS

PER SERVING: 165 calories (26% from fat, 59% from protein, 15% from carbohydrate); 24 g protein; 5 g total fat; 1 g saturated fat; 2 g monounsaturated fat; 1 g polyunsaturated fat; 6 g carbohydrate; 1 g fiber; 3 g sugar; 339 mg phosphorus; 18 mg calcium; 1 mg iron; 126 mg sodium; 529 mg potassium; 168 IU vitamin A; 41 mg ATE vitamin E; 12 mg vitamin C; 44 mg cholesterol; 159 g water

Oven-Fried Fish

The nice crunchy coating is low in fat and sodium, and it goes really well with oven-fried potatoes.

1 egg

2 tablespoons (30 ml) skim milk

½ cup (30 g) dried mashed potato flakes

¼ teaspoon (0.5 g) black pepper

1 pound (455 g) catfish fillets

Preheat oven to 325°F (170°C, or gas mark 3). Mix egg and milk together. Stir together potatoes and pepper. Dip fish in egg mixture, then potato flakes. Dip fish again in egg and then potato flakes. Place on baking sheet. Coat fish with nonstick vegetable oil spray. Bake for 15 minutes, or until fish flakes easily.

—Yield: 4 servings

NUTRITIONAL ANALYSIS

PER SERVING: 196 calories (43% from fat, 43% from protein, 14% from carbohydrate); 20 g protein; 9 g total fat; 2 g saturated fat; 4 g monounsaturated fat; 2 g polyunsaturated fat; 7 g carbohydrate; 1 g fiber; 0 g sugar; 269 mg phosphorus; 32 mg calcium; 1 mg iron; 100 mg sodium; 389 mg potassium; 130 IU vitamin A; 22 mg ATE vitamin E; 7 mg vitamin C; 104 mg cholesterol; 106 g water

Tuna Casserole

Ever have one of those nights where you can't think of a thing for dinner and end up pawing randomly through cookbooks looking for something that sounds good and that you have the ingredients for? This was the result. And it actually worked out well. The top layer is a quiche-like custard.

2 cups (330 g) cooked rice

4 eggs, divided

½ teaspoon (0.7 g) dried basil

1 tablespoon (10 g) onion, minced

7 ounces (200 g) water packed tuna

1 cup (235 ml) skim milk

4 ounces (115 g) Swiss cheese, shredded

Preheat oven to 350°F (180°C, or gas mark 4). Combine rice, 1 egg, basil, and onion. Press into the bottom of an 8 × 8-inch (20 × 20-cm) baking dish sprayed with nonstick vegetable oil spray. Spread tuna over the top. Combine remaining eggs, milk, and cheese and pour over the top. Bake for 40 to 45 minutes, or until a knife inserted near the center comes out clean.

—Yield: 4 servings

NUTRITIONAL ANALYSIS

PER SERVING: 285 calories (14% from fat, 48% from protein, 37% from carbohydrate); 33 g protein; 4 g total fat; 2 g saturated fat; 1 g monounsaturated fat; 1 g polyunsaturated fat; 26 g carbohydrate; 1 g fiber; 1 g sugar; 442 mg phosphorus; 417 mg calcium; 4 mg iron; 390 mg sodium; 419 mg potassium; 430 IU vitamin A; 57 mg ATE vitamin E; 1 mg vitamin C; 237 mg cholesterol; 219 g water

Tuna Noodle Casserole

This is traditional American comfort food.

1 tablespoon (15 ml) olive oil

2 tablespoons (16 g) flour

2 cups (470 ml) skim milk

¼ cup (30 g) low fat Cheddar cheese, shredded

3 cups (450 g) cooked egg noodles

10-ounce (280 g) package frozen peas, thawed

7 ounces (200 g) water-packed tuna

4 ounces (115 g) mushrooms, sliced

¼ cup (37 g) chopped green bell pepper

⅛ teaspoon (0.3 g) black pepper

½ cup (60 g) bread crumbs

Preheat oven to 375°F (190°C, or gas mark 5). Heat oil in a large skillet over low heat; add flour, stirring until smooth. Cook 1 minute, stirring constantly. Gradually add milk; cook over medium heat, stirring constantly, until mixture is thickened and bubbly. Stir in cheese; cook over low heat, stirring constantly, until cheese melts. Remove from heat. Combine cheese sauce, noodles, and next 5 ingredients (through black pepper). Spoon mixture into a 2-quart (1.9-L) casserole dish coated with nonstick vegetable oil spray. Sprinkle evenly with bread crumbs. Bake for 35 minutes, or until the casserole is bubbly and the top is browned.

—Yield: 6 servings

NUTRITIONAL ANALYSIS

PER SERVING: 277 calories (14% from fat, 28% from protein, 58% from carbohydrate); 19 g protein; 4 g total fat; 1 g saturated fat; 2 g monounsaturated fat; 1 g polyunsaturated fat; 40 g carbohydrate; 7 g fiber; 3 g sugar; 303 mg phosphorus; 174 mg calcium; 2 mg iron; 414 mg sodium; 424 mg potassium; 1254 IU vitamin A; 59 mg ATE vitamin E; 11 mg vitamin C; 13 mg cholesterol; 211 g water

Herbed Fish

Simple baked fish made flavorful by a combination of herbs and spices.

2 pounds (905 g) perch, or other firm white fish

1 tablespoon (15 ml) olive oil

½ teaspoon (1.5 g) garlic powder

½ teaspoon (0.3 g) dried marjoram

½ teaspoon (0.5 g) dried thyme

⅛ teaspoon (0.3 g) white pepper

2 bay leaves

½ cup (80 g) onion, chopped

½ cup (120 ml) white wine

Preheat oven to 350°F (180°C, or gas mark 4). Wash fish, pat dry, and place in 9 × 13-inch (23 × 33-cm) dish. Combine oil with garlic powder, marjoram, thyme, and white pepper. Drizzle over fish. Top with bay leaves and onion. Pour wine over all. Bake, uncovered, for 20 to 30 minutes, or until fish flakes easily with a fork.

—Yield: 4 servings

NUTRITIONAL ANALYSIS

PER SERVING: 277 calories (26% from fat, 69% from protein, 5% from carbohydrate); 43 g protein; 7 g total fat; 1 g saturated fat; 4 g monounsaturated fat; 1 g polyunsaturated fat; 3 g carbohydrate; 0 g fiber; 1 g sugar; 503 mg phosphorus; 253 mg calcium; 2 mg iron; 173 mg sodium; 675 mg potassium; 100 IU vitamin A; 27 mg ATE vitamin E; 3 mg vitamin C; 95 mg cholesterol; 222 g water

Brown Rice Tuna Bake

A variation on the traditional tuna casserole. Brown rice adds nutrients, and yogurt provides flavor and creaminess.

1¼ cups (238 g) uncooked brown rice

3 cups (710 ml) water

1 cup (100 g) chopped celery

½ cup (80 g) onion, finely diced

½ cup (115 g) plain fat-free yogurt

1 cup (235 ml) skim milk

¼ teaspoon (0.3 g) red pepper flakes

½ teaspoon (0.3 g) dried tarragon

14 ounces (395 g) water-packed canned tuna, drained

2 cups (280 g) frozen peas, thawed

¾ cup (90 g) low fat Cheddar cheese, shredded

Preheat oven to 350°F (180°C, or gas mark 4). Combine rice and water in large saucepan. Bring to a boil. Reduce heat, cover, and cook for 35 minutes. Remove from heat. Add celery, onion, yogurt, milk, red pepper flakes, and tarragon; mix well. Flake the tuna with a fork and add it and thawed peas to the rice mixture; mix well. Pour into 2-quart (1.9-L) casserole dish. Bake for 30 minutes. Top with shredded cheese.

—Yield: 6 servings

NUTRITIONAL ANALYSIS

PER SERVING: 321 calories (9% from fat, 37% from protein, 54% from carbohydrate); 29 g protein; 3 g total fat; 1 g saturated fat; 1 g monounsaturated fat; 1 g polyunsaturated fat; 42 g carbohydrate; 4 g fiber; 5 g sugar; 445 mg phosphorus; 209 mg calcium; 3 mg iron; 537 mg sodium; 526 mg potassium; 1231 IU vitamin A; 47 mg ATE vitamin E; 7 mg vitamin C; 25 mg cholesterol; 302 g water

CHAPTER 7

Main Dishes: Vegetarian

If you are the kind of person who thinks they don't like meat-less meals, you've come to the right place. Take a look through this chapter and I can almost guarantee you'll find something you like. And the great thing is vegetarian recipes have to be heart-healthy. It's nearly impossible to create a high fat one. They contain a variety of the vegetables that most of us struggle to eat enough of. And many contain the fiber of legumes and whole grains. We've made one night a week a meatless night and it's amazing how many things we have discovered that we like. Start here to do the same.

Grilled Stuffed Portobellos

These Mediterranean-flavored caps are best served with pasta or rice.

⅔ cup (120 g) plum tomato, chopped

2 ounces (55 g) part-skim mozzarella, shredded

1 teaspoon (5 ml) olive oil, divided

½ teaspoon (0.4 g) fresh rosemary

⅛ teaspoon (0.3 g) coarsely ground black pepper

¼ teaspoon (0.8 g) crushed garlic

4 portobello mushroom caps, about 4 to 5 inches (10 to 12.5 cm) each

2 tablespoons (30 ml) lemon juice

2 teaspoons (2.6 g) fresh parsley

Prepare grill. Combine the tomato, cheese, ½ teaspoon (2.5 ml) oil, rosemary, pepper, and garlic in a small bowl. Remove brown gills from the undersides of mushroom caps using a spoon, and discard. Remove stems; discard. Combine remaining ½ teaspoon oil (2.5 ml) and lemon juice in a small bowl. Brush over both sides of mushroom caps. Place the mushroom caps, stem sides down, on grill rack sprayed with nonstick vegetable oil spray, and grill for 5 minutes on each side or until soft. Spoon one-quarter of the tomato mixture into each mushroom cap. Cover and grill 3 minutes or until cheese is melted. Sprinkle with parsley.

—Yield: 4 servings

NUTRITIONAL ANALYSIS

PER SERVING: 75 calories (40% from fat, 29% from protein, 32% from carbohydrate); 6 g protein; 4 g total fat; 2 g saturated fat; 1 g monounsaturated fat; 0 g polyunsaturated fat; 6 g carbohydrate; 2 g fiber; 3 g sugar; 181 mg phosphorus; 122 mg calcium; 1 mg iron; 95 mg sodium; 490 mg potassium; 331 IU vitamin A; 18 mg ATE vitamin E; 8 mg vitamin C; 9 mg cholesterol; 115 g water

Grilled Portobello Mushrooms

This is a fairly simple recipe for grilled portobellos, but one that still provides a flavorful meat alternative.

4 portobello mushroom caps, cleaned and stems removed

¼ cup (60 ml) balsamic vinegar

1 tablespoon (15 ml) olive oil

1 teaspoon (0.7 g) dried basil

1 teaspoon (1 g) dried oregano

½ teaspoon (1.5 g) minced garlic

4 ounces (115 g) low fat Provolone cheese, sliced

Place the mushroom caps smooth side up in a shallow dish. Mix together vinegar, oil, basil, oregano, and garlic. Pour over the mushrooms. Let stand at room temperature for 15 minutes, turning twice. Preheat grill to medium-high heat. Brush grate with oil. Place mushrooms on the grill, reserving marinade for basting. Grill for 5 to 8 minutes on each side, or until tender. Brush with marinade frequently. Top with cheese during the last 2 minutes of grilling.

—Yield: 4 servings

NUTRITIONAL ANALYSIS

PER SERVING: 156 calories (53% from fat, 30% from protein, 17% from carbohydrate); 9 g protein; 7 g total fat; 3 g saturated fat; 4 g monounsaturated fat; 1 g polyunsaturated fat; 5 g carbohydrate; 1 g fiber; 2 g sugar; 252 mg phosphorus; 230 mg calcium; 1 mg iron; 254 mg sodium; 466 mg potassium; 283 IU vitamin A; 65 mg ATE vitamin E; 0 mg vitamin C; 20 mg cholesterol; 102 g water

Hawaiian Portobello Burgers

This recipe gives you a sandwich so flavorful you won't miss the meat.

2 portobello mushrooms, cleaned and stems removed

2 tablespoons (30 ml) Reduced Sodium Teriyaki Sauce (see recipe page 133)

2 slices pineapple

2 slices low fat Monterey Jack cheese

2 lettuce leaves

2 slices tomato

2 hamburger buns

1 tablespoon (14 g) low fat mayonnaise

Place mushrooms in a shallow dish. Spread teriyaki sauce over the mushrooms and marinate for 15 minutes. Grill the mushrooms and pineapple slices over low heat until tender. Add the cheese on top of the mushrooms and continue to grill briefly to melt cheese. Assemble burgers by placing 1 lettuce leaf and tomato slice on each bottom bun, then top with the mushrooms and pineapple. Spread each top bun with half of the mayonnaise.

—Yield: 2 servings

NUTRITIONAL ANALYSIS

PER SERVING: 248 calories (19% from fat, 25% from protein, 56% from carbohydrate); 17 g protein; 6 g total fat; 2 g saturated fat; 1 g monounsaturated fat; 1 g polyunsaturated fat; 39 g carbohydrate; 11 g fiber; 26 g sugar; 441 mg phosphorus; 276 mg calcium; 4 mg iron; 329 mg sodium; 1671 mg potassium; 4191 IU vitamin A; 17 mg ATE vitamin E; 29 mg vitamin C; 9 mg cholesterol; 909 g water

Bean and Tomato Curry

This makes a good side dish with something like a grilled chicken breast or loin pork chop, but you can also use it for a vegetarian meal. In that case, serve over rice or with pita bread.

1 tablespoon (15 ml) canola oil

1 teaspoon (3.7 g) mustard seed

1 teaspoon (2.5 g) cumin seeds

1 cup (160 g) onion, chopped

1 tablespoon (6 g) fresh ginger, peeled and chopped

½ teaspoon (1.5 g) chopped garlic

4 cups (720 g) canned no-salt-added tomatoes

2 cups (450 g) kidney beans, drained and rinsed

1 teaspoon (2 g) curry powder

Heat oil in large pot over medium heat and stir-fry the mustard and cumin seeds until they pop. Add onion, ginger, and garlic, and stir-fry until lightly colored. Add tomatoes with juice, beans, and curry powder. Simmer for about 20 minutes or until thick and saucy.

—Yield: 6 servings

NUTRITIONAL ANALYSIS

PER SERVING: 140 calories (19% from fat, 19% from protein, 62% from carbohydrate); 7 g protein; 3 g total fat; 0 g saturated fat; 2 g monounsaturated fat; 1 g polyunsaturated fat; 23 g carbohydrate; 6 g fiber; 5 g sugar; 131 mg phosphorus; 81 mg calcium; 4 mg iron; 163 mg sodium; 598 mg potassium; 196 IU vitamin A; 0 mg ATE vitamin E; 18 mg vitamin C; 0 mg cholesterol; 215 g water

TIP

To lower the amount of sodium, use no-salt-added beans or cooked dried beans.

Garbanzo Curry

Indian vegetarian slow cooker recipes like this curry will warm you up on a cold day. It's so easy, but it tastes as good as vegetarian Indian recipes you get at a restaurant.

2 tablespoons (30 ml) canola oil

1 cup (160 g) onion, diced

½ teaspoon (1.5 g) minced garlic

1 teaspoon (2.7 g) fresh ginger, peeled and grated

1 teaspoon (2.5 g) cumin

1 teaspoon (2 g) coriander

1 teaspoon (2.2 g) turmeric

2 cups (480 g) canned garbanzo beans, drained and rinsed

2 cups (360 g) canned no-salt-added tomatoes

½ teaspoon (1.2 g) garam masala

Heat oil in a heavy skillet. Sauté onion, garlic, ginger, cumin, coriander, and turmeric until onion becomes soft. Place onion mixture and remaining ingredients in a slow cooker and cook on low for 8 to 10 hours or on high for 4 to 5 hours.

—Yield: 4 servings

NUTRITIONAL ANALYSIS

PER SERVING: 246 calories (31% from fat, 12% from protein, 57% from carbohydrate); 8 g protein; 9 g total fat; 1 g saturated fat; 5 g monounsaturated fat; 3 g polyunsaturated fat; 37 g carbohydrate; 7 g fiber; 5 g sugar; 148 mg phosphorus; 93 mg calcium; 4 mg iron; 377 mg sodium; 524 mg potassium; 185 IU vitamin A; 0 mg ATE vitamin E; 20 mg vitamin C; 0 mg cholesterol; 233 g water

TIP

Garam masala is an Indian spice blend that you can find at larger grocery or specialty stores.

Tofu Curry

This is one of the simplest vegetarian meals you'll find. Serve the curry over rice with whatever condiments you like.

3 tablespoons (45 ml) olive oil, divided

12 ounces (340 g) firm tofu, drained and cubed

1 cup (113 g) zucchini, sliced

1 cup (70 g) mushrooms, sliced

1 cup (235 ml) fat free evaporated milk

2 teaspoons (4 g) curry powder

Heat 1 tablespoon (15 ml) oil in a large skillet or work. Fry tofu until the bottom gets golden, then carefully turn and fry the other sides. Remove to a plate. Heat remaining oil and stir-fry zucchini and mushrooms until crisp-tender. Add milk and curry powder and continue cooking until slightly thickened. Stir in tofu.

—Yield: 4 servings

NUTRITIONAL ANALYSIS

PER SERVING: 204 calories (55% from fat, 23% from protein, 22% from carbohydrate); 12 g protein; 13 g total fat; 2 g saturated fat; 8 g monounsaturated fat; 2 g polyunsaturated fat; 12 g carbohydrate; 1 g fiber; 9 g sugar; 232 mg phosphorus; 223 mg calcium; 2 mg iron; 109 mg sodium; 531 mg potassium; 325 IU vitamin A; 76 mg ATE vitamin E; 7 mg vitamin C; 3 mg cholesterol; 171 g water

TIP

The possibilities for vegetable combinations are almost endless. Feel free to experiment.

Zucchini Frittata

During the summer when the garden is producing I'm often looking for uses for zucchini, and this one is popular.

2 cups (250 g) shredded zucchini

2 tablespoons (30 ml) olive oil

½ cup (35 g) mushrooms, sliced

4 eggs, beaten

⅓ cup (37 g) Swiss cheese, shredded

Place the zucchini in a paper towel and squeeze out any excess moisture. Heat oil in a 10-inch (25-cm) skillet. Sauté the mushrooms briefly, then add the zucchini. Cook for 4 minutes, or until the squash is barely tender. Pour eggs over vegetables. Stir once quickly to coat vegetables. Cook over low heat until eggs begin to set. Sprinkle with the cheese. Place under the broiler until cheese browns. Let set for 2 to 3 minutes. Cut into wedges and serve.

—Yield: 4 servings

NUTRITIONAL ANALYSIS

PER SERVING: 144 calories (59% from fat, 32% from protein, 9% from carbohydrate); 12 g protein; 10 g total fat; 2 g saturated fat; 6 g monounsaturated fat; 2 g polyunsaturated fat; 3 g carbohydrate; 1 g fiber; 2 g sugar; 174 mg phosphorus; 149 mg calcium; 2 mg iron; 146 mg sodium; 310 mg potassium; 367 IU vitamin A; 4 mg ATE vitamin E; 11 mg vitamin C; 214 mg cholesterol; 125 g water

Pizza Omelet

When you have a taste for pizza, but don't have the time or want to make the effort to make it yourself, try this instead. This is a dinner-sized omelet for two.

4 eggs

2 tablespoons (30 g) fat free sour cream

2 tablespoons (30 ml) water

½ teaspoon (0.4 g) Italian seasoning

½ cup (35 g) mushrooms, sliced

¼ cup (40 g) onion, sliced

¼ cup (37 g) green bell pepper, coarsely chopped

¼ cup (60 ml) spaghetti sauce, heated

2 ounces (55 g) part-skim mozzarella, shredded

Whisk together egg, sour cream, water, and Italian seasoning until fluffy. Sauté mushrooms, onion, and green bell pepper until onion begins to get soft. Pour egg mixture into a heated nonstick skillet or omelet pan sprayed with nonstick vegetable oil spray. Lift the edges as it cooks to allow uncooked egg to run underneath. When it is nearly set, cover half the omelet with the vegetables and fold the other half over the top. Remove to plate. Top with heated sauce and cheese.

—Yield: 2 servings

NUTRITIONAL ANALYSIS

PER SERVING: 232 calories (39% from fat, 45% from protein, 16% from carbohydrate); 24 g protein; 9 g total fat; 4 g saturated fat; 3 g monounsaturated fat; 2 g polyunsaturated fat; 9 g carbohydrate; 2 g fiber; 3 g sugar; 334 mg phosphorus; 323 mg calcium; 3 mg iron; 547 mg sodium; 599 mg potassium; 856 IU vitamin A; 51 mg ATE vitamin E; 20 mg vitamin C; 435 mg cholesterol; 224 g water

Ricotta Omelet

This makes a nice summer dinner, with a salad and bread. You could also add some vegetables if you like.

4 eggs

¼ teaspoon (0.8 g) garlic powder

¼ teaspoon (0.5 g) black pepper

½ cup (125 g) low fat ricotta cheese

2 tablespoons (30 ml) olive oil

Beat the eggs with the garlic powder, pepper, and ricotta. Heat the oil in a skillet or omelet pan. Add the egg mixture, and swirl to distribute evenly. Cook until nearly set, lifting edge to allow uncooked egg to run underneath. Fold over, cover, and cook until done.

—Yield: 2 servings

NUTRITIONAL ANALYSIS

PER SERVING: 311 calories (66% from fat, 29% from protein, 6% from carbohydrate); 22 g protein; 23 g total fat; 6 g saturated fat; 12 g monounsaturated fat; 4 g polyunsaturated fat; 4 g carbohydrate; 0 g fiber; 1 g sugar; 266 mg phosphorus; 235 mg calcium; 3 mg iron; 299 mg sodium; 398 mg potassium; 689 IU vitamin A; 65 mg ATE vitamin E; 0 mg vitamin C; 440 mg cholesterol; 150 g water

Caribbean Vegetable Curry

A moderately spicy vegetarian curry meal. Adjust the amount of cayenne to your taste.

1 tablespoon (15 ml) olive oil

1 cup (160 g) thinly sliced onion

¾ teaspoon crushed garlic

1 apple, peeled, cored, and chopped

1½ teaspoons curry powder

1½ teaspoons grated lemon peel

1 teaspoon ginger

1 teaspoon coriander

⅛ teaspoon turmeric

⅛ teaspoon cayenne pepper

2 cups (344 g) cooked black-eyed peas, drained

2 cups (200 g) cooked kidney beans

⅓ cup (50 g) raisins

1 cup (230 g) plain fat-free yogurt

3 eggs, hard boiled and halved

3 cups (495 g) cooked rice

6 radishes, thinly sliced

¼ cup (25 g) sliced scallions

½ cup chopped fresh cilantro

¼ cup (37 g) chopped peanuts

Heat oil in skillet. Sauté onion, garlic, and apple until soft. Combine curry powder, lemon peel, ginger, coriander, turmeric, and cayenne pepper. Stir into onion mixture. Add black-eyed peas, undrained kidney beans, and raisins. Cover; simmer 5 minutes. Remove from heat, stir in yogurt. Place egg halves on rice. Spoon curry over. Top with radishes, scallions, cilantro, and peanuts.

—Yield: 6 servings

NUTRITIONAL ANALYSIS

PER SERVING: 218 g water; 524 calories (12% from fat, 22% from protein, 66% from carb); 29 g protein; 7 g total fat; 2 g saturated fat; 3 g monounsaturated fat; 1 g polyunsaturated fat; 89 g carbohydrate; 22 g fiber; 16 g sugar; 513 mg phosphorus; 238 mg calcium; 9 mg iron; 119 mg sodium; 1465 mg potassium; 495 IU vitamin A; 40 mg vitamin E; 13 mg vitamin C; 119 mg cholesterol

Tomato and Basil Quiche

If you want, you can put it in a crust, but we like it just as well without it.

1 tablespoon (15 ml) olive oil

1 cup (160 g) onion, sliced

2 cups (360 g) tomatoes, sliced

2 tablespoons (16 g) flour

2 teaspoons (1.4 g) dried basil

3 eggs

½ cup (120 ml) skim milk

½ teaspoon (1 g) black pepper

1 cup (110 g) Swiss cheese, shredded

Preheat oven to 400°F (200°C, or gas mark 6). Heat olive oil in a large skillet over medium heat. Sauté onion until soft; remove from skillet. Sprinkle tomato slices with flour and basil, then sauté 1 minute on each side. In a small bowl, whisk together eggs and milk. Season with pepper. Spread half the cheese in the bottom of a pie pan sprayed with nonstick vegetable oil spray. Layer onions over the cheese and top with tomatoes. Pour the egg mixture over the vegetables. Sprinkle the remaining cheese over the top. Bake for 10 minutes. Reduce heat to 350°F (180°C, or gas mark 4), and bake for 15 to 20 minutes, or until filling is puffed and golden brown. Serve warm.

—Yield: 4 servings

NUTRITIONAL ANALYSIS

PER SERVING: 188 calories (33% from fat, 38% from protein, 29% from carbohydrate); 18 g protein; 7 g total fat; 2 g saturated fat; 3 g monounsaturated fat; 1 g polyunsaturated fat; 14 g carbohydrate; 2 g fiber; 2 g sugar; 327 mg phosphorus; 408 mg calcium; 2 mg iron; 196 mg sodium; 391 mg potassium; 781 IU vitamin A; 32 mg ATE vitamin E; 23 mg vitamin C; 173 mg cholesterol; 192 g water

Bean and Cheddar Cheese Pie

Beans and cheese combine to make a filling and tasty meatless main dish with a southwestern accent.

¾ cup (93 g) flour

1½ cups (175 g) shredded Cheddar cheese, divided

1½ teaspoons baking powder

⅓ cup (80 ml) skim milk

1 egg, beaten

2 cups (328 g) cooked chickpeas, drained

2 cups (200 g) cooked kidney beans, drained

8 ounces (225 g) no-salt-added tomato sauce

½ cup (75 g) chopped green bell pepper

¼ cup (40 g) chopped onion

2 teaspoons chili powder

½ teaspoon dried oregano leaves

¼ teaspoon garlic powder

Heat oven to 375°F (190°C, gas mark 5) . Spray a 10-inch (25-cm) pie plate with nonstick vegetable oil spray. Mix flour, ½ cup (58 g) cheese, and baking powder in a medium bowl. Stir in milk and egg until blended. Spread over bottom and up sides of pie plate. Mix ½ cup (58 g) of the remaining cheese and the remaining ingredients; spoon into pie plate. Sprinkle with remaining cheese. Bake about 25 minutes or until edges are puffy and light brown. Let stand 10 minutes before cutting.

—Yield: 8 servings

NUTRITIONAL ANALYSIS

PER SERVING: 109 g water; 400 calories (23% from fat, 23% from protein, 54% from carb); 23 g protein; 10 g total fat; 6 g saturated fat; 3 g monounsaturated fat; 1 g polyunsaturated fat; 55 g carbohydrate; 15 g fiber; 3 g sugar; 438 mg phosphorus; 343 mg calcium; 6 mg iron; 464 mg sodium; 957 mg potassium; 648 IU vitamin A; 81 mg vitamin E; 16 mg vitamin C; 52 mg cholesterol

Artichoke Pie

A nice meatless meal with a kind of Italian flavor.

3 eggs

3 ounces (85 g) cream cheese with chives, softened

¾ teaspoon garlic powder

¼ teaspoon black pepper

1½ cups (225 g) shredded mozzarella cheese, divided

1 cup (250 g) ricotta cheese

½ cup (115 g) low-fat mayonnaise

1 can artichoke hearts

1 cup (164 g) cooked chickpeas

½ cup (50 g) sliced black olives

2 ounces (55 g) pimento, drained and diced

2 tablespoons fresh parsley

1 9-inch (23-cm) pie shell, unbaked

⅓ cup (33 g) grated Parmesan cheese

In a mixing bowl, beat eggs. Stir in cream cheese, garlic powder, and pepper. Stir in 1 cup (150 g) of mozzarella, the ricotta, and the mayonnaise. Quarter 2 artichoke hearts and set aside. Chop remaining artichoke hearts; fold into cheese mixture. Fold in chickpeas, olives, pimento, and parsley. Turn mixture into pastry shell. Bake in a 350°F (180°C, gas mark 4) oven for 30 minutes. Top with remaining mozzarella and the Parmesan cheese. Bake about 15 minutes more until set. Let stand for 10 minutes. Top with quartered artichokes.

—Yield: 8 servings

NUTRITIONAL ANALYSIS

PER SERVING: 128 g water; 371 calories (56% from fat, 19% from protein, 26% from carb); 17 g protein; 22 g total fat; 8 g saturated fat; 7 g monounsaturated fat; 2 g polyunsaturated fat; 23 g carbohydrate; 3 g fiber; 2 g sugar; 283 mg phosphorus; 288 mg calcium; 2 mg iron; 697 mg sodium; 282 mg potassium; 841 IU vitamin A; 122 mg vitamin E; 10 mg vitamin C; 130 mg cholesterol

Cheese Pie

This is an ideal vegetarian main dish, needing only a salad to make it a complete meal.

4 ounces (115 g) feta cheese

16 ounces (455 g) low fat ricotta cheese

4 eggs

¼ cup (30 g) flour

¾ cup (180 ml) skim milk

¼ teaspoon (0.5 g) black pepper

Preheat oven to 375°F (190°C, or gas mark 5). Spray an ovenproof skillet or glass baking dish with nonstick vegetable oil spray. Mix the cheeses together, then stir in the eggs, flour, milk, and pepper. Pour the batter into the prepared pan. Bake for 40 minutes, or until golden and set. Cut into wedges.

—Yield: 4 servings

NUTRITIONAL ANALYSIS

PER SERVING: 332 calories (47% from fat, 33% from protein, 20% from carbohydrate); 27 g protein; 17 g total fat; 10 g saturated fat; 5 g monounsaturated fat; 2 g polyunsaturated fat; 16 g carbohydrate; 0 g fiber; 2 g sugar; 439 mg phosphorus; 549 mg calcium; 2 mg iron; 597 mg sodium; 360 mg potassium; 875 IU vitamin A; 183 mg ATE vitamin E; 1 mg vitamin C; 272 mg cholesterol; 194 g water

Asparagus Strata

This can be either breakfast or dinner—fancy enough to serve guests, but easy enough to make often for family.

1 pound (455 g) asparagus

6 slices whole wheat bread

2 cups (225 g) shredded Cheddar cheese, divided

1 cup (150 g) cubed ham

5 eggs

¾ teaspoon Worcestershire sauce

¼ teaspoon garlic powder

1¾ cups (410 ml) skim milk

2 tablespoons (20 g) minced onion

⅛ teaspoon cayenne

Cut asparagus into 1-inch (2.5-cm) pieces, drop into boiling, salted water and cook rapidly for 4 minutes. Drain. If using frozen asparagus, thaw and drain. Trim crusts from bread. Fit into 7 × 11-inch (28-cm) baking dish sprayed with nonstick vegetable oil spray. Sprinkle 11/4 cups (145 g) Cheddar cheese over the bread slices and distribute the asparagus and ham. Beat the remaining ingredients, except the reserved cheese, together until blended. Pour over the layered ingredients, cover, and refrigerate at least 8 hours or overnight. Bake uncovered in 350°F (180°C, gas mark 4) oven for 30 minutes. Top with remaining cheese and continue baking for 10 minutes until center is firm. Allow to stand for 5 minutes before cutting.

—Yield: 8 servings

NUTRITIONAL ANALYSIS

PER SERVING: 158 g water; 303 calories (50% from fat, 29% from protein, 21% from carb); 22 g protein; 17 g total fat; 9 g saturated fat; 5 g monounsaturated fat; 1 g polyunsaturated fat; 16 g carbohydrate; 2 g fiber; 3 g sugar; 398 mg phosphorus; 378 mg calcium; 3 mg iron; 576 mg sodium; 413 mg potassium; 1051 IU vitamin A; 167 mg vitamin E; 6 mg vitamin C; 191 mg cholesterol

Fiber-Rich Casserole

This makes either a great side dish or a meatless meal. Serves 4 as a main dish, 6 as a side dish.

1½ cups (355 ml) chicken broth

1 cup (130 g) thinly sliced carrot

½ cup (100 g) pearl barley

2 cups (200 g) cooked kidney beans, drained

¼ cup (40 g) chopped onion

¼ cup fresh parsley

3 tablespoons (27 g) bulgur

⅛ teaspoon garlic powder

¼ cup (30 g) shredded Cheddar cheese

Mix all together except cheese. Put in 1-quart (1-L) dish. Bake covered at 350°F (180°C, gas mark 4) for 50 minutes. Uncover; sprinkle on cheese. Return to oven to melt cheese.

—Yield: 6 servings

NUTRITIONAL ANALYSIS

PER SERVING: 96 g water; 318 calories (9% from fat, 24% from protein, 67% from carb); 20 g protein; 3 g total fat; 1 g saturated fat; 1 g monounsaturated fat; 1 g polyunsaturated fat; 55 g carbohydrate; 20 g fiber; 3 g sugar; 360 mg phosphorus; 148 mg calcium; 6 mg iron; 259 mg sodium; 1099 mg potassium; 3856 IU vitamin A; 14 mg vitamin E; 8 mg vitamin C; 6 mg cholesterol

Eggplant and Fresh Mozzarella Bake

This again can be either a meal or a side dish with other Italian food. The fresh mozzarella adds a different flavor and has the benefit of being low in sodium.

6 ounces (170 g) fresh mozzarella

2 cups (470 ml) low sodium spaghetti sauce

1 eggplant, peeled and sliced

Preheat oven to 375°F (190°C, or gas mark 5). Slice mozzarella thinly and place on paper towels to soak up excess moisture. Cover the bottom of an 8 × 8-inch (20 × 20-cm) baking dish with spaghetti sauce, layer eggplant on top of sauce, then cheese on top of eggplant. Repeat layers, ending with a layer of sauce. Bake for 30 minutes or until bubbly and cheese is melted.

—Yield: 6 servings

NUTRITIONAL ANALYSIS

PER SERVING: 181 calories (41% from fat, 19% from protein, 39% from carbohydrate); 9 g protein; 9 g total fat; 3 g saturated fat; 4 g monounsaturated fat; 1 g polyunsaturated fat; 18 g carbohydrate; 5 g fiber; 12 g sugar; 180 mg phosphorus; 252 mg calcium; 1 mg iron; 202 mg sodium; 519 mg potassium; 669 IU vitamin A; 35 mg ATE vitamin E; 11 mg vitamin C; 18 mg cholesterol; 149 g water

Squash and Rice Bake

Another of those dishes that can be either a full meal or a side dish in a meal with meat. We like it both ways.

½ cup (95 g) rice

2 tablespoons (30 ml) olive oil

¼ teaspoon (0.8 g) minced garlic

½ teaspoon (0.5 g) dried thyme

4 cups (450 g) yellow squash, sliced

2 ounces (55 g) low fat Swiss cheese, shredded

Preheat oven to 350°F (180°C, or gas mark 4). Cook rice according to package directions. Heat oil in a large skillet. Sauté garlic for a few minutes. Add thyme and squash. Sauté for a few minutes more. Stir the rice and cheese into the mixture. Turn into a 2-quart (1.9-L) baking dish that has been coated with nonstick vegetable oil spray. Bake for 25 minutes or until heated through.

—Yield: 4 servings

NUTRITIONAL ANALYSIS

PER SERVING: 128 calories (53% from fat, 18% from protein, 29% from carbohydrate); 6 g protein; 8 g total fat; 1 g saturated fat; 5 g monounsaturated fat; 1 g polyunsaturated fat; 10 g carbohydrate; 1 g fiber; 3 g sugar; 140 mg phosphorus; 160 mg calcium; 1 mg iron; 40 mg sodium; 325 mg potassium; 252 IU vitamin A; 6 mg ATE vitamin E; 19 mg vitamin C; 5 mg cholesterol; 129 g water

Spinach-Stuffed Tomatoes

This is another of those recipes that would make a good side dish but could just as easily be the centerpiece of a vegetarian dinner.

10 ounces (280 g) fresh spinach

4 tomatoes

1 cup (115 g) part-skim mozzarella, divided

¼ cup (40 g) onion, finely chopped

¼ cup (25 g) Parmesan, grated

⅛ teaspoon (0.3 g) pepper

2 tablespoons (8 g) fresh parsley, minced

Preheat oven to 350°F (180°C, or gas mark 4). Steam or microwave spinach in a covered bowl until softened but still slightly crispy. Drain well and squeeze dry. Put in a large bowl. Slice and hollow out centers of tomatoes, reserving the pulp. Discard seeds. Chop pulp finely and add to spinach. Add ½ cup (60 g) mozzarella cheese, onion, Parmesan, and pepper to spinach mixture and blend well. Spoon evenly into tomato shells. Sprinkle with remaining mozzarella and parsley. Arrange in an 8-inch (20 cm) round glass or ceramic baking dish and bake for 6 minutes, or until heated through.

—Yield: 4 servings

NUTRITIONAL ANALYSIS

PER SERVING: 158 calories (38% from fat, 32% from protein, 30% from carbohydrate); 14 g protein; 7 g total fat; 4 g saturated fat; 2 g monounsaturated fat; 1 g polyunsaturated fat; 13 g carbohydrate; 4 g fiber; 1 g sugar; 252 mg phosphorus; 412 mg calcium; 2 mg iron; 355 mg sodium; 602 mg potassium; 9802 IU vitamin A; 42 mg ATE vitamin E; 44 mg vitamin C; 24 mg cholesterol; 230 g water

Zucchini Patties

These taste like crab cakes but without the crab.

2½ cups (310 g) grated zucchini

1 egg, beaten

1 cup (115 g) bread crumbs

¼ cup (60 g) minced onion

1 teaspoon (2.4 g) Old Bay Seasoning™

¼ cup (30 g) flour

2 tablespoons (30 ml) olive oil

In a large bowl, combine zucchini and egg. Stir in bread crumbs, minced onion, and seasoning. Mix well. Shape mixture into patties. Dredge in flour. In a medium skillet, heat oil over medium-high heat until hot. Fry patties in oil until golden brown on both sides.

—Yield: 6 servings

NUTRITIONAL ANALYSIS

PER SERVING: 150 calories (36% from fat, 13% from protein, 51% from carbohydrate); 5 g protein; 6 g total fat; 1 g saturated fat; 4 g monounsaturated fat; 1 g polyunsaturated fat; 19 g carbohydrate; 2 g fiber; 2 g sugar; 70 mg phosphorus; 49 mg calcium; 2 mg iron; 156 mg sodium; 171 mg potassium; 141 IU vitamin A; 0 mg ATE vitamin E; 9 mg vitamin C; 35 mg cholesterol; 65 g water

Thai Spinach and Noodle Bowl

Great for a lunch or light dinner, this soup is bursting with flavor.

4 cups low sodium chicken broth

2 ounces whole wheat spaghetti

⅛ teaspoon red pepper flakes

2 cups fresh spinach, coarsely chopped

¼ cup fresh basil

2 teaspoon ginger root, peeled and grated

In a medium saucepan bring the broth to a boil. Add the spaghetti and red pepper. Reduce the heat, cover and simmer until spaghetti is just tender. Remove from heat, stir in remaining ingredients, cover and let stand for 2 minutes.

—Yield: 4 servings

NUTRITIONAL ANALYSIS

PER SERVING: 97 calories (15% from fat, 28% from protein , 57% from carb); 8 g protein ; 2 g total fat; 0 g saturated fat; 1 g monounsaturated fat; 0 g polyunsaturated fat; 16 g carb; 2 g fiber; 0 g sugar; 127 mg phosphorus; 75 mg calcium; 86 mg sodium; 398 mg potassium; 1626 IU vitamin A; 0 mg ATE vitamin E; 6 mg vitamin C; 0 mg cholesterol

Vegetable Paella

This would be a good dish to try for those people who think they don't like vegetarian cooking. It has plenty of flavor and substance to satisfy.

2 tablespoons (30 ml) olive oil

1¼ cups (240 g) brown rice

1 cup (160 g) onion, sliced

2 cloves garlic, crushed

⅛ teaspoon (0.1 g) saffron

3 cups (710 ml) water

1 teaspoon (1.7 g) lemon peel

¼ teaspoon (0.5 g) freshly ground black pepper

2 cups (240 g) leeks, cut in 1-inch (2.5-cm) pieces

¼ cup (34 g) frozen peas, thawed

¼ cup (25 g) black olives

Heat the oil in a large, deep pan. Add the brown rice and onion slices and stir until the rice is coated and begins to turn opaque. Add the garlic, saffron, water, lemon peel, and pepper. Mix well, then bring to a boil. Mix again to distribute the saffron. Arrange the leeks, peas, and olives on top of the rice. Bring to a boil. Cover and simmer for 45 minutes. Serve straight from the pan.

—Yield: 4 servings

NUTRITIONAL ANALYSIS

PER SERVING: 335 calories (25% from fat, 7% from protein, 67% from carbohydrate); 6 g protein; 10 g total fat; 1 g saturated fat; 6 g monounsaturated fat; 1 g polyunsaturated fat; 57 g carbohydrate; 4 g fiber; 4 g sugar; 230 mg phosphorus; 66 mg calcium; 2 mg iron; 126 mg sodium; 291 mg potassium; 987 IU vitamin A; 0 mg ATE vitamin E; 10 mg vitamin C; 0 mg cholesterol; 271 g water

TIP

To add even more flavor and protein, sprinkle with nuts.

CHAPTER 8

Soups and Stews

What can we say about soups? They are almost always easy to cook, healthy, and delicious. In this chapter we have enough recipes that you could have a different one each week for a year and still have a number that you haven't tried. There are soups from around the country and around the world. There are spicy and refreshing ones. There are chowders and stews. And that's not to even mention all the extra heart-healthy bean and pea soups. So grab a soup and dig in.

Chicken Corn Chowder

A good soup for a cool fall day. Add bread and you have a meal.

6 potatoes, peeled and diced

1½ cups (195 g) sliced carrot

1 cup (160 g) chopped onion

4 cups (950 ml) low-sodium chicken broth

12 ounces (340 g) frozen corn

2 cups (280 g) cooked, diced chicken

1 cup (235 ml) skim milk

¼ teaspoon garlic powder

½ teaspoon black pepper

1 cup (225 g) instant mashed potatoes

Cook potatoes, carrot, and onion in broth until soft. Add corn and chicken. Cook 5 minutes longer. Add milk, garlic powder, pepper, and mashed potatoes. Stir until potatoes are dissolved. Heat through.

—Yield: 6 servings

NUTRITIONAL ANALYSIS

PER SERVING: 548 g water; 498 calories (10% from fat, 21% from protein, 69% from carb); 27 g protein; 6 g total fat; 2 g saturated fat; 2 g monounsaturated fat; 2 g polyunsaturated fat; 89 g carbohydrate; 9 g fiber; 8 g sugar; 391 mg phosphorus; 117 mg calcium; 2 mg iron; 169 mg sodium; 1716 mg potassium; 5617 IU vitamin A; 32 mg vitamin E; 39 mg vitamin C; 42 mg cholesterol

Italian Chicken Soup

One more cook-ahead meal for your slow cooker. This one is good either as a full meal or just to have on hand for lunches.

1 pound (455 g) boneless chicken breasts, cubed

4 cups (950 ml) low-sodium chicken broth

2 cups (480 g) low-sodium tomatoes

4 ounces (115 g) mushrooms, sliced

½ cup (65 g) sliced carrot

½ cup (56 g) sliced zucchini

½ cup (62 g) frozen green beans

6 ounces (170 g) frozen spinach

½ teaspoon garlic powder

1 teaspoon basil

½ teaspoon oregano

Combine ingredients and place in slow cooker. Cover and cook on low 8 to 10 hours or on high 4 to 5 hours.

—Yield: 6 servings

NUTRITIONAL ANALYSIS

PER SERVING: 305 g water; 78 calories (17% from fat, 40% from protein, 43% from carb); 9 g protein; 2 g total fat; 0 g saturated fat; 1 g monounsaturated fat; 0 g polyunsaturated fat; 10 g carbohydrate; 3 g fiber; 4 g sugar; 133 mg phosphorus; 73 mg calcium; 2 mg iron; 101 mg sodium; 568 mg potassium; 5706 IU vitamin A; 1 mg vitamin E; 23 mg vitamin C; 7 mg cholesterol

Mexican Chicken Soup

A flavorful Mexican chicken noodle soup. Serve with cornmeal bread for a complete meal.

1½ pounds (675 g) boneless chicken breasts, cut in bite-size pieces

1 cup (150 g) green bell pepper, cut in strips

1 cup (160 g) diced onion

½ teaspoon minced garlic

2 cups (480 g) no-salt-added canned tomatoes

4 ounces (115 g) chopped green chiles

2 cups (475 ml) low-sodium chicken broth

2 tablespoons (28 ml) vinegar

1 teaspoon oregano

10 ounces (280 g) frozen corn

2 cups (342 g) cooked pinto beans, drained

2 ounces (55 g) egg noodles

Mix all ingredients together, except noodles, in Dutch oven. Simmer until chicken is cooked through and vegetables are tender, about 30 minutes. Add noodles and cook until they are done, about 10 minutes.

—Yield: 6 servings

NUTRITIONAL ANALYSIS

PER SERVING: 385 g water; 304 calories (8% from fat, 46% from protein, 46% from carb); 36 g protein; 3 g total fat; 1 g saturated fat; 1 g monounsaturated fat; 1 g polyunsaturated fat; 36 g carbohydrate; 9 g fiber; 5 g sugar; 395 mg phosphorus; 88 mg calcium; 4 mg iron; 188 mg sodium; 940 mg potassium; 252 IU vitamin A; 7 mg vitamin E; 39 mg vitamin C; 66 mg cholesterol

Smoked Chicken Minestrone

Not a very traditional minestrone. I was just looking for something with beans in it and a way to use up the last of a smoked chicken. If you don't have smoked chicken, regular chicken will also work.

½ pound (225 g) dry cannellini beans

½ pound (225 g) dry chickpeas

2 smoked chicken thighs

2 cups (475 ml) low-sodium chicken broth

¼ cup (40 g) chopped onion

⅓ cup (43 g) sliced carrot

1 cup (113 g) sliced zucchini

½ teaspoon garlic powder

1 teaspoon basil

1 teaspoon oregano

2 cups (480 g) no-salt-added canned tomatoes

Soak beans and drain. Simmer chicken in broth and enough water to cover until meat separates from bones. Cool, skim off fat, and remove meat from bones. Return meat to broth. Add other ingredients and simmer 1 to 1½ hours, until beans are tender. Add additional water as needed. Garnish with Parmesan cheese.

—Yield: 4 servings

NUTRITIONAL ANALYSIS

PER SERVING: 386 g water; 229 calories (8% from fat, 33% from protein, 59% from carb); 20 g protein; 2 g total fat; 1 g saturated fat; 1 g monounsaturated fat; 1 g polyunsaturated fat; 35 g carbohydrate; 9 g fiber; 5 g sugar; 353 mg phosphorus; 124 mg calcium; 4 mg iron; 781 mg sodium; 914 mg potassium; 2044 IU vitamin A; 0 mg vitamin E; 21 mg vitamin C; 17 mg cholesterol

Amish Chicken Soup

When I was growing up along the Maryland/Pennsylvania border, Amish chicken corn soup was always one of the highlights at volunteer fire company carnivals and suppers. This soup has a similar flavor.

4 cups (946 ml) low sodium chicken broth

2 cups (220 g) chicken, cooked and chopped

½ cup (50 g) celery, chopped

½ cup (65 g) carrot, sliced

½ cup (80 g) onion, chopped

1 tablespoon (0.4 g) dried parsley

¼ teaspoon (0.8 g) garlic powder

2 cups (470 ml) water

12 ounces (340 g) egg noodles

Place all ingredients in a large kettle and simmer until noodles are tender (see package directions for approximate time).

—Yield: 8 servings

NUTRITIONAL ANALYSIS

PER SERVING: 148 calories (22% from fat, 37% from protein, 41% from carbohydrate); 14 g protein; 4 g total fat; 1 g saturated fat; 1 g monounsaturated fat; 1 g polyunsaturated fat; 15 g carbohydrate; 3 g fiber; 1 g sugar; 144 mg phosphorus; 20 mg calcium; 1 mg iron; 49 mg sodium; 262 mg potassium; 1456 IU vitamin A; 6 mg ATE vitamin E; 2 mg vitamin C; 31 mg cholesterol; 248 g water

Chicken Barley Soup

A nice change from chicken and noodle or rice soup featuring barley.

3 pound (1¼ kg) chicken, cut up

2 quarts (1.9 L) water

1½ cups (195 g) diced carrot

1 cup (120 g) diced celery

1 cup (200 g) pearl barley

½ cup (60 g) chopped onion

1 bay leaf

½ teaspoon poultry seasoning

½ teaspoon black pepper

½ teaspoon dried sage

Cook chicken in water until tender. Cool broth and skim off fat. Bone chicken and cut into bite-size pieces; return to kettle along with remaining ingredients. Return to heat and bring to a boil. Simmer covered for at least 1 hour until vegetables are tender and barley is done, adding more water if needed. Remove bay leaf and serve.

—Yield: 6 servings

NUTRITIONAL ANALYSIS

PER SERVING: 546 g water; 400 calories (18% from fat, 54% from protein, 28% from carb); 53 g protein; 8 g total fat; 2 g saturated fat; 2 g monounsaturated fat; 2 g polyunsaturated fat; 27 g carbohydrate; 7 g fiber; 3 g sugar; 493 mg phosphorus; 69 mg calcium; 3 mg iron; 224 mg sodium; 829 mg potassium; 5595 IU vitamin A; 36 mg vitamin E; 9 mg vitamin C; 159 mg cholesterol

Chicken Vegetable Barley Soup

This soup is full of both flavor and nutrition, low in fat, and high in fiber.

4 cups (946 ml) low sodium chicken broth

4 cups (720 g) canned no-salt-added tomatoes

3 cups (710 ml) water

3 cups (480 g) onions, chopped

¾ cup (98 g) carrot, chopped

1⅔ cups (280 g) frozen corn, thawed

1 cup (150 g) red bell pepper, chopped

1 cup (165 g) frozen lima beans, thawed

½ cup (50 g) celery, chopped

¼ cup (56 g) lentils

¼ cup (50 g) pearl barley

¼ cup (50 g) split peas

1½ tablespoons (3 g) dried sage

2 cups (220 g) cooked chicken breast, diced

Combine all ingredients except chicken in large, heavy pot or Dutch oven. Bring to boil over medium-high heat. Reduce heat to medium. Simmer for 45 minutes, or until all vegetables and legumes are tender and soup is thick, stirring occasionally. Stir in chicken and heat through.

—Yield: 8 servings

NUTRITIONAL ANALYSIS

PER SERVING: 222 calories (11% from fat, 33% from protein, 55% from carbohydrate); 20 g protein; 3 g total fat; 1 g saturated fat; 1 g monounsaturated fat; 1 g polyunsaturated fat; 32 g carbohydrate; 7 g fiber; 9 g sugar; 256 mg phosphorus; 89 mg calcium; 3 mg iron; 109 mg sodium; 864 mg potassium; 2913 IU vitamin A; 2 mg ATE vitamin E; 44 mg vitamin C; 30 mg cholesterol; 479 g water

Chicken Barley Chowder

A simple, creamy soup of chicken and barley, perfect for a cold day.

2 tablespoons (28 ml) olive oil

½ cup (60 g) minced celery

¾ cup (120 g) minced onion

1 tablespoon flour

½ teaspoon black pepper

6 cups (1.4 L) low-sodium chicken broth

1 cup (200 g) pearl barley

1 pound (455 g) cooked boneless chicken breast, shredded

½ cup (120 ml) fat-free evaporated milk

Heat oil in heavy saucepan. Sauté celery and onion; sprinkle with flour and pepper. Gradually stir in broth and barley. Add chicken. Simmer covered for about an hour, stirring occasionally until barley is tender. Remove from heat and add milk.

—Yield: 4 servings

NUTRITIONAL ANALYSIS

PER SERVING: 499 g water; 452 calories (23% from fat, 37% from protein, 41% from carb); 42 g protein; 12 g total fat; 2 g saturated fat; 6 g monounsaturated fat; 2 g polyunsaturated fat; 47 g carbohydrate; 9 g fiber; 6 g sugar; 528 mg phosphorus; 148 mg calcium; 4 mg iron; 236 mg sodium; 995 mg potassium; 218 IU vitamin A; 45 mg vitamin E; 4 mg vitamin C; 67 mg cholesterol

Pork Stew

It's nice to have dinner finished when you get home once in a while. You can serve this over rice or noodles or just have it with a big slice of freshly baked bread (the delay bake option on the bread machine works so well with the slow cooker).

1 pound (455 g) pork loin

¾ cup (120 g) onion, sliced

2 cups (360 g) canned no-salt-added tomatoes

½ cup (75 g) green bell pepper, coarsely chopped

2 cups (470 ml) low sodium chicken broth

1 cup (70 g) mushrooms, quartered

1 tablespoon (0.4 g) dried parsley

1 teaspoon (1 g) dried thyme

¼ cup (15 g) fresh cilantro, chopped

¼ cup (30 g) flour

Cube pork. Layer all ingredients except the flour in a slow cooker, reserving half the chicken broth. Cook on low for 6 to 8 hours. Stir the flour into the remaining chicken broth. Add to slow cooker. Turn to high and cook an additional 30 minutes, or until slightly thickened.

—Yield: 4 servings

NUTRITIONAL ANALYSIS

PER SERVING: 242 calories (35% from fat, 35% from protein, 30% from carbohydrate); 22 g protein; 10 g total fat; 4 g saturated fat; 4 g monounsaturated fat; 1 g polyunsaturated fat; 18 g carbohydrate; 3 g fiber; 70 mg calcium; 3 mg iron; 91 mg sodium; 801 mg potassium; 1073 IU vitamin A; 54 mg vitamin C; 52 mg cholesterol

Chowder from the Sea

This one came about on a weekend when I didn't want to spend my day cooking and I knew everyone was going to be available for dinner at a different time. The answer: the slow cooker and a fish and shrimp soup that people could ladle up whenever they were ready.

½ pound (225 g) cod or other white fish, cubed

½ pound (225 g) shrimp, peeled

4 potatoes, shredded

1 cup (110 g) shredded carrot

½ cup (80 g) finely chopped onion

½ cup (75 g) finely chopped red bell pepper

½ cup (60 g) finely chopped celery

2 cups (475 ml) low-sodium chicken broth

1 cup (235 ml) skim milk

1 teaspoon seafood seasoning

Place fish and shrimp in slow cooker. Add potato and vegetables. Pour broth over meat and vegetables. Add milk and seasoning. Stir to mix. Cook on low 8 to 10 hours.

—Yield: 6 servings

NUTRITIONAL ANALYSIS

PER SERVING: 378 g water; 289 calories (5% from fat, 30% from protein, 65% from carb); 22 g protein; 2 g total fat; 0 g saturated fat; 0 g monounsaturated fat; 1 g polyunsaturated fat; 48 g carbohydrate; 5 g fiber; 4 g sugar; 295 mg phosphorus; 115 mg calcium; 2 mg iron; 186 mg sodium; 1161 mg potassium; 4209 IU vitamin A; 55 mg vitamin E; 35 mg vitamin C; 91 mg cholesterol

Indian Vegetable Soup

A great vegetarian meal. The amount of ginger gives it a sneaky sort of spiciness. I prefer mild curry powder, but if you want something even hotter you could use hot curry powder.

1 eggplant, peeled and cubed

1 pound (455 g) potatoes, cubed

2 cups (360 g) canned no-salt-added tomatoes

1½ cups (360 g) cooked garbanzo beans

1 cup (160 g) onion, coarsely chopped

1½ teaspoons (3 g) curry powder

1½ teaspoons (2.7 g) ground ginger

1 teaspoon (2 g) ground coriander

¼ teaspoon (0.5 g) black pepper

4 cups (946 ml) low sodium vegetable broth

In a slow cooker combine the eggplant, potatoes, tomatoes, garbanzo beans, and onion. Sprinkle curry powder, ginger, coriander, and pepper over top. Pour the broth over all. Cover and cook on low for 8 to 10 hours or on high for 4 to 5 hours.

—Yield: 6 servings

NUTRITIONAL ANALYSIS

PER SERVING: 196 calories (9% from fat, 18% from protein, 73% from carbohydrate); 9 g protein; 2 g total fat; 0 g saturated fat; 1 g monounsaturated fat; 1 g polyunsaturated fat; 38 g carbohydrate; 8 g fiber; 6 g sugar; 193 mg phosphorus; 76 mg calcium; 3 mg iron; 246 mg sodium; 969 mg potassium; 146 IU vitamin A; 0 mg ATE vitamin E; 21 mg vitamin C; 0 mg cholesterol; 426 g water

Winter Vegetable Soup

A good meal for a winter's evening. With no potatoes or pasta, it's also low in carbohydrates for an entire meal. Using a lean cut of meat like round steak also makes it low in fat.

1 pound (455 g) beef round steak

2 cups (470 ml) low sodium beef broth

2 cups (360 g) canned no-salt-added tomatoes

1 cup (150 g) turnips, diced

6 ounces (170 g) frozen green beans, thawed

6 ounces (170 g) frozen broccoli, thawed

6 ounces (170 g) frozen cauliflower, thawed

½ cup (65 g) carrot, sliced

½ cup (80 g) onion, diced

½ cup (50 g) celery, diced

Combine all ingredients in a slow cooker and cook on low for 8 to 10 hours or high 4 to 5 hours. Remove meat and cut into bite-sized pieces or shred. Return to slow cooker and stir until warmed through.

—Yield: 4 servings

NUTRITIONAL ANALYSIS

PER SERVING: 317 calories (19% from fat, 59% from protein, 23% from carbohydrate); 47 g protein; 7 g total fat; 2 g saturated fat; 2 g monounsaturated fat; 1 g polyunsaturated fat; 18 g carbohydrate; 7 g fiber; 8 g sugar; 377 mg phosphorus; 119 mg calcium; 6 mg iron; 188 mg sodium; 1135 mg potassium; 3451 IU vitamin A; 0 mg ATE vitamin E; 82 mg vitamin C; 102 mg cholesterol; 493 g water

Vegetarian Minestrone

You can either use canned beans for this or cook your own from dried beans.

½ cup (80 g) onion, chopped

½ cup (65 g) carrot, diced

1 cup (113 g) zucchini, sliced

2 cloves garlic, crushed

2 cups (470 ml) low sodium chicken broth

2 cups (450 g) canned great northern beans, no-salt-added

1 teaspoon (0.7 g) dried basil

1 teaspoon (1 g) dried oregano

2 cups (360 g) canned no-salt-added tomatoes

6 ounces (170 g) fresh spinach

Parmesan cheese (optional)

Sauté onions, carrot, zucchini, and garlic until tender. Add to a soup pot with the remaining ingredients and simmer for 1 to 1½ hours. Add additional water if needed. Garnish with Parmesan cheese, if desired.

—Yield: 6 servings

NUTRITIONAL ANALYSIS

PER SERVING: 149 calories (7% from fat, 26% from protein, 68% from carbohydrate); 10 g protein; 1 g total fat; 0 g saturated fat; 0 g monounsaturated fat; 0 g polyunsaturated fat; 27 g carbohydrate; 7 g fiber; 4 g sugar; 189 mg phosphorus; 133 mg calcium; 3 mg iron; 75 mg sodium; 727 mg potassium; 5370 IU vitamin A; 0 mg ATE vitamin E; 15 mg vitamin C; 0 mg cholesterol; 279 g water

Corn Chowder

This is great just the way it is, or you can add some cooked chicken or ground turkey if you like. We had it just like this, with breadsticks and nothing else.

1 tablespoon (15 ml) olive oil

1 cup (160 g) onion, chopped

½ cup (50 g) celery, sliced

½ cup (65 g) carrot, sliced

2 tablespoons (16 g) flour

2 cups (475 ml) low sodium chicken broth

4 cups (945 ml) skim milk

2 potatoes, peeled and diced

3 cups (410 g) frozen corn, thawed

½ teaspoon (1 g) black pepper

Heat the oil in a large Dutch oven. Add the onion, celery, and carrots and cook over medium heat until just soft. Sprinkle on the flour and cook for 3 minutes, stirring frequently. Stir in the broth and milk. Add the potatoes and corn. Simmer for 25 minutes or until potatoes are tender. Sprinkle with pepper.

—Yield: 6 servings

NUTRITIONAL ANALYSIS

PER SERVING: 278 calories (12% from fat, 18% from protein, 70% from carbohydrate); 13 g protein; 4 g total fat; 1 g saturated fat; 2 g monounsaturated fat; 1 g polyunsaturated fat; 52 g carbohydrate; 5 g fiber; 6 g sugar; 346 mg phosphorus; 268 mg calcium; 2 mg iron; 148 mg sodium; 1148 mg potassium; 2176 IU vitamin A; 100 mg ATE vitamin E; 18 mg vitamin C; 3 mg cholesterol; 427 g water

Cream of Broccoli Soup

I suppose this really should be called cream of vegetable, but the broccoli seems to dominate.

20 ounces (560 g) frozen mixed vegetables

10 ounces (280 g) frozen broccoli, chopped fine

8 slices low-sodium bacon

¼ cup (40 g) chopped onion

¼ cup (30 g) whole wheat pastry flour

4 cups (950 ml) skim milk

Boil frozen mixed vegetables and broccoli. Set aside to drain. Fry bacon until crispy. Set aside bacon. Pour enough bacon grease in soup pan to cover bottom of pan. Simmer onion until clear. Mix in flour, then add milk. Stir well. Add vegetables and bacon. Simmer until soup is thickened. Salt and pepper to taste. This soup has better flavor when eaten the next day.

—Yield: 6 servings

NUTRITIONAL ANALYSIS

PER SERVING: 276 g water; 219 calories (21% from fat, 28% from protein, 51% from carb); 15 g protein; 5 g total fat; 2 g saturated fat; 2 g monounsaturated fat; 1 g polyunsaturated fat; 28 g carbohydrate; 6 g fiber; 4 g sugar; 331 mg phosphorus; 278 mg calcium; 2 mg iron; 363 mg sodium; 616 mg potassium; 4907 IU vitamin A; 101 mg vitamin E; 24 mg vitamin C; 15 mg cholesterol

Borscht

A traditional Russian or eastern European soup, but one you don't see that often in the United States. Which is a shame, because it tastes good and is nutritious.

2 cups (140 g) finely shredded cabbage

½ cup (80 g) chopped onion

16 ounces (455 g) beets

3 cups (355 ml) low-sodium chicken broth

3 tablespoons (42 g) unsalted butter

2 teaspoons caraway seeds

1 teaspoon sugar

3 tablespoons (45 ml) lemon juice

Cook cabbage about 10 minutes in boiling water. Sauté onion in a soup pot a few minutes without browning. Drain and chop beets, reserving liquid. Add chicken broth to onion, and when it comes to a boil, add cabbage and the water in which it cooked. Add chopped beets, butter, beet juice, caraway seeds, and sugar and simmer for 10 minutes. Add lemon juice. Serve with sour cream.

—Yield: 6 servings

NUTRITIONAL ANALYSIS

PER SERVING: 231 g water; 113 calories (50% from fat, 13% from protein, 38% from carb); 4 g protein; 7 g total fat; 4 g saturated fat; 2 g monounsaturated fat; 0 g polyunsaturated fat; 12 g carbohydrate; 3 g fiber; 7 g sugar; 67 mg phosphorus; 38 mg calcium; 2 mg iron; 190 mg sodium; 306 mg potassium; 229 IU vitamin A; 48 mg vitamin E; 19 mg vitamin C; 15 mg cholesterol

Russian Vegetable Soup

This soup has a little bit of everything in it, and that really gives it a spark of flavor.

1 pound (455 g) mixed dried beans

1 pound (455 g) ham hocks

3 quarts (2.8 L) water

2 tablespoons (28 ml) olive oil

1 cup (160 g) diced onion

1 cup (120 g) diced celery

½ cup (75 g) diced green bell pepper

1 teaspoon crushed garlic

2 cups (260 g) diced carrot

2 cups (300 g) diced rutabaga

2 cups (142 g) diced broccoli

1 cup (200 g) pearl barley

2 tablespoons dried parsley

1 tablespoon black pepper

1 teaspoon basil

1 teaspoon coriander

1 teaspoon nutmeg

Soak beans overnight. Drain, then add the beans, ham, and water to the pot. Bring to a boil, then let it simmer for an hour. (Can be refrigerated overnight at this point to skin off grease.) Remove meat from ham bones and return to pot. Heat oil in a skillet and sauté onion, celery, bell pepper, and garlic until softened, about 5 minutes. Add to pot. Simmer for another hour. Add carrot, rutabaga, broccoli, barley, and herbs. Simmer for another hour.

—Yield: 8 servings

NUTRITIONAL ANALYSIS

PER SERVING: 522 g water; 421 calories (14% from fat, 29% from protein, 57% from carb); 32 g protein; 7 g total fat; 1 g saturated fat; 3 g monounsaturated fat; 1 g polyunsaturated fat; 62 g carbohydrate; 16 g fiber; 7 g sugar; 439 mg phosphorus; 215 mg calcium; 8 mg iron; 551 mg sodium; 1726 mg potassium; 5713 IU vitamin A; 0 mg vitamin E; 42 mg vitamin C; 35 mg cholesterol

Bean Soup with Dumplings

Whole wheat dumplings give this soup extra flavor and nutrition.

1 pound (455 g) dried navy beans

8 ounces (225 g) no-salt-added tomato sauce

2 cups (360 g) chopped tomato

1 cup (160 g) chopped onion

3 quarts (2.8 L) water

4 potatoes, diced

¾ cup (90 g) whole wheat flour

2 teaspoons baking powder

1 egg, beaten

2 tablespoons (28 ml) skim milk

Use large soup pot. Add beans, tomato sauce, tomato, and onion. Cover with water and cook on low until beans are tender, about 2 hours. Add additional water if necessary. Add potatoes. Let cook about 1 additional hour. Sift the flour and baking powder together. Add the egg and milk and mix well. Drop in bean soup. Cover and cook at medium boil for 15 minutes. Do not take the lid off the pan until the 15 minutes are up.

—Yield: 8 servings

NUTRITIONAL ANALYSIS

PER SERVING: 630 g water; 271 calories (6% from fat, 16% from protein, 78% from carb); 11 g protein; 2 g total fat; 0 g saturated fat; 0 g monounsaturated fat; 1 g polyunsaturated fat; 55 g carbohydrate; 9 g fiber; 4 g sugar; 293 mg phosphorus; 146 mg calcium; 4 mg iron; 419 mg sodium; 1285 mg potassium; 394 IU vitamin A; 13 mg vitamin E; 31 mg vitamin C; 26 mg cholesterol

Chunky Pea Soup

Something a little more than most split pea soups, with turnips and lots of other vegetables adding more than the usual substance and flavor.

1 cup (225 g) dried yellow split peas

1 cup (225 g) dried green split peas

7 cups (1.6 L) cold water

2 cups (130 g) sliced carrot

2 cups (300 g) peeled, diced turnip

2 cups (320 g) peeled, chopped onion

1 cup (100 g) chopped celery

½ cup (97 g) rice

¾ pound (340 g) ham

Sort and rinse peas. Add cold water, bring to boil. Cook for 1 hour. Add vegetables and rice and cook for 1 additional hour. Cut ham into small cubes and add for last 20 minutes of cooking.

—Yield: 6 servings

NUTRITIONAL ANALYSIS

PER SERVING: 471 g water; 388 calories (13% from fat, 30% from protein, 56% from carb); 30 g protein; 6 g total fat; 2 g saturated fat; 2 g monounsaturated fat; 1 g polyunsaturated fat; 56 g carbohydrate; 20 g fiber; 12 g sugar; 419 mg phosphorus; 97 mg calcium; 4 mg iron; 698 mg sodium; 1194 mg potassium; 7347 IU vitamin A; 0 mg vitamin E; 17 mg vitamin C; 23 mg cholesterol

Split Pea Soup

This soup has great flavor, even without the traditional ham, which adds more sodium than I can have. It also has a large helping of soluble fiber to help clean out your blood vessels.

1 cup (160 g) onion, chopped

½ cup (60 g) celery, chopped

½ cup (65 g) carrot, sliced

2 tablespoons (30 ml) olive oil

1½ cups (295 g) split peas

6 cups (1.4 L) low sodium chicken broth

½ teaspoon (0.5 g) dried thyme

½ teaspoon (0.4 g) dried basil

1 teaspoon (2 g) black pepper

Heat oil in a large Dutch oven over medium-high heat and sauté onion, celery, and carrot until onion is soft. Add remaining ingredients. Bring to a boil, then reduce heat and simmer for 1 hour, or until peas are very soft. Mash peas with a spoon against the side of the pot until you reach the desired consistency.

—Yield: 8 servings

NUTRITIONAL ANALYSIS

PER SERVING: 115 calories (34% from fat, 23% from protein, 43% from carbohydrate); 7 g protein; 5 g total fat; 1 g saturated fat; 3 g monounsaturated fat; 1 g polyunsaturated fat; 13 g carbohydrate; 4 g fiber; 3 g sugar; 101 mg phosphorus; 25 mg calcium; 1 mg iron; 66 mg sodium; 365 mg potassium; 1384 IU vitamin A; 0 mg ATE vitamin E; 2 mg vitamin C; 0 mg cholesterol; 229 g water

TIP

If you prefer a smoother soup, process in batches in a blender or food processor until smooth.

Lentil and Barley Soup

Lentil and barley make a great combination, both in terms of flavor and nutrition. This hearty soup proves that, tasting great and packing 10 grams of fiber while remaining low in sodium and saturated fat.

¼ cup (60 ml) olive oil

½ teaspoon garlic

½ cup (80 g) diced onion

1 cup (110 g) shredded carrot

½ cup (50 g) sliced celery

1 teaspoon basil

3 quarts (2.8 L) water

1 pound (455 g) lentils

½ cup (100 g) pearl barley

½ teaspoon black pepper

¼ teaspoon garlic powder

¼ cup (60 ml) red wine

Heat oil in Dutch oven. Add garlic, onion, carrot, celery, and basil and cook until tender on low to medium heat, about 10 to 15 minutes. Add water, cover, and bring to boil. Add lentils, barley, pepper, garlic powder, and red wine. Reduce heat and simmer until beans are tender, about 1 hour.

—Yield: 6 servings

NUTRITIONAL ANALYSIS

PER SERVING: 566 g water; 245 calories (36% from fat, 15% from protein, 49% from carb); 9 g protein; 10 g total fat; 1 g saturated fat; 7 g monounsaturated fat; 1 g polyunsaturated fat; 30 g carbohydrate; 10 g fiber; 3 g sugar; 192 mg phosphorus; 48 mg calcium; 3 mg iron; 34 mg sodium; 462 mg potassium; 3608 IU vitamin A; 0 mg vitamin E; 4 mg vitamin C; 0 mg cholesterol

Lentil Brown Rice Soup

A hearty soup of lentils and rice.

¾ cup (75 g) chopped celery

¾ cup (120 g) chopped onion

2 tablespoons (28 ml) olive oil

6 cups (1.4 L) water

¾ cup (144 g) lentils

4 cups (1 kg) no-salt-added canned tomatoes

½ teaspoon garlic powder

¼ teaspoon black pepper

¾ cup (142 g) brown rice

½ teaspoon rosemary

1 tablespoon (15 ml) Worcestershire sauce

½ cup (55 g) shredded carrot

Sauté celery and onion in oil in a Dutch oven. Add water and lentils. Cook 20 minutes. Add remaining ingredients, except carrot. Simmer 45 to 60 minutes. Add carrot. Cook 5 minutes more.

—Yield: 6 servings

NUTRITIONAL ANALYSIS

PER SERVING: 447 g water; 199 calories (24% from fat, 11% from protein, 64% from carb); 6 g protein; 6 g total fat; 1 g saturated fat; 4 g monounsaturated fat; 1 g polyunsaturated fat; 33 g carbohydrate; 5 g fiber; 6 g sugar; 168 mg phosphorus; 80 mg calcium; 3 mg iron; 73 mg sodium; 566 mg potassium; 2048 IU vitamin A; 0 mg vitamin E; 22 mg vitamin C; 0 mg cholesterol

Healthy Chili

A healthier version of chili that doesn't suffer at all in the taste department. Low in fat, high in fiber, but still just as tasty.

1 pound (455 g) ground turkey

4 cups (684 g) cooked pinto beans, undrained

18 ounces (510 g) no-salt-added tomato sauce

6 ounces (170 g) no-salt-added tomato paste

2 cups (475 ml) vegetable juice, such as V8

2 tablespoons chili powder

1 teaspoon cumin

1 teaspoon cinnamon

½ cup (70 g) bulgur

Brown turkey and drain. Add remaining ingredients. Simmer 30 minutes. Stir often.

—Yield: 6 servings

NUTRITIONAL ANALYSIS

PER SERVING: 295 g water; 410 calories (12% from fat, 35% from protein, 53% from carb); 37 g protein; 6 g total fat; 2 g saturated fat; 1 g monounsaturated fat; 2 g polyunsaturated fat; 56 g carbohydrate; 16 g fiber; 11 g sugar; 438 mg phosphorus; 120 mg calcium; 7 mg iron; 337 mg sodium; 1614 mg potassium; 1840 IU vitamin A; 0 mg vitamin E; 35 mg vitamin C; 57 mg cholesterol

TIP

Serve with grated cheese if desired and cornbread.

Black Bean Chili

This could be the perfect chili. Not only does it taste great, but it's good for you, high in fiber, and low in fat. And it cooks in only about 20 minutes. Plus, it makes a great, different-tasting way to use up leftover turkey.

1 cup (250 g) dried black beans

1 tablespoon (15 ml) canola oil

1 cup (160 g) onion, chopped

½ cup (75 g) red bell pepper, cubed

1 teaspoon (3 g) minced garlic

2 jalapeño peppers, seeded and chopped

2 cups (360 g) canned no-salt-added tomatoes

2 tablespoons (15 g) chili powder

1 teaspoon (2.5 g) cumin

1 teaspoon (2 g) coriander

1 teaspoon (0.6 g) dried marjoram

¼ teaspoon (0.3 g) red pepper flakes

¼ teaspoon (0.6 g) cinnamon

2 cups (225 g) cooked turkey breast, cubed

⅓ cup fresh (20 g) cilantro, coarsely chopped

4 teaspoons (8 g) low fat Cheddar cheese, shredded

Soak and cook black beans according to package directions. Heat oil in a 3-quart (2.8-L) saucepan and sauté onion, bell pepper, garlic, and jalapeño peppers until crisp-tender. Add all other ingredients except turkey, cilantro, and cheese. Bring to a boil, then simmer for 10 to 15 minutes. Stir in turkey and cilantro and cook until heated throughout. To serve, ladle into bowls and top with cheese.

—Yield: 4 servings

NUTRITIONAL ANALYSIS

PER SERVING: 153 calories (27% from fat, 17% from protein, 56% from carbohydrate); 7 g protein; 5 g total fat; 1 g saturated fat; 2 g monounsaturated fat; 2 g polyunsaturated fat; 23 g carbohydrate; 8 g fiber; 6 g sugar; 133 mg phosphorus; 97 mg calcium; 3 mg iron; 77 mg sodium; 608 mg potassium; 2208 IU vitamin A; 2 mg ATE vitamin E; 46 mg vitamin C; 1 mg cholesterol; 207 g water

CHAPTER 9

Breads

Delicious breads are one of those things that can be really bad for your heart healthy diet as most of them are high in fat and sodium and mostly empty calories from white flour and white sugar. We've attacked that problem head on, creating a long list of healthy quick breads and yeast breads for you to choose from. There are biscuits, cornbread, coffee cakes, and more!

Making traditional loaves in a bread machine is incredibly simple and almost foolproof. All of the yeast bread recipes were made in a bread machine, and I can't recommend them enough. You dump the ingredients in, turn it on, and come back a couple of hours later to freshly baked bread.

There are also many ways to make bread by hand, of course. You can find many other methods, including some that reduce the amount of kneading by combining some of the ingredients with a mixer or food processor. Generally speaking, you can use any recipe or method that you like, simply substituting the ingredients as recommended for those other methods.

Lower-Fat Restaurant-Style Biscuits

This recipe has the flakiness and the buttery flavor typical of biscuits served at fast food chicken restaurants, but without the fat and sodium.

2 cups (250 g) flour

1 tablespoon (13.8 g) baking powder

4 tablespoons (56 g) unsalted butter, divided

2 ounces (55 g) fat-free sour cream

½ cup (120 ml) club soda, at room temperature

Preheat oven to 375°F (190°C, or gas mark 5). Stir flour and baking powder together. Cut in 2 tablespoons (28 g) butter with a pastry blender or two knives until mixture resembles coarse crumbs. Mix sour cream and club soda into flour mixture. Turn out onto a lightly floured surface and knead lightly. Roll or pat to ½-inch (1.3-cm) thickness. Cut into 6 biscuits with a biscuit cutter or sharp knife. Place biscuits in an 8 × 8-inch (20 × 20-cm) baking dish sprayed with nonstick vegetable oil spray. Melt remaining butter and pour over the top. Bake for 20 to 25 minutes, or until golden brown.

—Yield: 6 servings

NUTRITIONAL ANALYSIS

PER SERVING: 232 calories (32% from fat, 9% from protein, 59% from carbohydrate); 5 g protein; 8 g total fat; 6 g saturated fat; 2 g monounsaturated fat; 0 g polyunsaturated fat; 33 g carbohydrate; 1 g fiber; 0 g sugar; 109 mg phosphorus; 158 mg calcium; 2 mg iron; 335 mg sodium; 66 mg potassium; 435 IU vitamin A; 101 mg ATE vitamin E; 0 mg vitamin C; 14 mg cholesterol; 34 g water

Lower-Fat Cornbread

Cornbread goes well with a lot of things. (It's also great re-heated with a little honey or syrup for breakfast.) I've found here, like with a lot of recipes, that reducing the amount of fat called for doesn't really affect the end product at all.

1 cup (140 g) cornmeal

1 cup (125 g) flour

¼ cup (50 g) sugar

1 tablespoon (13.8 g) baking powder

2 tablespoons (28 g) unsalted butter

1 cup (235 ml) skim milk

1 egg

Preheat oven to 425°F (220°C, or gas mark 7). Mix together cornmeal, flour, sugar, and baking powder. Cut in butter until mixture resembles coarse crumbs. Stir milk and egg together and add to dry ingredients, stirring until just mixed. Place in a 9-inch (23-cm) square pan sprayed with nonstick vegetable oil spray and bake for 20 to 25 minutes.

—Yield: 12 servings

NUTRITIONAL ANALYSIS

PER SERVING: 133 calories (17% from fat, 11% from protein, 73% from carbohydrate); 4 g protein; 2 g total fat; 1 g saturated fat; 0 g monounsaturated fat; 0 g polyunsaturated fat; 24 g carbohydrate; 1 g fiber; 4 g sugar; 81 mg phosphorus; 103 mg calcium; 1 mg iron; 165 mg sodium; 88 mg potassium; 189 IU vitamin A; 35 mg ATE vitamin E; 0 mg vitamin C; 35 mg cholesterol; 26 g water

Blueberry Muffins

These are a real breakfast treat. And you won't even notice that they are fat-free.

1½ cups (180 g) flour

6 tablespoons (75 g) sugar, divided

2½ teaspoons (11.5 g) baking powder

1 teaspoon (2.3 g) cinnamon, divided

1 egg

¾ cup (180 ml) skim milk

⅓ cup (80 ml) applesauce

½ cup (73 g) blueberries

Preheat oven to 400°F (200°C, or gas mark 6). Stir together flour, 4 tablespoons (50 g) sugar, baking powder, and ½ teaspoon (1.2 g) cinnamon. Make a well in the center. Stir together milk, egg, and applesauce. Add all at once to dry ingredients. Stir until just moistened. Stir in blueberries. Spoon into greased or paper-lined muffin cups. Mix together remaining cinnamon and sugar. Sprinkle over the tops of the muffins. Bake for 20 minutes.

—Yield: 12 servings

NUTRITIONAL ANALYSIS

PER SERVING: 99 calories (4% from fat, 12% from protein, 85% from carbohydrate); 3 g protein; 0 g total fat; 0 g saturated fat; 0 g monounsaturated fat; 0 g polyunsaturated fat; 21 g carbohydrate; 1 g fiber; 8 g sugar; 63 mg phosphorus; 86 mg calcium; 1 mg iron; 120 mg sodium; 73 mg potassium; 56 IU vitamin A; 9 mg ATE vitamin E; 1 mg vitamin C; 17 mg cholesterol; 31 g water

Cranberry Orange Muffins

Easy to make and a good, healthy way to start the day.

1¾ cups (215 g) flour

¼ cup (50 g) sugar

2½ tablespoons (7 g) baking powder

1 egg

¼ cup (60 ml) orange juice

2 tablespoons (30 ml) canola oil

¼ cup (60 ml) applesauce

½ cup (75 g) dried cranberries

Preheat oven to 400°F (200°C, or gas mark 6). Stir together flour, sugar, and baking powder. Combine egg, orange juice, oil, and applesauce. Add all at once to dry ingredients. Stir until just mixed. Fold in cranberries. Fill 12 greased or paper-lined muffin cups. Bake for 20 to 25 minutes.

—Yield: 12 servings

NUTRITIONAL ANALYSIS

PER SERVING: 129 calories (19% from fat, 8% from protein, 73% from carbohydrate); 3 g protein; 3 g total fat; 0 g saturated fat; 1 g monounsaturated fat; 1 g polyunsaturated fat; 24 g carbohydrate; 1 g fiber; 8 g sugar; 90 mg phosphorus; 176 mg calcium; 1 mg iron; 315 mg sodium; 53 mg potassium; 24 IU vitamin A; 0 mg ATE vitamin E; 2 mg vitamin C; 17 mg cholesterol; 17 g water

Pasta Fritters

A different sort of use for leftover pasta.

2 cups (280 g) leftover spaghetti
¼ cup (25 g) chopped scallions
½ cup (56 g) shredded zucchini
⅓ cup (78 ml) canola oil
1 egg
1 cup (120 g) whole wheat pastry flour
⅛ teaspoon black pepper
1 cup (235 ml) water

About 35 minutes before serving, coarsely chop cooked spaghetti, chop scallions, and shred zucchini; set aside. In 12-inch (30-cm) skillet, over high heat, heat canola oil until very hot. Meanwhile prepare batter. In medium bowl, with wire whisk or fork, mix egg, flour, pepper, and water. Stir in spaghetti mixture. Drop mixture into hot oil in skillet by ¼ cups into 4 mounds about 2 inches (5 cm) apart. With pancake turner, flatten each to make 3-inch (7.5-cm) pancake. Cook fritters until golden brown on both sides; drain fritters on paper towels. Keep warm. Repeat with remaining mixture, adding more oil if needed.

—Yield: 6 servings

NUTRITIONAL ANALYSIS

PER SERVING: 92 g water; 254 calories (48% from fat, 10% from protein, 42% from carb); 6 g protein; 14 g total fat; 1 g saturated fat; 8 g monounsaturated fat; 4 g polyunsaturated fat; 28 g carbohydrate; 5 g fiber; 1 g sugar; 132 mg phosphorus; 24 mg calcium; 2 mg iron; 21 mg sodium; 152 mg potassium; 123 IU vitamin A; 15 mg vitamin E; 3 mg vitamin C; 35 mg cholesterol

Banana Pumpkin Muffins

These moist pumpkin muffins have a spiced brown sugar topping.

½ cup (112 g) pureed banana
½ cup (123 g) canned pumpkin
½ cup (100 g) sugar
¼ cup (60 ml) skim milk
¼ cup (60 ml) canola oil
1 egg
1¾ cups (210 g) whole wheat pastry flour
2 teaspoons baking powder
1 teaspoon pumpkin pie spice

TOPPING:
½ cup (115 g) packed brown sugar
½ cup (40 g) rolled oats
½ teaspoon pumpkin pie spice

Mix pureed banana, pumpkin, sugar, milk, oil, and egg until well blended. Combine flour, baking powder, and pumpkin pie spice. Spoon into muffin tins coated with nonstick vegetable oil spray. Top each with 1 tablespoon of the sugar-spice mixture. Bake in preheated 375°F (190°C, gas mark 5) oven for 20 minutes or until toothpick inserted into muffin comes out clean.

—Yield: 12 servings

NUTRITIONAL ANALYSIS

PER SERVING: 19 g water; 195 calories (26% from fat, 7% from protein, 67% from carb); 4 g protein; 6 g total fat; 1 g saturated fat; 3 g monounsaturated fat; 2 g polyunsaturated fat; 34 g carbohydrate; 3 g fiber; 18 g sugar; 112 mg phosphorus; 74 mg calcium; 1 mg iron; 96 mg sodium; 151 mg potassium; 1629 IU vitamin A; 11 mg vitamin E; 0 mg vitamin C; 18 mg cholesterol

Apple Pinwheels

These little apple rolls are another good weekend breakfast—sweet, but low in fat.

2 cups (250 g) sifted flour

4 teaspoons (18.4 g) baking powder

4 tablespoons (56 g) unsalted butter, divided

¾ cup (180 ml) skim milk

4 cups (600 g) apple, peeled and sliced

1 teaspoon (2.3 g) cinnamon

1¼ cups (285 g) brown sugar, divided

Preheat oven to 425°F (220°C, or gas mark 7). Sift flour with baking powder. Cut in 2 tablespoons (28 g) butter with two spatulas or a pastry blender. Add milk, mixing quickly and lightly. Turn onto a lightly floured surface. Roll into an oblong sheet ¼-inch (0.6-cm) thick. Melt remaining 2 tablespoons (28 g) butter and brush over dough. Cover with apples. Mix together cinnamon and 1 cup (225 g) of the brown sugar and sprinkle over the apple. Roll up like a jelly roll. Cut into 12 slices. Sprinkle remaining ¼ cup (60 g) brown sugar over baking sheet sprayed with nonstick vegetable oil spray. Place rolls, cut sides down, on pan. Bake for 25 minutes.

—Yield: 12 servings

NUTRITIONAL ANALYSIS

PER SERVING: 221 calories (16% from fat, 5% from protein, 79% from carbohydrate); 3 g protein; 4 g total fat; 3 g saturated fat; 1 g monounsaturated fat; 0 g polyunsaturated fat; 44 g carbohydrate; 1 g fiber; 26 g sugar; 83 mg phosphorus; 140 mg calcium; 2 mg iron; 181 mg sodium; 165 mg potassium; 214 IU vitamin A; 45 mg ATE vitamin E; 2 mg vitamin C; 10 mg cholesterol; 49 g water

Banana Sticky Buns

Am I the only one that seems to always have bananas at that use-or-throw-away stage? I hate throwing things away, so I went looking for a different recipe to use bananas and found this one.

¾ cup (75 g) unsalted pecans

¼ cup (56 g) unsalted butter

⅓ cup (75 g) plus ¼ cup (60 g) brown sugar, divided

2 cups (250 g) flour

1 tablespoon (13.8 g) baking powder

6 tablespoons (90 ml) applesauce

⅔ cup (150 g) mashed bananas

Preheat oven to 375°F (190°C, or gas mark 5). Divide pecans, butter, and ⅓ cup (75 g) brown sugar between 12 muffin cups. Bake for 5 minutes, or until butter is melted. Combine flour and baking powder. Stir in applesauce and banana until mixture forms a soft dough. On a lightly floured surface, knead dough a few times until it holds together. Roll or press dough into a 9 × 12-inch (23 × 30-cm) rectangle. Spread remaining ¼ cup (60 g) brown sugar over dough. Roll up from long side. Slice into 12 rolls. Place each in a muffin cup. Bake for 12 to 15 minutes, or until golden. Allow to cool 1 minute before inverting onto a serving platter.

—Yield: 12 servings

NUTRITIONAL ANALYSIS

PER SERVING: 212 calories (37% from fat, 6% from protein, 58% from carbohydrate); 3 g protein; 9 g total fat; 6 g saturated fat; 2 g monounsaturated fat; 02 g polyunsaturated fat; 31 g carbohydrate; 2 g fiber; 13 g sugar; 75 mg phosphorus; 89 mg calcium; 2 mg iron; 168 mg sodium; 142 mg potassium; 214 IU vitamin A; 46 mg ATE vitamin E; 1 mg vitamin C; 12 mg cholesterol; 20 g water

Pumpkin Bread

If you have some leftover pumpkin when you make pumpkin pie, you can make it into pumpkin bread. This makes a great breakfast without even needing any toppings on it.

3 cups (600 g) sugar

1 cup (235 ml) applesauce

4 eggs

16 ounces canned or cooked fresh pumpkin

3½ cups (438 g) flour

4 teaspoons (18.4 g) baking soda

1 teaspoon (4.6 g) baking powder

2 teaspoons (4.6 g) cinnamon

1 teaspoon (1.8 g) ground ginger

⅔ cup (160 ml) water

Preheat oven to 350°F (180°C, or gas mark 4). Cream sugar and applesauce. Add eggs and pumpkin; mix well. Sift together flour, baking soda, baking powder, cinnamon, and ginger. Add to pumpkin mixture alternately with water. Mix well after each addition. Divide batter evenly between two well-greased and floured glass 9 × 5-inch (23 × 12.5-cm) loaf pans. Bake for 1½ hours, or until knife inserted near center comes out clean. Let stand for 10 minutes. Remove from pans to cool.

—Yield: 24 servings

NUTRITIONAL ANALYSIS

PER SERVING: 184 calories (3% from fat, 7% from protein, 90% from carbohydrate); 3 g protein; 1 g total fat; 0 g saturated fat; 0 g monounsaturated fat; 0 g polyunsaturated fat; 42 g carbohydrate; 1 g fiber; 27 g sugar; 44 mg phosphorus; 28 mg calcium; 1 mg iron; 250 mg sodium; 103 mg potassium; 2983 IU vitamin A; 0 mg ATE vitamin E; 1 mg vitamin C; 35 mg cholesterol; 43 g water

Nut Bread

Another good use for recipe bananas, this provides grab-and-go breakfast for most of the week when I make it.

1¾ cups (210 g) whole wheat pastry flour

1¼ teaspoons baking powder

1 teaspoon baking soda

⅔ cup (133 g) sugar

½ cup (112 g) unsalted butter

2 eggs

2 tablespoons (28 ml) skim milk

1 cup (225 g) mashed banana

¼ cup (28 g) chopped pecans

Stir together flour, baking powder, and baking soda. In a mixing bowl, cream sugar and butter with electric mixer until light. Add eggs and milk, beating until smooth. Add dry ingredients and banana alternately, beating until smooth after each addition. Stir in pecans. Turn batter into 9 × 4 × 2-inch (23 × 10 × 5-cm) loaf pan coated with nonstick vegetable oil spray. Bake at 350°F (180°C, gas mark 4) for 60 to 65 minutes until knife inserted near center comes out clean. Cool 10 minutes before removing from pan.

—Yield: 12 servings

NUTRITIONAL ANALYSIS

PER SERVING: 27 g water; 218 calories (42% from fat, 7% from protein, 51% from carb); 4 g protein; 11 g total fat; 5 g saturated fat; 3 g monounsaturated fat; 1 g polyunsaturated fat; 29 g carbohydrate; 3 g fiber; 14 g sugar; 104 mg phosphorus; 48 mg calcium; 1 mg iron; 67 mg sodium; 167 mg potassium; 302 IU vitamin A; 78 mg vitamin E; 2 mg vitamin C; 60 mg cholesterol

Italian Wheat Bread

This great bread recipe came from subscriber Pat. This could also be taken out of the machine at the end of the dough cycle and shaped into a more traditional Italian loaf.

3 tablespoons (45 ml) olive oil

1 cup (235 ml) warm water

1½ cups (185 g) whole wheat flour

1½ cups (185 g) bread flour

1½ teaspoons (6 g) yeast

Place all ingredients in the bread machine pan in the order specified by the manufacturer. Process on the white or French bread cycle.

—Yield: 12 servings

NUTRITIONAL ANALYSIS

PER SERVING: 144 calories (24% from fat, 12% from protein, 64% from carbohydrate); 4 g protein; 4 g total fat; 1 g saturated fat; 3 g monounsaturated fat; 1 g polyunsaturated fat; 23 g carbohydrate; 2 g fiber; 0 g sugar; 75 mg phosphorus; 9 mg calcium; 1 mg iron; 2 mg sodium; 88 mg potassium; 2 IU vitamin A; 0 mg ATE vitamin E; 0 mg vitamin C; 0 mg cholesterol; 24 g water

Whole Wheat French Bread

This is particularly good with soup or a bean dish. You can bake it either in the bread machine or in the oven, as I do here.

¾ teaspoon (3 g) yeast

1 tablespoon (15 ml) honey

1 cup (235 ml) water

2 cups (250 g) whole wheat flour

1½ cups (185 g) bread flour

Place all ingredients in the bread machine pan in the order specified by the manufacturer. Process on the dough cycle. Remove the dough from the machine. Shape into a tapered loaf. Place on a greased baking sheet, cover with a towel, and let rise until doubled, about 30 minutes. Preheat oven to 400°F (200°C, or gas mark 6). Cut diagonal slices about ¼ inch (0.4 cm) long across the top of the loaf with a sharp knife. Brush with cold water. Bake for 15 to 20 minutes, or until done.

—Yield: 12 servings

NUTRITIONAL ANALYSIS

PER SERVING: 136 calories (4% from fat, 14% from protein, 82% from carbohydrate); 5 g protein; 1 g total fat; 0 g saturated fat; 0 g monounsaturated fat; 0 g polyunsaturated fat; 28 g carbohydrate; 3 g fiber; 2 g sugar; 89 mg phosphorus; 10 mg calcium; 2 mg iron; 2 mg sodium; 104 mg potassium; 2 IU vitamin A; 0 mg ATE vitamin E; 0 mg vitamin C; 0 mg cholesterol; 24 g water

Sesame Wheat Bread

A good sandwich bread, with a little crunch and the flavor of sesame seeds.

1½ cups (355 ml) water

2 tablespoons (28 g) unsalted butter

1½ cups (185 g) bread flour

1½ cups (185 g) whole wheat flour

1 cup (187 g) uncooked multigrain cereal

¼ cup (30 g) sesame seeds

3 tablespoons (45 g) brown sugar

1½ teaspoons (6 g) yeast

Place all ingredients in the bread machine pan in the order specified by the manufacturer. Process on the whole wheat cycle.

—Yield: 12 servings

NUTRITIONAL ANALYSIS

PER SERVING: 211 calories (15% from fat, 12% from protein, 73% from carbohydrate); 6 g protein; 4 g total fat; 3 g saturated fat; 1 g monounsaturated fat; 0 g polyunsaturated fat; 39 g carbohydrate; 3 g fiber; 3 g sugar; 105 mg phosphorus; 39 mg calcium; 2 mg iron; 25 mg sodium; 127 mg potassium; 102 IU vitamin A; 23 mg ATE vitamin E; 0 mg vitamin C; 10 mg cholesterol; 35 g water

Whole Wheat Beer Bread

This bread is good with soups and chili and makes excellent toast. The flavor of the bread will change, depending on type of beer used.

1½ cups (187 g) all-purpose flour

1½ cups (180 g) whole wheat flour

4½ teaspoons (20 g) baking powder

1 tablespoon baking soda

⅓ cup (75 g) brown sugar

12 ounces (355 ml) beer

Preheat oven to 350°F (180°C, gas mark 4). Coat a 9 × 5-inch (23 × 13-cm) loaf pan with nonstick vegetable oil spray. In a large mixing bowl, combine all-purpose flour, whole wheat flour, baking powder, baking soda, and brown sugar. Pour in beer; stir until a stiff batter is formed. It may be necessary to mix dough with your hands. Scrape dough into prepared loaf pan. Bake in preheated oven for 50 to 60 minutes, until a toothpick inserted into center of the loaf comes out clean.

—Yield: 12 servings

NUTRITIONAL ANALYSIS

PER SERVING: 30 g water; 140 calories (3% from fat, 11% from protein, 86% from carb); 4 g protein; 0 g total fat; 0 g saturated fat; 0 g monounsaturated fat; 0 g polyunsaturated fat; 30 g carbohydrate; 2 g fiber; 6 g sugar; 111 mg phosphorus; 115 mg calcium; 2 mg iron; 187 mg sodium; 105 mg potassium; 1 IU vitamin A; 0 mg vitamin E; 0 mg vitamin C; 0 mg cholesterol

Buttermilk Wheat Bread

Another great bread with a nice hot bowl of soup or stew for dinner. The buttermilk gives it an almost sourdough flavor. It's also good toasted.

1 cup (235 ml) buttermilk

¼ cup (60 ml) water

1 tablespoon (14 g) unsalted butter

1½ cups (185 g) whole wheat flour

1½ cups (185 g) bread flour

1 tablespoon (13 g) sugar

1 teaspoon (4 g) yeast

Place all ingredients in the bread machine in the order specified by the manufacturer. Process on the whole wheat cycle.

—Yield: 12 servings

NUTRITIONAL ANALYSIS

PER SERVING: 134 calories (11% from fat, 14% from protein, 74% from carbohydrate); 5 g protein; 2 g total fat; 2 g saturated fat; 0 g monounsaturated fat; 0 g polyunsaturated fat; 25 g carbohydrate; 2 g fiber; 2 g sugar; 92 mg phosphorus; 32 mg calcium; 1 mg iron; 33 mg sodium; 117 mg potassium; 57 IU vitamin A; 13 mg ATE vitamin E; 0 mg vitamin C; 4 mg cholesterol; 27 g water

Onion and Garlic Wheat Bread

Looking for a bread with a little more flavor to stand up to some of your spicier meals? This may be just the one.

½ cup (80 g) finely chopped onion

½ teaspoon finely chopped garlic

1 tablespoon sugar

½ cup (60 g) whole wheat flour

2½ cups (342 g) bread flour

1½ tablespoons nonfat dry milk

1½ teaspoons yeast

¾ cup (175 ml) water

1½ tablespoons (21 g) unsalted butter

Place ingredients in bread machine in order specified by manufacturer. Process on white bread cycle.

—Yield: 12 servings

NUTRITIONAL ANALYSIS

PER SERVING: 25 g water; 143 calories (13% from fat, 13% from protein, 74% from carb); 5 g protein; 2 g total fat; 1 g saturated fat; 0 g monounsaturated fat; 0 g polyunsaturated fat; 27 g carbohydrate; 2 g fiber; 2 g sugar; 59 mg phosphorus; 15 mg calcium; 2 mg iron; 5 mg sodium; 79 mg potassium; 58 IU vitamin A; 16 mg vitamin E; 1 mg vitamin C; 4 mg cholesterol

Whole Wheat Flatbread

Make your own flatbread for roll-ups or other filled sandwiches.

1½ teaspoons yeast

¾ cup (180 ml) water, warm (100–110°F or 38–43°C)

1½ cups (205 g) bread flour

1½ cups (180 g) whole wheat flour

2 tablespoons (28 g) unsalted butter, melted

In small bowl dissolve yeast in warm water. Let stand 5 minutes. Place flours in bowl of food processor. Turn on machine and slowly add yeast-water mixture. Keep machine running until dough just forms a ball. Place ball in bowl coated with nonstick vegetable oil spray. Cover with towel and let rise 1 hour in warm place. Punch down dough and turn out on lightly floured surface. Roll dough into a log about 1½ inches (4 cm) thick. Cut log vertically into 12 equal pieces. Roll each piece into a 6-inch (15-cm) circle. In large cast-iron or heavy skillet over high heat, cook breads one at a time, 1 to 2 minutes until they begin to form bubbles. With tongs, turn and cook other side 1 to 2 minutes, until golden brown. Brush with melted butter. Store tightly wrapped in the refrigerator for 1 week. To reheat, cook in microwave on high 1 minute on microwave-safe dish lightly covered with plastic wrap.

—Yield: 12 servings

NUTRITIONAL ANALYSIS

PER SERVING: 19 g water; 131 calories (17% from fat, 13% from protein, 70% from carb); 4 g protein; 3 g total fat; 1 g saturated fat; 1 g monounsaturated fat; 0 g polyunsaturated fat; 23 g carbohydrate; 2 g fiber; 0 g sugar; 76 mg phosphorus; 9 mg calcium; 1 mg iron; 2 mg sodium; 89 mg potassium; 61 IU vitamin A; 16 mg vitamin E; 0 mg vitamin C; 5 mg cholesterol

Potato Rolls

We like these for Thanksgiving. They are tender and flavorful and the leftovers are just right for a small turkey sandwich for lunch the next day.

½ cup prepared mashed potatoes

¼ cup skim milk

¼ cup canola oil

1 egg

¼ cup sugar

4 cups bread flour

2¼ teaspoons yeast

Place ingredients in bread machine in order specified by manufacturer. Process on dough cycle. When done, remove from bread machine pan and punch down. Separate into 15 balls. Place rolls in 12 × 17-inch baking pan or on cookie sheet. Cover with towel and allow to rise until doubled, about ½ hour. Bake at 350°F (175°C) until golden brown, about 20 minutes.

—Yield: 15 servings

NUTRITIONAL ANALYSIS

PER SERVING: 16 g water; 195 calories (24% from fat, 11% from protein, 65% from carb); 5 g protein; 5 g total fat; 1 g saturated fat; 3 g monounsaturated fat; 1 g polyunsaturated fat; 32 g carbohydrate; 1 g fiber; 4 g sugar; 57 mg phosphorus; 15 mg calcium; 0 mg iron; 10 mg sodium; 81 mg potassium; 41 IU vitamin A; 11 mg vitamin E; 0 mg vitamin C; 15 mg cholesterol

CHAPTER 10

Desserts

Sometimes you want a "real" dessert, say cake or pie. This chapter has a number of cakes, featuring lower fat versions of some traditional favorites. It also contains some healthier desserts and rice pudding.

These cookies, tarts, cakes, and other sweet treats are healthier than most. They contain whole grains, fruits, nuts, and a diverse amount of whole and heart-friendly ingredients. If you're looking for something refreshing, it's hard to go wrong when you start with the nutrition of fresh fruit, and you may find that your family appreciates something a little different.

So, indulge yourself guiltlessly, and have something sweet.

Apple Cookies

A nice, soft, chewy cookie . . . and it includes things that are good for you.

2 cups (240 g) whole wheat pastry flour

1 teaspoon baking soda

1 teaspoon cinnamon

½ teaspoon cloves

½ teaspoon nutmeg

½ cup (112 g) unsalted butter

1¼ cups (210 g) firmly packed brown sugar

1 egg

1 cup (110 g) chopped pecans

1 cup (125 g) finely chopped apple

1 cup (145 g) raisins

¼ cup (60 ml) skim milk

Sift flour with baking soda, cinnamon, cloves, and nutmeg. In a large mixing bowl, cream butter and brown sugar; beat in egg until well-blended. Stir in half of flour and spice mixture, then stir in pecans, apple, and raisins. Blend in milk, then remaining flour mixture. Drop by rounded tablespoons of dough, about 2 inches (5 cm) apart, onto baking sheets coated with nonstick vegetable oil spray. Bake at 375°F (190°C, gas mark 5) for 12 to 15 minutes, or until done.

—Yield: 36 servings

NUTRITIONAL ANALYSIS

PER SERVING: 8 g water; 114 calories (38% from fat, 5% from protein, 56% from carb); 2 g protein; 5 g total fat; 2 g saturated fat; 2 g monounsaturated fat; 1 g polyunsaturated fat; 17 g carbohydrate; 1 g fiber; 11 g sugar; 44 mg phosphorus; 18 mg calcium; 1 mg iron; 7 mg sodium; 110 mg potassium; 94 IU vitamin A; 24 mg vitamin E; 0 mg vitamin C; 13 mg cholesterol

Crunchy Orange Cookies

A different kind of oatmeal cookie, with a nice, unexpected orange flavor.

1 cup (225 g) unsalted butter

1 cup (200 g) sugar

2 eggs

¼ cup (60 ml) orange juice

1 teaspoon vanilla extract

2 teaspoons grated orange peel

2 cups (240 g) whole wheat pastry flour

1 teaspoon baking soda

2 cups (160 g) quick-cooking oats

1 cup (145 g) raisins

½ cup (55 g) chopped pecans

Cream butter and sugar until light. Beat in eggs, juice, vanilla, and orange peel. Add dry ingredients and mix well. Stir in by hand oats, raisins, and pecans. Drop by teaspoon on baking sheet coated with nonstick vegetable oil spray. Bake at 375°F (190°C, gas mark 5) for 10 to 15 minutes.

—Yield: 42 servings

NUTRITIONAL ANALYSIS

PER SERVING: 6 g water; 117 calories (44% from fat, 7% from protein, 49% from carb); 2 g protein; 6 g total fat; 3 g saturated fat; 2 g monounsaturated fat; 1 g polyunsaturated fat; 15 g carbohydrate; 1 g fiber; 7 g sugar; 52 mg phosphorus; 10 mg calcium; 1 mg iron; 5 mg sodium; 80 mg potassium; 151 IU vitamin A; 40 mg vitamin E; 1 mg vitamin C; 23 mg cholesterol

Good-for-You Chocolate Chip Cookies

Oatmeal chocolate chip cookies that you'll never suspect have been made more healthy.

¼ cup (55 g) unsalted butter

⅔ cup (150 g) packed brown sugar

¼ cup (85 g) honey

1 egg

1 teaspoon vanilla extract

¼ cup (60 ml) skim milk

1 teaspoon baking soda

½ teaspoon baking powder

1 cup (82 g) granola

¾ cup (60 g) quick-cooking oats

2 cups (240 g) whole wheat pastry flour

1 cup (175 g) chocolate chips

Cream together butter and brown sugar. Mix in honey, egg, vanilla, and milk. Then mix in baking soda and baking powder. Add granola, oats, and flour. Mix all ingredients. Stir in chocolate chips. Place on nonstick baking sheet by teaspoons. Bake at 325°F (170°C, gas mark 3) for 10 minutes.

—Yield: 36 servings

NUTRITIONAL ANALYSIS

PER SERVING: 4 g water; 100 calories (28% from fat, 8% from protein, 64% from carb); 2 g protein; 3 g total fat; 2 g saturated fat; 1 g monounsaturated fat; 0 g polyunsaturated fat; 17 g carbohydrate; 1 g fiber; 9 g sugar; 54 mg phosphorus; 24 mg calcium; 1 mg iron; 25 mg sodium; 78 mg potassium; 61 IU vitamin A; 16 mg vitamin E; 0 mg vitamin C; 10 mg cholesterol

White Chocolate–Cranberry Cookies

These were inspired by cookies that were served as a snack at a training session I had at work. I was looking for a soft cookie with white chocolate chips and dried cranberries.

½ cup (112 g) shortening

1 cup (225 g) brown sugar

1 egg

1 teaspoon vanilla extract

1¾ cups (210 g) whole wheat pastry flour

1 teaspoon baking soda

¼ cup (60 ml) buttermilk

½ cup (87 g) white chocolate chips

½ cup (60 g) dried cranberries

Beat shortening until light. Add sugar and beat until fluffy. Beat in egg and vanilla. Stir together dry ingredients. Add alternately with buttermilk. Beat until smooth. Stir in chips and cranberries. Drop about 2 inches (5 cm) apart on baking sheet coated with nonstick vegetable oil spray. Bake at 375°F (190°C, gas mark 5) 8 to 10 minutes, until lightly browned.

—Yield: 36 servings

NUTRITIONAL ANALYSIS

PER SERVING: 4 g water; 91 calories (37% from fat, 5% from protein, 57% from carb); 1 g protein; 4 g total fat; 1 g saturated fat; 2 g monounsaturated fat; 1 g polyunsaturated fat; 13 g carbohydrate; 1 g fiber; 9 g sugar; 33 mg phosphorus; 15 mg calcium; 0 mg iron; 9 mg sodium; 75 mg potassium; 14 IU vitamin A; 4 mg vitamin E; 0 mg vitamin C; 6 mg cholesterol

TIP

If you like softer cookies like these, replace the butter with shortening like butter-flavored Crisco and the white sugar with brown in your favorite recipes.

Chocolate Peanut Cookies

This a quick and easy treat. It only makes 6 cookies, but the nonbake method makes it possible to stir up a batch whenever you want them. (I've found you can cheat on the 30 minutes and take them out of the freezer a little early too.)

1⅝ ounces (45 g) chocolate candy bar

4 tablespoons (64 g) crunchy peanut butter

1 cup (60 g) lightly sweetened bran cereal, such as Fiber One

Melt the chocolate bar and peanut butter in microwave until smooth, checking at 30-second intervals. Be careful not to burn. Stir to mix melted chocolate and peanut butter. Add cereal and gently toss until coated. Drop on waxed paper or foil, making 6 cookies. Freeze for 30 minutes, then put in resealable plastic bags and refrigerate.

—Yield: 6 servings

NUTRITIONAL ANALYSIS

PER SERVING: 1 g water; 124 calories (49% from fat, 10% from protein, 41% from carb); 4 g protein; 8 g total fat; 2 g saturated fat; 4 g monounsaturated fat; 2 g polyunsaturated fat; 15 g carbohydrate; 6 g fiber; 5 g sugar; 100 mg phosphorus; 53 mg calcium; 2 mg iron; 93 mg sodium; 169 mg potassium; 17 IU vitamin A; 4 mg vitamin E; 2 mg vitamin C; 2 mg cholesterol

Oat Bran Cookies

The old favorite oatmeal raisin cookies updated to be even healthier with the addition of oat bran.

1 cup (235 ml) canola oil

1 teaspoon (5 ml) vanilla

2 eggs

1½ cups (340 g) packed brown sugar

2 cups (160 g) quick-cooking or rolled oats

2 cups (200 g) oat bran

1 cup (125 g) flour

½ teaspoon (2.3 g) baking soda

1 cup (165 g) raisins

Preheat oven to 350°F (180°C, or gas mark 4). Mix oil, vanilla, eggs, and sugar together in a large bowl. Combine dry ingredients and stir into sugar mixture. Stir in raisins. Drop onto a baking sheet coated with nonstick vegetable oil spray. Bake for 15 minutes, or until lightly browned.

—Yield: 48 servings

NUTRITIONAL ANALYSIS

PER SERVING: 122 calories (39% from fat, 6% from protein, 55% from carbohydrate); 2 g protein; 5 g total fat; 0 g saturated fat; 3 g monounsaturated fat; 2 g polyunsaturated fat; 17 g carbohydrate; 1 g fiber; 9 g sugar; 55 mg phosphorus; 16 mg calcium; 1 mg iron; 28 mg sodium; 97 mg potassium; 28 IU vitamin A; 6 mg ATE vitamin E; 0 mg vitamin C; 6 mg cholesterol; 4 g water

Mudball Cookies

The name may not sound too appetizing, but wait until you taste them.

1 cup (80 g) quick-cooking oats
½ cup (55 g) broken pecans
½ cup (45 g) instant cocoa mix
½ cup (130 g) peanut butter
½ cup (170 g) honey
1 cup (72 g) graham cracker crumbs

Mix oats, nut pieces, and instant cocoa mix in a large bowl. Add peanut butter and honey. Mix everything in the bowl until it looks like mud. Place graham cracker crumbs on a sheet of waxed paper. Take 1 teaspoon of cookie mixture at a time and roll in your hands to make a ball. Roll the cookie balls in the cracker crumbs and place on a paper plate or baking sheet. Store in the refrigerator.

—Yield: 24 servings

NUTRITIONAL ANALYSIS

PER SERVING: 2 g water; 111 calories (41% from fat, 8% from protein, 51% from carb); 2 g protein; 5 g total fat; 1 g saturated fat; 2 g monounsaturated fat; 1 g polyunsaturated fat; 15 g carbohydrate; 1 g fiber; 9 g sugar; 49 mg phosphorus; 12 mg calcium; 1 mg iron; 78 mg sodium; 73 mg potassium; 2 IU vitamin A; 0 mg vitamin E; 0 mg vitamin C; 0 mg cholesterol

Whole Wheat Sunflower Seed Cookies

Crunchy sweet nuggets of goodness.

4 tablespoons (55 g) unsalted butter
½ cup (170 g) honey
1½ cups (180 g) whole wheat pastry flour
1 cup (68 g) nonfat dry milk
½ teaspoon baking soda
2 tablespoons (28 ml) water
2 eggs
½ teaspoon vanilla extract
1 cup (175 g) chocolate chips
½ cup (72 g) sunflower seeds
¼ cup (37 g) chopped peanuts

Combine all ingredients. Drop by teaspoon onto baking sheet coated with nonstick vegetable oil spray. Bake in 350°F (180°C, gas mark 4) oven for 12 minutes.

—Yield: 48 servings

NUTRITIONAL ANALYSIS

PER SERVING: 4 g water; 68 calories (39% from fat, 11% from protein, 50% from carb); 2 g protein; 3 g total fat; 1 g saturated fat; 1 g monounsaturated fat; 1 g polyunsaturated fat; 9 g carbohydrate; 1 g fiber; 6 g sugar; 55 mg phosphorus; 28 mg calcium; 0 mg iron; 17 mg sodium; 70 mg potassium; 81 IU vitamin A; 23 mg vitamin E; 0 mg vitamin C; 13 mg cholesterol

Fudgy Brownies

Quick brownie recipe, with a fiber boost not just from the whole wheat flour, but from the cocoa.

1 cup (225 g) unsalted butter

½ cup (45 g) cocoa powder

2 cups (400 g) sugar

4 eggs

2 teaspoons vanilla extract

1 cup (120 g) whole wheat pastry flour

Heat oven to 350°F (180°C, gas mark 4). In microwave, melt butter and cocoa together, stirring once or twice. When melted, add sugar, eggs, and vanilla. Stir to mix well, then add flour. Pour into 13 × 9-inch (33 × 23-cm) pan coated with nonstick vegetable oil spray. Bake 25 minutes.

—Yield: 18 servings

NUTRITIONAL ANALYSIS

PER SERVING: 13 g water; 224 calories (46% from fat, 5% from protein, 49% from carb); 3 g protein; 12 g total fat; 7 g saturated fat; 3 g monounsaturated fat; 1 g polyunsaturated fat; 29 g carbohydrate; 2 g fiber; 23 g sugar; 67 mg phosphorus; 15 mg calcium; 1 mg iron; 20 mg sodium; 84 mg potassium; 376 IU vitamin A; 102 mg vitamin E; 0 mg vitamin C; 80 mg cholesterol

Granola Bars

You can add unsalted nuts to this if you want or substitute chocolate chips or other dried fruit for the raisins to vary the flavor.

3 cups (240 g) quick-cooking oats

½ cup (115 g) brown sugar

¼ cup (28 g) wheat germ

½ cup (112 g) unsalted butter

¼ cup (60 ml) corn syrup

¼ cup (85 g) honey

½ cup (75 g) raisins

½ cup (40 g) sweetened coconut

Combine the oats, sugar, and wheat germ. Cut in the butter until the mixture is crumbly. Stir in the corn syrup and honey. Add the raisins and coconut. Press into a 9-inch (23-cm) square pan coated with nonstick vegetable oil spray. Bake in a 350°F (180°C, gas mark 4) oven for 20 to 25 minutes. Let cool 10 minutes, then cut into bars.

—Yield: 27 servings

NUTRITIONAL ANALYSIS

PER SERVING: 4 g water; 153 calories (30% from fat, 8% from protein, 61% from carb); 3 g protein; 5 g total fat; 3 g saturated fat; 1 g monounsaturated fat; 1 g polyunsaturated fat; 24 g carbohydrate; 2 g fiber; 10 g sugar; 107 mg phosphorus; 17 mg calcium; 1 mg iron; 9 mg sodium; 129 mg potassium; 105 IU vitamin A; 28 mg vitamin E; 0 mg vitamin C; 9 mg cholesterol

Sweet Potato Pie

You'll be hard pressed to tell the difference between this and pumpkin pie.

FOR CRUST:

⅓ cup (80 ml) canola oil

1⅓ cups (165 g) flour

2 tablespoons (30 ml) cold water

FOR FILLING:

2 cups (650 g) cooked and mashed sweet potatoes

¾ cup (150 g) sugar

½ teaspoon (0.9 g) ground ginger

½ teaspoon (1.1 g) nutmeg

½ teaspoon (1.2 g) cinnamon

2 eggs

1½ cups (355 ml) fat-free evaporated milk

1 teaspoon (5 ml) vanilla

Preheat oven to 400°F (200°C, or gas mark 6).

To make the crust: Add oil to flour and mix well with a fork. Sprinkle water over and mix well. With your hands, press dough into a ball and flatten. Roll between two pieces of waxed paper. Remove the top piece of waxed paper, invert over pie plate, and remove the other piece of waxed paper. Press into place.

To make the filling: Combine sweet potatoes, sugar, ginger, nutmeg, and cinnamon in a mixing bowl. Add eggs and mix well. Add milk and vanilla and combine. Pour into pie shell. Bake for 45 to 50 minutes, or until knife inserted near the center comes out clean.

—Yield: 8 servings

NUTRITIONAL ANALYSIS

PER SERVING: 345 calories (26% from fat, 10% from protein, 64% from carbohydrate); 9 g protein; 10 g total fat; 1 g saturated fat; 3 g monounsaturated fat; 5 g polyunsaturated fat; 55 g carbohydrate; 3 g fiber; 29 g sugar; 162 mg phosphorus; 175 mg calcium; 2 mg iron; 106 mg sodium; 426 mg potassium; 13153 IU vitamin A; 57 mg ATE vitamin E; 11 mg vitamin C; 52 mg cholesterol; 123 g water

Pumpkin Custard

This is basically a pumpkin pie without the crust. This recipe is also a little less sweet than most pies.

2 eggs

1 tablespoon sugar

1 cup (235 ml) skim milk

2 cups (490 g) pumpkin, cooked or canned

1 teaspoon cinnamon

1 teaspoon ginger

Beat the eggs and combine with the sugar. Add the milk and pumpkin and mix well. Add the spices and pour into an 8-inch (20-cm) pie pan. Bake in a moderate oven for 50 to 60 minutes. Test by inserting a knife near the edge. When it comes out clean, the custard is finished. Cut into 6 equal portions when chilled. This custard will keep the pie-wedge shape without a crust.

—Yield: 6 servings

NUTRITIONAL ANALYSIS

PER SERVING: 125 g water; 81 calories (23% from fat, 23% from protein, 54% from carb); 5 g protein; 2 g total fat; 1 g saturated fat; 1 g monounsaturated fat; 0 g polyunsaturated fat; 11 g carbohydrate; 3 g fiber; 5 g sugar; 111 mg phosphorus; 94 mg calcium; 2 mg iron; 55 mg sodium; 271 mg potassium; 12885 IU vitamin A; 51 mg vitamin E; 4 mg vitamin C; 80 mg cholesterol

Crumb-Topped Cherry Cobbler

A quick and easy cobbler recipe, low in fat.

21-ounce (595-g) can cherry pie filling

2 tablespoons (28 g) unsalted butter

½ cup (40 g) quick-cooking oats

¼ cup (30 g) flour

½ cup (100 g) sugar

2 tablespoons (16 g) chopped pecans

Preheat oven to 350°F (180°C, or gas mark 4). Spray a 2-quart (1.9-L) casserole dish with nonstick vegetable oil spray. Pour cherry pie filling into prepared dish. Mix butter, oats, flour, sugar, and pecans. Crumble over cherry pie filling. Bake for 20 to 25 minutes.

—Yield: 8 servings

NUTRITIONAL ANALYSIS

PER SERVING: 205 calories (19% from fat, 3% from protein, 77% from carbohydrate); 2 g protein; 4 g total fat; 3 g saturated fat; 1 g monounsaturated fat; 0 g polyunsaturated fat; 40 g carbohydrate; 1 g fiber; 13 g sugar; 46 mg phosphorus; 15 mg calcium; 1 mg iron; 44 mg sodium; 111 mg potassium; 303 IU vitamin A; 34 mg ATE vitamin E; 3 mg vitamin C; 6 mg cholesterol; 55 g water

Ambrosia

A lighter dessert, the sort of refreshing end you might want with a heavy meal or something like a spicy curry. But it still contains 5 grams of fiber per serving.

4 cups orange slices

2 cups (300 g) sliced banana

1 cup (110 g) coarsely chopped pecans

2 ounces (57 g) coconut

In a large glass bowl, arrange alternate layers of orange slices, banana, pecans, and coconut. Sprinkle a small amount of orange juice between layers if desired. Repeat layers. Chill several hours.

—Yield: 8 servings

NUTRITIONAL ANALYSIS

PER SERVING: 122 g water; 218 calories (47% from fat, 5% from protein, 48% from carb); 3 g protein; 12 g total fat; 3 g saturated fat; 6 g monounsaturated fat; 3 g polyunsaturated fat; 28 g carbohydrate; 5 g fiber; 16 g sugar; 70 mg phosphorus; 49 mg calcium; 1 mg iron; 2 mg sodium; 443 mg potassium; 246 IU vitamin A; 0 mg vitamin E; 53 mg vitamin C; 0 mg cholesterol

Apple and Banana Fritters

A search for something for breakfast that would use up some overripe bananas was rewarded with the this recipe. They are incredibly light and very tasty. Sprinkle with confectioners' sugar or dip in honey if you don't mind adding a few more calories to the ones they already have.

1 cup (120 g) whole wheat pastry flour

1 tablespoon sugar

1 tablespoon baking powder

½ cup (120 ml) skim milk

1 egg

1 tablespoon (15 ml) canola oil

½ cup (75 g) chopped banana

½ cup (62 g) chopped apple

½ teaspoon nutmeg

Stir together flour, sugar, and baking powder. Combine the milk, egg, and oil. Add banana, apple, and nutmeg. Stir into dry ingredients, stirring until just moistened. Drop by tablespoons into hot oil. Fry for 2 to 3 minutes on a side until golden brown. Drain.

—Yield: 4 servings

NUTRITIONAL ANALYSIS

PER SERVING: 74 g water; 212 calories (23% from fat, 13% from protein, 64% from carb); 7 g protein; 6 g total fat; 1 g saturated fat; 3 g monounsaturated fat; 1 g polyunsaturated fat; 36 g carbohydrate; 5 g fiber; 8 g sugar; 249 mg phosphorus; 267 mg calcium; 2 mg iron; 405 mg sodium; 311 mg potassium; 157 IU vitamin A; 38 mg vitamin E; 3 mg vitamin C; 60 mg cholesterol

Pear Pie

Delicious as is or with a little dollop of whipped topping.

1⅓ cup whole wheat flour

⅓ cup canola oil

2 tablespoons cold water

½ cup (100 g) sugar

3 tablespoons (24 g) flour

1 teaspoon cinnamon

1 teaspoon lemon peel

5 cups pears, peeled and sliced

1 tablespoon unsalted butter

1 tablespoon (15 ml) lemon juice

Add oil to flour and mix well with fork. Sprinkle water over and mix well. With hands press into ball and flatten. Roll between two pieces in waxed paper. Remove top waxed paper, invert over pan, and remove other paper. Press into place. Combine sugar, flour, cinnamon, and lemon peel in mixing bowl. Arrange pears in layers in the prepared crust, sprinkling sugar mixture over each layer. Dot with butter. Sprinkle with lemon juice. Bake at 450°F (230°C) for 10 minutes. Reduce temperature to 350°F (175°C), and bake for an additional 35 to 40 minutes.

—Yield: 8 servings

NUTRITIONAL ANALYSIS

PER SERVING: 80 g water; 281 calories (34% from fat, 5% from protein, 62% from carb); 3 g protein; 11 g total fat; 2 g saturated fat; 6 g monounsaturated fat; 3 g polyunsaturated fat; 4 g carbohydrate; 6 g fiber; 23 g sugar; 84 mg phosphorus; 216 mg calcium; 0 mg iron; 2 mg sodium; 212 mg potassium; 71 IU vitamin A; 12 mg vitamin E; 6 mg vitamin C; 4 mg cholesterol

Chocolate Cherry Cake

This is a great special occasion cake (Valentine's Day comes immediately to mind).

2 cups (240 g) whole wheat pastry flour

1½ cups (300 g) sugar

1¼ teaspoons baking soda

1 teaspoon baking powder

3 tablespoons nonfat dry milk powder

⅔ cup (135 g) shortening

⅓ cup (30 g) cocoa powder

1 can cherry pie filling

2 eggs

1 teaspoon almond extract

Combine all ingredients. Pour into greased and floured 13 × 9-inch (33 × 23-cm) pan. Bake at 350°F (180°C, gas mark 4) until done, about 30 minutes.

—Yield: 16 servings

NUTRITIONAL ANALYSIS

PER SERVING: 34 g water; 260 calories (33% from fat, 5% from protein, 62% from carb); 4 g protein; 10 g total fat; 3 g saturated fat; 4 g monounsaturated fat; 2 g polyunsaturated fat; 42 g carbohydrate; 3 g fiber; 19 g sugar; 98 mg phosphorus; 42 mg calcium; 1 mg iron; 52 mg sodium; 151 mg potassium; 131 IU vitamin A; 15 mg vitamin E; 1 mg vitamin C; 30 mg cholesterol

Brown Rice Pudding

Quick rice pudding recipe that uses leftover rice. (I tend to make a lot of rice when I cook it so I can use it in all these recipes calling for leftovers.)

2 cups (440 g) cooked brown rice

1½ cups (355 ml) skim milk

½ cup (170 g) honey

1 cup (145 g) golden raisins

1 tablespoon unsalted butter

1 teaspoon cinnamon

In medium saucepan, combine rice, milk, honey, and raisins and bring to boil. Reduce heat and simmer 20 minutes, stirring frequently. Remove from heat and stir in butter and cinnamon.

—Yield: 4 servings

NUTRITIONAL ANALYSIS

PER SERVING: 168 g water; 426 calories (8% from fat, 7% from protein, 85% from carb); 8 g protein; 4 g total fat; 2 g saturated fat; 1 g monounsaturated fat; 0 g polyunsaturated fat; 96 g carbohydrate; 4 g fiber; 60 g sugar; 235 mg phosphorus; 174 mg calcium; 2 mg iron; 66 mg sodium; 543 mg potassium; 277 IU vitamin A; 80 mg vitamin E; 3 mg vitamin C; 9 mg cholesterol

Red Velvet Cake

This is one of those old-time traditional cakes, updated to provide a little extra fiber by using whole wheat flour.

2½ cups (300 g) whole wheat pastry flour

1½ cups (300 g) sugar

2 teaspoons cocoa powder

1 teaspoon baking soda

2 eggs

½ cup (120 ml) canola oil

½ cup (120 ml) buttermilk

2 tablespoons (28 ml) red food coloring

1 teaspoon vanilla extract

ICING:

¼ cup (55 g) unsalted butter

4 cups (400 g) confectioners' sugar

½ teaspoon vanilla extract

8 ounces (225 g) cream cheese

1 cup (110 g) chopped pecans

Mix together the first four ingredients in a large bowl. Blend eggs with a fork, add oil, and blend again. Add the dry ingredients and mix with whisk till smooth. Add and blend in buttermilk, food coloring, and vanilla. Pour into 3 greased and floured 8-inch (20-cm) cake pans. Bake at 350°F (180°C, gas mark 4) for 30 minutes. Cool for 10 minutes and gently remove from pan. Icing: Mix ingredients until light and fluffy.

—Yield: 16 servings

NUTRITIONAL ANALYSIS

PER SERVING: 23 g water; 457 calories (39% from fat, 6% from protein, 55% from carb); 7 g protein; 20 g total fat; 6 g saturated fat; 9 g monounsaturated fat; 4 g polyunsaturated fat; 65 g carbohydrate; 3 g fiber; 49 g sugar; 137 mg phosphorus; 40 mg calcium; 1 mg iron; 63 mg sodium; 184 mg potassium; 317 IU vitamin A; 85 mg vitamin E; 0 mg vitamin C; 53 mg cholesterol

Easy Pumpkin Cupcakes

Use a cake mix and canned pumpkin pie filling to make these tasty cupcakes quick and easy to prepare.

1 package yellow cake mix

2 cups (490 g) pumpkin pie mix

2 eggs

6 ounces (170 g) butterscotch chips

Mix all ingredients together and place in greased or lined cupcake pan. Bake at 350°F (180°C, gas mark 4) for 15 to 20 minutes.

—Yield: 24 servings

NUTRITIONAL ANALYSIS

PER SERVING: 20 g water; 65 calories (12% from fat, 5% from protein, 83% from carb); 1 g protein; 1 g total fat; 0 g saturated fat; 0 g monounsaturated fat; 0 g polyunsaturated fat; 14 g carbohydrate; 2 g fiber; 7 g sugar; 19 mg phosphorus; 14 mg calcium; 0 mg iron; 93 mg sodium; 38 mg potassium; 1897 IU vitamin A; 8 mg vitamin E; 1 mg vitamin C; 20 mg cholesterol

CHAPTER 11

Sauces, Condiments, Mixes, and Spice Blends

It's sometimes hard to find healthy commercial products in this category. Most sauces and dressings and a number of spice blends contain high amounts of sodium. Sauces and mixes tend to contain more fat than you'd want and sometimes still contain trans fats. But these are items that it is easy to create healthy versions of ahead of time so you can just grab them and use them when you need to. We have a wide variety of items in this chapter including Asian sauces, salad dressings and various other sauces and condiments. We also have a few spice blends that are targeted for grilling, but can be used on your favorite meat no matter how you are cooking it. And we end up with some healthy pancake and biscuit mixes.

Reduced-Sodium Soy Sauce

Soy sauce, even the reduced-sodium kinds, contains more sodium than many people's diets can stand. A teaspoonful often contains at least a quarter of the daily amount of sodium that is recommended for a healthy adult. If you have heart disease or are African American, the recommendation is even less. This sauce gives you real soy sauce flavor while holding the sodium to a level that should fit in most people's diets.

4 tablespoons (24 g) sodium-free beef bouillon

¼ cup (60 ml) cider vinegar

2 tablespoons (30 ml) molasses

1½ cups (355 ml) boiling water

⅛ teaspoon (0.3 g) black pepper

⅛ teaspoon (0.2 g) ground ginger

¼ teaspoon (0.8 g) garlic powder

¼ cup (60 ml) reduced-sodium soy sauce

Combine ingredients, stirring to blend thoroughly. Pour into jars. Cover and seal tightly. Keeps indefinitely if refrigerated.

—Yield: 48 servings

NUTRITIONAL ANALYSIS

PER SERVING: 6 calories (13% from fat, 11% from protein, 76% from carbohydrate); 0 g protein; 0 g total fat; 0 g saturated fat; 0 g monounsaturated fat; 0 g polyunsaturated fat; 1 g carbohydrate; 0 g fiber; 1 g sugar; 3 mg phosphorus; 4 mg calcium; 0 mg iron; 52 mg sodium; 19 mg potassium; 3 IU vitamin A; 0 mg ATE vitamin E; 0 mg vitamin C; 0 mg cholesterol; 10 g water

Reduced-Sodium Teriyaki Sauce

The story on this recipe is the same as the soy sauce. In this case, you can sometimes find commercial teriyaki sauces that aren't too high in sodium, but this one is much lower and, to my mind, tastes just as good, if not better.

1 cup (235 ml) Reduced-Sodium Soy Sauce (see recipe on this page)

1 tablespoon (15 ml) sesame oil

2 tablespoons (30 ml) mirin wine

½ cup (100 g) sugar

2 cloves garlic, crushed

two ⅛-inch (31-mm) slices ginger root

Dash black pepper

Combine all ingredients in a saucepan and heat until the sugar is dissolved. Store in the refrigerator.

—Yield: 20 servings

NUTRITIONAL ANALYSIS

PER SERVING: 37 calories (2% from fat, 0% from protein, 98% from carbohydrate); 0 g protein; 1 g total fat; 0 g saturated fat; 0 g monounsaturated fat; 2 g polyunsaturated fat; 84 g carbohydrate; 0 g fiber; 7 g sugar; 10 mg phosphorus; 7 mg calcium; 0 mg iron; 83 mg sodium; 32 mg potassium; 5 IU vitamin A; 0 mg ATE vitamin E; 0 mg vitamin C; 0 mg cholesterol; 17 g water

TIP

Mirin is a sweet Japanese rice wine; you can substitute sherry or sake.

Lower Fat Peppercorn Dressing

This is my favorite dressing recipe. It's similar to a ranch dressing, but with a little extra pop from the peppercorns.

1 cup (225 g) low fat mayonnaise

1 cup (235 ml) low fat buttermilk

2 teaspoons (0.2 g) dried parsley

1 teaspoon (3 g) onion powder

¼ teaspoon (0.8 g) garlic powder

¼ teaspoon (0.3 g) dried dill

1 teaspoon (1.7 g) black peppercorns, coarsely cracked

Mix all ingredients together well. Refrigerate overnight before using.

—Yield: 16 servings

NUTRITIONAL ANALYSIS

PER SERVING: 51 calories (87% from fat, 1% from protein, 12% from carbohydrate); 0 g protein; 5 g total fat; 1 g saturated fat; 0 g monounsaturated fat; 0 g polyunsaturated fat; 2 g carbohydrate; 0 g fiber; 1 g sugar; 10 mg phosphorus; 3 mg calcium; 0 mg iron; 120 mg sodium; 13 mg potassium; 42 IU vitamin A; 0 mg ATE vitamin E; 0 mg vitamin C; 5 mg cholesterol; 8 g water

TIP

You can crack the peppercorns by putting them in a plastic bag and beating on them with a mallet or rolling pin, so you might want to try this recipe on a day when you are feeling a need to release some frustration.

Onion Ranch Dressing

This dressing is better if you make it ahead of time and let it sit at least overnight so the herbs soften and the flavor develops.

½ cup (120 ml) buttermilk

1 cup (225 g) low fat mayonnaise

1 teaspoon (3 g) onion powder

1 teaspoon (0.1 g) dried parsley

1½ teaspoons (6 g) sugar

½ teaspoon (1.5 g) garlic powder

½ teaspoon (1.5 g) dry mustard

¼ teaspoon (0.2 g) dried thyme

¼ teaspoon (0.2 g) dried basil

¼ teaspoon (0.3 g) dried oregano

¼ teaspoon (0.3 g) dried rosemary

¼ teaspoon (0.2 g) dried sage

¼ teaspoon (0.5 g) freshly ground black pepper

Mix all the ingredients together. Store in the refrigerator in a tightly covered jar.

—Yield: 12 servings

NUTRITIONAL ANALYSIS

PER SERVING: 75 calories (81% from fat, 3% from protein, 16% from carbohydrate); 1 g protein; 7 g total fat; 1 g saturated fat; 0 g monounsaturated fat; 0 g polyunsaturated fat; 3 g carbohydrate; 0 g fiber; 2 g sugar; 22 mg phosphorus; 16 mg calcium; 0 mg iron; 170 mg sodium; 32 mg potassium; 53 IU vitamin A; 1 mg ATE vitamin E; 0 mg vitamin C; 7 mg cholesterol; 20 g water

Low Fat Cheese Sauce

A low fat, full-flavored cheese sauce you can use over vegetables or for macaroni and cheese. The cream cheese gives it an extra richness.

2 cups (475 ml) skim milk

2 tablespoons (16 g) cornstarch

1 cup (120 g) low fat Cheddar cheese, shredded

8 ounces (225 g) fat free cream cheese, cubed

Combine the milk and the cornstarch in a saucepan. Bring slowly to almost the boiling point, stirring constantly. Cook at this temperature until the milk begins to thicken. Remove from heat and stir in the cheeses. Let stand until the cheese melts, then stir or whisk until smooth.

—Yield: 4 servings

NUTRITIONAL ANALYSIS

PER SERVING: 123 calories (20% from fat, 43% from protein, 37% from carbohydrate); 13 g protein; 3 g total fat; 2 g saturated fat; 1 g monounsaturated fat; 0 g polyunsaturated fat; 11 g carbohydrate; 0 g fiber; 0 g sugar; 298 mg phosphorus; 313 mg calcium; 0 mg iron; 275 mg sodium; 246 mg potassium; 318 IU vitamin A; 95 mg ATE vitamin E; 1 mg vitamin C; 9 mg cholesterol; 131 g water

Creamy Lemon Sauce

Another fat-free sauce, this one is great heated over fish or broccoli or as a topping for fruit.

1 cup (230 g) fat-free sour cream

1 teaspoon (1.7 g) grated lemon peel

2 tablespoons (30 ml) lemon juice

½ teaspoon (2 g) sugar

In a medium bowl, combine sour cream, lemon peel, lemon juice, and sugar; mix until well blended.

—Yield: 6 servings

NUTRITIONAL ANALYSIS

PER SERVING: 57 calories (0% from fat, 32% from protein, 68% from carbohydrate); 1 g protein; 0 g total fat; 0 g saturated fat; 0 g monounsaturated fat; 0 g polyunsaturated fat; 3 g carbohydrate; 0 g fiber; 1 g sugar; 39 mg phosphorus; 43 mg calcium; 0 mg iron; 17 mg sodium; 59 mg potassium; 151 IU vitamin A; 40 mg ATE vitamin E; 3 mg vitamin C; 16 mg cholesterol; 37 g water

Reduced-Fat Creamy Chicken Sauce

An easy white sauce recipe. The chicken broth and onion give it additional flavor.

2 tablespoons (20 g) onion, minced

½ cup (120 ml) low sodium chicken broth

⅓ cup (40 g) flour

2 cups (475 ml) skim milk

½ cup (120 ml) dry white wine

1 teaspoon (2 g) chicken bouillon

Cook onion and broth in a 1-quart (946-ml) saucepan until liquid is almost all cooked away. In a small bowl, whisk flour with the milk. Add to the onion mixture in the saucepan and continue to cook, whisking, until sauce begins to thicken. Add wine and bouillon and whisk to combine.

—Yield: 4 servings

NUTRITIONAL ANALYSIS

PER SERVING: 120 calories (6% from fat, 27% from protein, 67% from carbohydrate); 7 g protein; 1 g total fat; 0 g saturated fat; 0 g monounsaturated fat; 0 g polyunsaturated fat; 16 g carbohydrate; 0 g fiber; 1 g sugar; 165 mg phosphorus; 183 mg calcium; 1 mg iron; 91 mg sodium; 289 mg potassium; 250 IU vitamin A; 75 mg ATE vitamin E; 2 mg vitamin C; 2 mg cholesterol; 170 g water

TIP

This makes a good base for an Italian sauce, with the addition of some Italian seasoning and Parmesan cheese.

Cottage Cheese Sauce

This sounds a little strange, but it makes a nice creamy sauce with just a little cheese flavor, and it's fat-free.

1 cup (226 g) nonfat cottage cheese

1 cup (235 ml) skim milk

2 tablespoons (30 ml) water

2 tablespoons (16 g) cornstarch

In blender, blend cottage cheese and milk. Pour into a saucepan and heat almost to a boil. Set aside. Add the water to the cornstarch and mix to a paste. Add to cottage cheese mixture in saucepan and stir well. Cook 10 minutes, stirring constantly until thickened.

—Yield: 4 servings

NUTRITIONAL ANALYSIS

PER SERVING: 71 calories (4% from fat, 51% from protein, 45% from carbohydrate); 9 g protein; 0 g total fat; 0 g saturated fat; 0 g monounsaturated fat; 0 g polyunsaturated fat; 8 g carbohydrate; 0 g fiber; 1 g sugar; 107 mg phosphorus; 100 mg calcium; 0 mg iron; 42 mg sodium; 124 mg potassium; 136 IU vitamin A; 41 mg ATE vitamin E; 1 mg vitamin C; 4 mg cholesterol; 92 g water

Cabernet Sauce

This sauce is great served over steak. If you pan-fry the steak, you could use the same pan for the sauce, adding extra flavor.

¼ cup (40 g) onion, chopped

¾ cup (53 g) mushrooms, sliced

1 tablespoon (8 g) flour

½ cup (120 ml) cabernet sauvignon

¼ cup (60 ml) low sodium chicken broth

1 tablespoon (2.7 g) dried thyme

Spray a medium-sized nonstick skillet with olive oil spray. Over medium heat, sauté onions and mushrooms until softened, about 4 to 5 minutes. Add flour to the skillet and mix with vegetables until dissolved. Raise the heat and add the wine. Cook 1 minute. Add the broth and thyme. Cook 4 minutes to reduce liquid and thicken. Add pepper to taste. Spoon sauce over steak.

—Yield: 2 servings

NUTRITIONAL ANALYSIS

PER SERVING: 87 calories (8% from fat, 19% from protein, 73% from carbohydrate); 2 g protein; 0 g total fat; 0 g saturated fat; 0 g monounsaturated fat; 0 g polyunsaturated fat; 9 g carbohydrate; 1 g fiber; 2 g sugar; 58 mg phosphorus; 40 mg calcium; 3 mg iron; 14 mg sodium; 230 mg potassium; 57 IU vitamin A; 0 mg ATE vitamin E; 3 mg vitamin C; 0 mg cholesterol; 122 g water

Roasted Red Pepper Sauce

I developed this sauce when I had a good crop of red Italian peppers in the garden. It's a simple sauce that is great over pasta or chicken.

4 red bell peppers
½ cup (115 g) fat-free sour cream
¼ teaspoon (0.5 g) black pepper
½ teaspoon (1.6 g) garlic powder

Preheat broiler. Place peppers on a baking sheet and broil until the skin blackens and blisters, turning frequently. Place in a paper bag and seal until cooled to loosen skin. Remove skin and place peppers in a blender or food processor and process until smooth. Add remaining ingredients; blend well. May be heated or used cold over meat or pasta.

—Yield: 6 servings

NUTRITIONAL ANALYSIS

PER SERVING: 48 calories (7% from fat, 18% from protein, 75% from carbohydrate); 1 g protein; 0 g total fat; 0 g saturated fat; 0 g monounsaturated fat; 0 g polyunsaturated fat; 6 g carbohydrate; 2 g fiber; 3 g sugar; 40 mg phosphorus; 27 mg calcium; 0 mg iron; 11 mg sodium; 187 mg potassium; 2408 IU vitamin A; 20 mg ATE vitamin E; 95 mg vitamin C; 8 mg cholesterol; 85 g water

Tofu Mayonnaise

This recipe makes a low fat, almost sodium-free, egg-free mayo—or mayo substitute, I suppose, is more accurate. At any rate, it works well for dishes like potato or tuna salads where there tend to be other flavors that predominate, because it isn't quite the same flavor as real mayonnaise.

½ pound (225 g) firm tofu
½ teaspoon (1.5 g) dry mustard
⅛ teaspoon (0.3 g) cayenne pepper
2 tablespoons (30 ml) fresh lemon juice
2 tablespoons (30 ml) olive oil
2 tablespoons (30 ml) water

In a food processor or blender, process tofu, mustard, cayenne pepper, and lemon juice until mixed. With machine still running add oil very slowly and then add water. Blend until smooth. Stop the machine a few times during processing and scrape the sides. Keeps up to 3 months when refrigerated in an airtight container.

—Yield: 12 servings

NUTRITIONAL ANALYSIS

PER SERVING: 32 calories (76% from fat, 16% from protein, 8% from carbohydrate); 1 g protein; 3 g total fat; 0 g saturated fat; 2 g monounsaturated fat; 1 g polyunsaturated fat; 1 g carbohydrate; 0 g fiber; 0 g sugar; 17 mg phosphorus; 6 mg calcium; 0 mg iron; 7 mg sodium; 41 mg potassium; 8 IU vitamin A; 0 mg ATE vitamin E; 1 mg vitamin C; 0 mg cholesterol; 21 g water

Beer Mop

You can use this on any grilled or smoked meat, but it is particularly good on pork.

12 ounces (355 ml) beer

½ cup (120 ml) cider vinegar

¼ cup (60 ml) olive oil

½ teaspoon (1.5 g) minced garlic

1 tablespoon (9 g) onion powder

1 tablespoon (15 ml) Worcestershire sauce

1 tablespoon (8 g) The Wild Rub or The Mild Rub (see recipes on this page)

Combine ingredients in a saucepan and heat. Use warm on grilling or smoking meat.

—Yield: 24 servings

NUTRITIONAL ANALYSIS

PER SERVING: 29 calories (83% from fat, 2% from protein, 15% from carbohydrate); 0 g protein; 2 g total fat; 0 g saturated fat; 2 g monounsaturated fat; 0 g polyunsaturated fat; 1 g carbohydrate; 0 g fiber; 0 g sugar; 4 mg phosphorus; 2 mg calcium; 0 mg iron; 7 mg sodium; 15 mg potassium; 1 IU vitamin A; 0 mg ATE vitamin E; 1 mg vitamin C; 0 mg cholesterol; 18 g water

The Mild Rub

A sweeter, less spicy rub for grilling and smoking.

½ cup (56 g) paprika

2 tablespoons (13 g) freshly ground black pepper

⅓ cup (75 g) brown sugar

2 tablespoons (15 g) chili powder

2 tablespoons (18 g) onion powder

2 tablespoons (18 g) garlic powder

Mix well, and store in a cool, dark place.

—Yield: 22 servings

NUTRITIONAL ANALYSIS

PER SERVING: 28 calories (13% from fat, 9% from protein, 78% from carbohydrate); 1 g protein; 0 g total fat; 0 g saturated fat; 0 g monounsaturated fat; 0 g polyunsaturated fat; 6 g carbohydrate; 1 g fiber; 4 g sugar; 15 mg calcium; 1 mg iron; 10 mg sodium; 105 mg potassium; 1527 IU vitamin A; 0 mg ATE vitamin E; 3 mg vitamin C; 0 mg cholesterol

The Wild Rub

A traditional southern dry rub for barbecue, typically rubbed into the meat and allowed to flavor it overnight in the refrigerator before long, low heat cooking.

½ cup (56 g) paprika

3 tablespoons (19 g) freshly ground black pepper

¼ cup (60 g) brown sugar

2 tablespoons (15 g) chili powder

2 tablespoons (18 g) onion powder

2 tablespoons (18 g) garlic powder

2 teaspoons (3.6 g) cayenne pepper

Mix well, and store in a cool, dark place.

—Yield: 22 servings

NUTRITIONAL ANALYSIS

PER SERVING: 26 calories (15% from fat, 10% from protein, 76% from carbohydrate); 1 g protein; 1 g total fat; 0 g saturated fat; 0 g monounsaturated fat; 0 g polyunsaturated fat; 6 g carbohydrate; 2 g fiber; 3 g sugar; 15 mg calcium; 1 mg iron; 10 mg sodium; 109 mg potassium; 1595 IU vitamin A; 0 mg ATE vitamin E; 3 mg vitamin C; 0 mg cholesterol; 1 g water

Homestyle Pancake Mix

Make up a batch of this mix and you'll always be ready to make pancakes in a flash.

6 cups (720 g) whole wheat pastry flour

1½ cups (210 g) cornmeal

½ cup (100 g) sugar

1½ cups (102 g) nonfat dry milk

2 tablespoons (28 g) baking powder

Combine all ingredients and store in tightly covered jar. To cook, add 1 cup water to 1 cup mix; use less water if you want a thicker pancake. Stir only until lumps disappear. Lightly coat a nonstick skillet or griddle with nonstick vegetable oil spray and preheat until drops of cold water bounce and sputter. Drop batter to desired size and cook until bubbles form and edges begin to dry. Turn only once.

—Yield: 16 servings

NUTRITIONAL ANALYSIS

PER SERVING: 7 g water; 256 calories (4% from fat, 14% from protein, 82% from carb); 9 g protein; 1 g total fat; 0 g saturated fat; 0 g monounsaturated fat; 0 g polyunsaturated fat; 55 g carbohydrate; 6 g fiber; 10 g sugar; 272 mg phosphorus; 196 mg calcium; 3 mg iron; 221 mg sodium; 314 mg potassium; 187 IU vitamin A; 45 mg vitamin E; 0 mg vitamin C; 1 mg cholesterol

Reduced-Fat Whole Wheat Biscuit Mix

Similar to the regular baking mix, but with the nutritional boost of whole grain flour. I use this one almost all the time in place of the white flour one.

4 cups (500 g) flour

2 cups (250 g) whole wheat flour

3 tablespoons (41.5 g) baking powder

⅓ cup (75 g) unsalted butter

Stir flours and baking powder together. Cut in butter with pastry blender or two knives until mixture resembles coarse crumbs. Store in a container with a tight-fitting lid.

—Yield: 12 servings

NUTRITIONAL ANALYSIS

PER SERVING: 266 calories (19% from fat, 11% from protein, 70% from carbohydrate); 7 g protein; 7 g total fat; 4 g saturated fat; 1 g monounsaturated fat; 1 g polyunsaturated fat; 47 g carbohydrate; 4 g fiber; 0 g sugar; 103 mg phosphorus; 220 mg calcium; 3 mg iron; 422 mg sodium; 132 mg potassium; 268 IU vitamin A; 61 mg ATE vitamin E; 0 mg vitamin C; 10 mg cholesterol; 8 g water

About the Author

Dick Logue is the author of several cookbooks and founder of the website www.lowsodiumcooking.com. After being diagnosed with congestive heart failure more than ten years ago, Dick threw himself into the process of creating healthy versions of his favorite recipes. A cook since the age of twelve, he grows his own vegetables, bakes his own bread, and cans a variety of foods. He is the author of *500 Low-Sodium Recipes*, *500 Low-Cholesterol Recipes*, *500 High-Fiber Recipes*, *500 Low-Glycemic-Index Recipes*, *500 Heart-Healthy Slow Cooker Recipes*, *500 400-Calorie Recipes*, and *500 15-Minute Low-Sodium Recipes*. He lives in La Plata, Maryland.

Index

A

almonds
Apricot Chews, 36
Chicken and Snow Peas, 45
Chicken Polynesian, 46
Ambrosia, 128
Amish Chicken Soup, 101
Antipasto on a Skewer, 28
apples
Apple and Banana Fritters, 129
Apple and Pork Chop Skillet, 69
Apple Cookies, 122
Apple Cranberry Stuffed Pork Roast, 73
Apple Pinwheels, 115
Caribbean Vegetable Curry, 91
Cinnamon Apple Omelet, 14
Pork and Apple Curry, 70
Apricot Chews, 36
Artichoke Pie, 93
Asian Tuna Bites, 27
Asparagus, Chicken with, 48
Asparagus Strata, 94

B

bacon
Brisket of Beef with Beans, 57
Cream of Broccoli Soup, 106
Snowy Day Breakfast Casserole, 12
Spinach Quiche, 14
Turkey Vegetable Sauté, 52
Baked Chicken Nuggets, 44
Baked Swordfish with Vegetables, 83

bananas
Ambrosia, 128
Apple and Banana Fritters, 129
Banana Bites, 36
Banana Melon Smoothies, 23
Banana Pumpkin Muffins, 114
Banana Sticky Buns, 115
Bananaberry Breakfast Shake, 22
Banana-Peach-Blueberry Smoothie, 21
Cranberry Orange Smoothie, 23
Nut Bread, 116
Raspberry-Banana Smoothie, 22
Barbecue Pork Chops, 66
barley, pearl
Beef and Barley Stew, 63
Beef Barley Skillet, 57

Chicken Barley Chowder, 102
Chicken Barley Soup, 101
Chicken Vegetable Barley Soup, 102
Cholent, 59
Fiber-Rich Casserole, 94
Lentil and Barley Soup, 109
Russian Vegetable Soup, 107
beans and legumes
    Bean and Cheddar Cheese Pie, 92
    Bean and Tomato Curry, 88
    Bean Soup with Dumplings, 107
    Black Bean Chili, 110
    Black Bean Tortilla Pinwheels, 30
    Brisket of Beef with Beans, 57
    Chicken and Bean Skillet, 48
    Chicken and Black Beans, 49
    Chicken and Snow Peas, 45
    Chunky Pea Soup, 108
    Cornbread-Topped Bean Casserole,
        59
    Garbanzo Curry, 89
    Healthy Chili, 110
    Lentil and Barley Soup, 109
    Lentil Brown Rice Soup, 109
    Pork and Chickpea Stir-Fry, 69
    Pork Chop and Bean Skillet, 68
    Smoked Chicken Minestrone, 100
    Split Pea Soup, 108
    Three Bean Casserole, 60
    Vegetarian Minestrone, 105
beef
    Beef and Barley Stew, 63
    Beef Barley Skillet, 57
    Beef Paprikash, 62
    Beef Stroganoff, 58
    Brisket of Beef with Beans, 57
    Cholent, 59
    Cornbread-Topped Bean Casserole,
        59
    Country Beef Stew, 63
    German Meatballs, 55
    Ground Beef Stroganoff, 58
    Pot Roast with Root Vegetables, 62
    Reduced-Fat Meatballs, 56
    Sauerbraten, 61
    Skillet Nachos, 31
    Steak Bites, 26
    Stuffed Banana Peppers, 56–57
    Tex-Mex Meat Loaf, 55
    Three Bean Casserole, 60
    Western Casserole, 60
    Winter Vegetable Soup, 104
beer
    Beer Mop, 138
    Whole Wheat Beer Bread, 118
Biscuit Mix, Reduced-Fat Whole
    Wheat, 139
Biscuits, Lower-Fat Restaurant-Style,
    112

Black Bean Chili, 110
Black Bean Tortilla Pinwheels, 30
blueberries
    Banana-Peach-Blueberry Smoothie,
        21
    Blueberry Muffins, 113
Boneless Buffalo Wings, 25
Borscht, 106
Brisket of Beef with Beans, 57
broccoli
    Broccoli Bites, 35
    Cream of Broccoli Soup, 106
Brown Rice Pudding, 130
Brown Rice Tuna Bake, 85
Buttermilk Pancakes, Whole Milk, 19
Buttermilk Wheat Bread, 119

C
Cabernet Sauce, 136–137
Caribbean Vegetable Curry, 91
cashews
    Breakfast Couscous, 21
Cedar Planked Salmon, 79
Cheddar cheese
    Asparagus Strata, 94
    Bean and Cheddar Cheese Pie, 92
    Black Bean Chili, 110
    Breakfast Wraps, 15
    Brown Rice Tuna Bake, 85
    Cheese Crisps, 37
    Cornbread-Topped Bean Casserole,
        59
    Easy Breakfast Strata, 17
    Fiber-Rich Casserole, 94
    Low Fat Cheese Sauce, 135
    Quiche Nibblers, 28
    Sausage Frittata, 16
    Shepherd's Pie with Cornbread
        Crust, 53
    Skillet Nachos, 31
    Snowy Day Breakfast Casserole, 12
    Spinach Quiche, 14
    Tuna Noodle Casserole, 84
    Western Casserole, 60
Cheese Crisps, 37
Cheese Pie, 93
Cherry Cake, Chocolate, 130
Cherry Cobbler, Crumb-Topped, 128
chicken
    Amish Chicken Soup, 101
    Baked Chicken Nuggets, 44
    Boneless Buffalo Wings, 25
    Chicken and Bean Skillet, 48
    Chicken and Black Beans, 49
    Chicken and Mushroom Quesadil-
        las, 33
    Chicken and Snow Peas, 45
    Chicken Barley Chowder, 102
    Chicken Barley Soup, 101

Chicken Corn Chowder, 99
Chicken Polynesian, 46
Chicken Pot Pie, 51
Chicken Vegetable Barley Soup, 102
Chicken Wings Nibblers, 25
Chicken with Asparagus, 48
Chicken-Pasta Stir-Fry, 50–51
Grilled Chicken and Vegetables, 41
Grilled Marinated Chicken Breasts,
    41
Grilled Roaster, 40
Honey Mustard Fruit Sauced
    Chicken, 44
Indian-Flavored Chicken, 49
Italian Chicken Kabobs, 42
Italian Chicken Soup, 99
Lemon Rosemary Chicken, 46
Lemon Thyme Chicken, 42
Maple Glazed Chicken, 45
Mexican Chicken Soup, 100
Moroccan Chicken, 47
Oven-Fried Chicken, 43
Potato-Coated Oven-Fried
    Chicken, 43
Pulled Chicken, 47
Reduced Fat Chicken and
    Dumplings, 50
Rotisserie-Flavored Chicken
    Breasts, 40
Smoked Chicken Minestrone, 100
Stir-Fried Chicken and Brown Rice,
    51
Taco Chicken Wings, 26
Chickpea Stir-Fry, Pork and, 69
Chickpea-Stuffed Eggs, 35
chocolate
    Chocolate Cherry Cake, 130
    Chocolate Peanut Cookies, 124
    Chocolate-Raspberry Smoothie, 22
    Good-for-You Chocolate Chip
        Cookies, 123
    White Chocolate–Cranberry
        Cookies, 123
    Whole Wheat Sunflower Seed
        Cookies, 125
Cholent, 59
Chowder from the Sea, 103
Chunky Pea Soup, 108
Cinnamon Apple Omelet, 14
Corn Chowder, 105
Corn Chowder, Chicken, 99
Cornbread, Lower-Fat, 112
Cornbread Crust, Shepherd's Pie with,
    53
Cornbread-Topped Bean Casserole, 59
Cornmeal Pancakes, 19
Cottage Cheese Sauce, 136

Country Beef Stew, 63
Couscous, Breakfast, 21
cranberries/cranberry juice
    Apple Cranberry Stuffed Pork
        Roast, 73
    Cranberry Orange Muffins, 113
    Cranberry Orange Smoothie, 23
    Oat Bran–Berry Smoothie, 23
    White Chocolate–Cranberry
        Cookies, 123
Cream of Broccoli Soup, 106
Creamy Lemon Sauce, 135
Crostini with Mushrooms, 32
Crumb-Topped Cherry Cobbler, 128
Crunchy Orange Cookies, 122

D

Date Chews, 36

E

Easy Breakfast Strata, 17
Easy Pumpkin Cupcakes, 131
Eggplant and Fresh Mozzarella Bake, 95
eggs
    Asparagus Strata, 94
    Breakfast Skillet, 13
    Breakfast Wraps, 15
    Chickpea-Stuffed Eggs, 35
    Cinnamon Apple Omelet, 14
    Cornmeal Pancakes, 19
    Easy Breakfast Strata, 17
    Frittata, 15
    Latkes, 18
    Pasta Frittata, 17
    Pizza Omelet, 90
    Quiche Nibblers, 28
    Ricotta Omelet, 91
    Sausage Frittata, 16
    Snowy Day Breakfast Casserole, 12
    Spinach Quiche, 14
    Tomato and Basil Quiche, 92
    Vegetable Frittata, 16
    Whole Milk Buttermilk Pancakes,
        19
    Zucchini Frittata, 90
    Zucchini Pancakes, 18–19

F

Fat-Free Potato Skins, 34
Fiber-Rich Casserole, 94
fish and seafood
    Asian Tuna Bites, 27
    Baked Swordfish with Vegetables,
        83
    Brown Rice Tuna Bake, 85
    Cedar Planked Salmon, 79
    Chowder from the Sea, 103
    Greek Islands Fish, 82
    Grilled Salmon and Vegetables, 78

Grilled Salmon Fillets, 78
Grilled Swordfish, 82–83
Grilled Tuna Steaks, 75
Grilled Tuna with Honey Mustard
    Marinade, 76
Herbed Fish, 85
Lemon Baked Salmon, 80–81
Maple Salmon, 77
Marinated Tuna Steaks, 76
Mediterranean Salmon, 80
Mediterranean Tilapia, 82
Oven-Fried Fish, 83
Oven-Steamed Salmon and
    Vegetables, 81
Poached Salmon, 77
Salmon with Dill, 81
Salmon with Honey Mustard Glaze,
    80
Thyme Roasted Salmon, 79
Tuna Casserole, 84
Tuna Noodle Casserole, 84
Tuna Steaks, 75
Frittata, 15
Fruit Sauced Chicken, Honey Mustard,
    44
Fudgy Brownies, 126

G

Garbanzo Curry, 89
Garlic Pita Toasts, Parmesan-, 38
Garlic Wheat Bread, Onion and, 119
German Meatballs, 55
Glazed Pork Roast, 71
Good-for-You Chocolate Chip Cookies,
    123
Granola Bars, 126
Greek Islands Fish, 82
Grilled Chicken and Vegetables, 41
Grilled Marinated Chicken Breasts, 41
Grilled Pork Chops, 65
Grilled Portobello Mushrooms, 87
Grilled Roaster, 40
Grilled Salmon and Vegetables, 78
Grilled Salmon Fillets, 78
Grilled Stuffed Portobellos, 87
Grilled Swordfish, 82–83
Grilled Tuna Steaks, 75
Grilled Tuna with Honey Mustard
    Marinade, 76
Ground Beef Stroganoff, 58

H

ham
    Asparagus Strata, 94
    Chunky Pea Soup, 108
    Russian Vegetable Soup, 107
Hawaiian Kabobs, 68
Hawaiian Portobello Burgers, 88
Healthy Chili, 110

Herbed Fish, 85
Homestyle Pancake Mix, 139
Honey Mustard Fruit Sauced Chicken,
    44

I

Indian Vegetable Soup, 104
Indian-Flavored Chicken, 49
Italian Chicken Kabobs, 42
Italian Chicken Soup, 99
Italian Wheat Bread, 117

L

Latkes, 18
Lemon Baked Salmon, 80–81
Lemon Rosemary Chicken, 46
Lemon Sauce, Creamy, 135
Lemon Thyme Chicken, 42
Lentil and Barley Soup, 109
Lentil Brown Rice Soup, 109
Low Fat Cheese Sauce, 135
Lower Fat Peppercorn Dressing, 134
Lower-Fat Cornbread, 112
Lower-Fat Restaurant-Style Biscuits,
    112

M

Maple Glazed Chicken, 45
Maple Salmon, 77
Marinated Tuna Steaks, 76
Mediterranean Salmon, 80
Mediterranean Tilapia, 82
Melon Smoothies, Banana, 23
Mexican Chicken Soup, 100
Mexican Pinwheels, 29
Mild Rub, The, 138
Monterey Jack cheese
    Black Bean Tortilla Pinwheels, 30
    Chicken and Mushroom Quesadil-
        las, 33
    Hawaiian Portobello Burgers, 88
    Mexican Pinwheels, 29
    Spinach Quiche, 14
Moroccan Chicken, 47
mozzarella cheese
    Antipasto on a Skewer, 28
    Artichoke Pie, 93
    Eggplant and Fresh Mozzarella
        Bake, 95
    Grilled Stuffed Portobellos, 87
    Pizza Omelet, 90
    Pizza Pitas, 32
    Spinach-Stuffed Tomatoes, 96
    Turkey Cocktail Meatballs, 27
    Veggie Pizza Bites, 31
Mudball Cookies, 125
Multigrain Pancakes, 20
mushrooms
    Antipasto on a Skewer, 28

Baked Swordfish with Vegetables, 83
Beef Stroganoff, 58
Cabernet Sauce, 136–137
Chicken and Mushroom Quesadillas, 33
Crostini with Mushrooms, 32
German Meatballs, 55
Grilled Portobello Mushrooms, 87
Grilled Stuffed Portobellos, 87
Ground Beef Stroganoff, 58
Hawaiian Portobello Burgers, 88
Italian Chicken Kabobs, 42
Italian Chicken Soup, 99
Mediterranean Salmon, 80
Oven-Steamed Salmon and Vegetables, 81
Pizza Omelet, 90
Pork Loin Roast with Asian Vegetables, 72
Pork Stew, 103
Spinach Quiche, 14
Tofu Curry, 89
Tuna Noodle Casserole, 84
Turkey Vegetable Sauté, 52
Vegetable Frittata, 16
Vegetable Omelet, 13
Western Casserole, 60
Zucchini Frittata, 90

N

National Nutrient Database for Standard Reference, 10
New York Goodwich Roll-Ups, 30
Nut Bread, 116

O

oats/oat bran
Banana Pumpkin Muffins, 114
Crumb-Topped Cherry Cobbler, 128
Crunchy Orange Cookies, 122
Good-for-You Chocolate Chip Cookies, 123
Granola Bars, 126
Mudball Cookies, 125
Multigrain Pancakes, 20
Oat Bran Cookies, 124
Oat Bran Pancakes, 20
Oat Bran–Berry Smoothie, 23
Wheat Germ Crackers, 37
Onion and Garlic Wheat Bread, 119
Onion Ranch Dressing, 134
oranges/orange juice
Ambrosia, 128
Banana Bites, 36
Breakfast Couscous, 21
Chicken Polynesian, 46
Cranberry Orange Muffins, 113

Cranberry Orange Smoothie, 23
Crunchy Orange Cookies, 122
Pork Loin Roast, 70
Southern Pork Chops, 66
Oven-Fried Chicken, 43
Oven-Fried Fish, 83
Oven-Steamed Salmon and Vegetables, 81

P

Parmesan cheese
Artichoke Pie, 93
Broccoli Bites, 35
Italian Chicken Kabobs, 42
Parmesan-Garlic Pita Toasts, 38
Pasta Frittata, 17
Potato-Coated Oven-Fried Chicken, 43
Reduced-Fat Meatballs, 56
Spinach-Stuffed Tomatoes, 96
Vegetarian Minestrone, 105
Veggie Pizza Bites, 31
pasta and noodles
Amish Chicken Soup, 101
Chicken-Pasta Stir-Fry, 50–51
Ground Beef Stroganoff, 58
Mexican Chicken Soup, 100
Pasta Frittata, 17
Pasta Fritters, 114
Thai Spinach and Noodle Bowl, 97
Tuna Noodle Casserole, 84
Turkey-Stuffed Zucchini, 53
Western Casserole, 60
peanuts/peanut butter
Caribbean Vegetable Curry, 91
Chocolate Peanut Cookies, 124
Mudball Cookies, 125
Whole Wheat Sunflower Seed Cookies, 125
Pear Pie, 129
peas
Beef Paprikash, 62
Brown Rice Tuna Bake, 85
Chicken and Snow Peas, 45
Chicken Pot Pie, 51
Indian-Flavored Chicken, 49
Pork Loin Roast with Asian Vegetables, 72
Stir-Fried Chicken and Brown Rice, 51
Tuna Noodle Casserole, 84
Vegetable Paella, 97
peas, split
Chicken Vegetable Barley Soup, 102
Cholent, 59
Chunky Pea Soup, 108
Split Pea Soup, 108
pecans
Ambrosia, 128

Apple Cookies, 122
Banana Sticky Buns, 115
Crumb-Topped Cherry Cobbler, 128
Crunchy Orange Cookies, 122
Date Chews, 36
Mudball Cookies, 125
Nut Bread, 116
Red Velvet Cake, 131
Southern Pork Chops, 66
pineapple
Chicken Polynesian, 46
Hawaiian Kabobs, 68
Hawaiian Portobello Burgers, 88
Pineapple-Stuffed Pork Chops, 67
pineapple juice
Turkey Cocktail Meatballs, 27
pitas
Parmesan-Garlic Pita Toasts, 38
Pita Chips, 37
Pizza Pitas, 32
Spicy Pita Dippers, 38
Pizza Omelet, 90
Pizza Pitas, 32
Poached Salmon, 77
pork
Apple and Pork Chop Skillet, 69
Apple Cranberry Stuffed Pork Roast, 73
Barbecue Pork Chops, 66
Cornbread-Topped Bean Casserole, 59
Glazed Pork Roast, 71
Grilled Pork Chops, 65
Hawaiian Kabobs, 68
Pineapple-Stuffed Pork Chops, 67
Pork and Apple Curry, 70
Pork and Chickpea Stir-Fry, 69
Pork Chop and Bean Skillet, 68
Pork Loin Roast, 70
Pork Loin Roast with Asian Vegetables, 72
Pork Stew, 103
Potstickers, 34
Skillet Pork Chops, 65
Southern Pork Chops, 66
Stuffed Pork Chops, 67
Stuffed Pork Roast, 71
Pot Roast with Root Vegetables, 62
potatoes
Bean Soup with Dumplings, 107
Beef Paprikash, 62
Breakfast Potatoes, 18
Breakfast Skillet, 13
Breakfast Wraps, 15
Chicken Corn Chowder, 99
Chicken Pot Pie, 51
Cholent, 59

Chowder from the Sea, 103
Corn Chowder, 105
Fat-Free Potato Skins, 34
Frittata, 15
Indian Vegetable Soup, 104
Latkes, 18
Oven-Fried Fish, 83
Oven-Steamed Salmon and
    Vegetables, 81
Pot Roast with Root Vegetables, 62
Potato Rolls, 120
Potato-Coated Oven-Fried
    Chicken, 43
Reduced Fat Chicken and
    Dumplings, 50
Shepherd's Pie with Cornbread
    Crust, 53
Snowy Day Breakfast Casserole, 12
Potstickers, 34
Provolone cheese
    Grilled Portobello Mushrooms, 87
Pulled Chicken, 47
pumpkin
    Banana Pumpkin Muffins, 114
    Easy Pumpkin Cupcakes, 131
    Pumpkin Bread, 116
    Pumpkin Custard, 127

Q

Quiche Nibblers, 28

R

raspberries
    Chocolate-Raspberry Smoothie, 22
    Raspberry-Banana Smoothie, 22
Red Pepper Sauce, Roasted, 137
Red Velvet Cake, 131
Reduced Fat Chicken and Dumplings,
    50
Reduced-Fat Creamy Chicken Sauce,
    136
Reduced-Fat Meatballs, 56
Reduced-Fat Whole Wheat Biscuit Mix,
    139
Reduced-Sodium Soy Sauce, 133
Reduced-Sodium Teriyaki Sauce, 133
rice
    Brown Rice Pudding, 130
    Brown Rice Tuna Bake, 85
    Caribbean Vegetable Curry, 91
    Chunky Pea Soup, 108
    Grilled Salmon and Vegetables, 78
    Lentil Brown Rice Soup, 109
    Pork and Chickpea Stir-Fry, 69
    Squash and Rice Bake, 95
    Stir-Fried Chicken and Brown Rice,
    51
    Tuna Casserole, 84
    Turkey-Stuffed Zucchini, 53

Vegetable Paella, 97
Ricotta Omelet, 91
Roasted Red Pepper Sauce, 137
Rotisserie-Flavored Chicken Breasts, 40
Russian Vegetable Soup, 107

S

Salmon with Dill, 81
Salmon with Honey Mustard Glaze, 80
Sauerbraten, 61
sausage
    Breakfast Wraps, 15
    Easy Breakfast Strata, 17
    Sausage Frittata, 16
    Turkey Breakfast Sausage, 12
Shepherd's Pie with Cornbread Crust,
    53
Skillet Nachos, 31
Skillet Pork Chops, 65
Smoked Chicken Minestrone, 100
Snowy Day Breakfast Casserole, 12
Southern Pork Chops, 66
Spicy Pita Dippers, 38
spinach
    Spinach Quiche, 14
    Spinach-Stuffed Tomatoes, 96
    Thai Spinach and Noodle Bowl, 97
Squash and Rice Bake, 95
Steak Bites, 26
Stir-Fried Chicken and Brown Rice, 51
strawberries
    Bananaberry Breakfast Shake, 22
    Oat Bran–Berry Smoothie, 23
Stuffed Banana Peppers, 56–57
Stuffed Pork Chops, 67
Stuffed Pork Roast, 71
Sunflower Seed Cookies, Whole Wheat,
    125
Sweet Potato Pie, 127
Swiss cheese
    Squash and Rice Bake, 95
    Stuffed Banana Peppers, 56–57
    Tomato and Basil Quiche, 92
    Tuna Casserole, 84
    Turkey Skillet Pie, 52
    Turkey-Stuffed Zucchini, 53
    Vegetable Frittata, 16
    Vegetable Omelet, 13
    Zucchini Frittata, 90

T

Taco Chicken Wings, 26
Tex-Mex Meat Loaf, 55
Thai Spinach and Noodle Bowl, 97
Three Bean Casserole, 60
Thyme Roasted Salmon, 79
tofu
    Banana Melon Smoothies, 23
    Tofu Curry, 89

Tofu Mayonnaise, 137
Tomato and Basil Quiche, 92
Tomato Curry, Bean and, 88
Tomatoes, Spinach-Stuffed, 96
Tuna Casserole, 84
Tuna Noodle Casserole, 84
Tuna Steaks, 75
turkey
    Black Bean Chili, 110
    Breakfast Wraps, 15
    Grilled Tuna Steaks, 75
    Healthy Chili, 110
    Sausage Frittata, 16
    Shepherd's Pie with Cornbread
        Crust, 53
    Turkey Breakfast Sausage, 12
    Turkey Cocktail Meatballs, 27
    Turkey Skillet Pie, 52
    Turkey Vegetable Sauté, 52
    Turkey-Stuffed Zucchini, 53
Tuscan Bruschetta, 33

V

Vegetable Frittata, 16
Vegetable Omelet, 13
Vegetable Paella, 97
Vegetarian Minestrone, 105
Veggie Pizza Bites, 31

W

Western Casserole, 60
Wheat Germ Crackers, 37
White Chocolate–Cranberry Cookies,
    123
Whole Milk Buttermilk Pancakes, 19
Whole Wheat Beer Bread, 118
Whole Wheat Flatbread, 120
Whole Wheat French Bread, 117
Whole Wheat Sunflower Seed Cookies,
    125
Wild Rub, The
    Beer Mop, 138
    recipe, 138
Winter Vegetable Soup, 104

Z

zucchini
    Turkey-Stuffed Zucchini, 53
    Zucchini Frittata, 90
    Zucchini Pancakes, 18–19
    Zucchini Patties, 96